Praise for *Exodus, Reckoning, Sacrifice*

'One of the most original, learned and surprising treatments of Brexit I have seen, interpreting it through the symbolic language of myth. Such a welcome change from the usual Brexit debate. I recommend it most warmly.'

Timothy Garton Ash, author of *Free Speech: Ten Principles for a Connected World*

'Whether we live Brexit as a drama about to slip into a tragedy, a comedy or a heroic epic, here is a highly unusual book that dares say that there is something yet more important: that we use the Brexit odyssey to make sense of our European togetherness. A single urgency marks this endeavour – that we treat Brexit as a theatre of recognition, that we be generous and gracious in hearing our rivals' stories as stories that matter. Reader, fear not that you will be subjected to academic instruction, confronted with the rights and wrongs of the political saga, or the hows and whys of European integration. You will be simply reminded of tools already at your possession – the archetypal, time-immemorial stories from the Greek, Roman and Biblical traditions that are stubbornly settled in our collective imagination. Enjoy the best of treats – a story told in the long-lost style of insightful and informed reflection that was typical of the Enlightenment, when a writer's erudition supplied both edification and amusement – enticing a craving to hear more. Alas, the book is short.'

Albena Azmanova, author of *The Scandal of Reason*

'This book is essential reading, for a lot more is going on in Brexit than meets the eye. Hopes of escape, freedom and even self-sacrifice are buried in mythological memories bound into people's identification with their country and its future. Kalypso Nicolaidis has bravely gone where none has so far dared and has extended her exceptional empathy and intelligence to the imagined powers of escaping and embracing Europe from which none of us can escape.'

Anthony Barnett, author of *The Lure of Greatness*

'Dazzling, tolerant, wise, pyrotechnic, thoroughly up-to-date yet steeped in millennia-old story patterns, this book is a must-read for anyone tempted to believe that Brexit – or, for that matter, ancient mythology – is a simple matter. Like the Hebrew and Greek myths which she evokes, Professor Nicolaidis offers no easy solutions. This is a book which neither Remainers nor Leavers can afford to ignore.'

Richard Buxton, author of *Myths and Tragedies in their Ancient Greek Contexts*

'Kalypso Nicolaidis offers a striking and pithy exploration, aptly recast as epic Greek and Biblical tragedy and as Socratic dialogue, of how the case for Brexit became a mêlée of myths, both eviscerating and tantalizing. Amidst the plethora of writings on Brexit, her brilliant and highly entertaining narrative stands out as a chastening and revealing account of human hope, hubris, ardour and folly. Nicolaidis tells her rich and finely crafted tale with subtlety, imagination, great historical insight, and compassion for all involved – the British tribes and their continental counterparts – and tenders her own vision for the future.'

Michael Freeden, author of *The Political Theory of Political Thinking:*
The Anatomy of a Practice

'We understand the present through the stories we have heard from the past. Kalypso Nicolaidis weaves an analysis of many stories into a profound, insightful and often strangely lyrical account of the most bizarre episode in recent British history. The result is a new and different understanding of the phenomenon known as Brexit, showing how competing memories and narratives intertwine as each individual draws on memory to comprehend the weirdness of reality. It is an impressive, important book, an antidote to those who think that rationality rules, or that myths have lost their power.'

Iain Pears, author of *Arcadia*

'Truth is the poetic residue of reality and Kalypso Nicolaidis brings us the truth within the Brexit mess. Believe it or not she does it with joy. Read this book to refresh your faith in humankind and see how today's confusion echoes through time.'

Ece Temelkuran, author of *How to Lose a Country*

'This is a book about Brexit which will not make you yawn. Different, imaginative, thought-provoking.'

J. H. H. Weiler, author of *The Constitution of Europe*

'I have known Kalypso Nicolaidis over the last three decades not only as one of the greatest experts on the EU, but one capable of engaging with it through countless angles, from policy wonk to storyteller. This book is the ultimate expression of her passionate, life-long commitment and a beacon on the road of our never-ending Brexit.'

Shirley Williams, author of *God and Caesar: Personal Reflections on*
Politics and Religion

EXODUS

RECKONING

SACRIFICE

First published in 2019

Unbound

6th Floor Mutual House, 70 Conduit Street, London W1S 2GF

www.unbound.com

Text Design by PDQ

A CIP record for this book is available from the British Library

ISBN 978-1-78352-809-7 (hardback)
ISBN 978-1-78352-810-3 (ebook)

Printed in Great Britain by CPI Group (UK)

1 3 5 7 9 8 6 4 2

EXODUS

Kalypso Nicolaidis

RECKONING

Three Meanings of Brexit

SACRIFICE

unbound

To Simon, Ari and Daphne

Contents

Preface

Do you remember how Ulysses, the cleverest of them all, was defined by his ambivalence even more than by his cunning? We meet him on his island of Ithaca at the beginning of Homer's *Iliad* as old Palamedes begs him to join the Greek expedition against Troy. We are told how Ulysses, determined to stay put with his young wife Penelope and three-month-old son Telemachus, colludes with his people and pretends to have gone mad by ploughing his field backwards and sowing it with salt while singing to the winds, and how Palamedes unveils the stratagem by laying Ulysses' newborn son in the way of the plough. The rest is history. If Ulysses' ploy had succeeded, there would be no hero's *Odyssey* for sure. But wouldn't Penelope have been better off?

To each epoch its ambivalent Odyssey. Brexit is only beginning and yet this political odyssey of ours is already replete with flawed heroes and monsters, acts of courage and trickery, misjudgements and delusions, terrible tempests and dead calm. Albeit torn apart, the British ship of state has managed to stay afloat as continental horizons recede into the distance, and Europe's early 'we already miss you' recedes into the past. From wherever you are watching, you may have called this political drama a bewildering mess. But admit it: what an extraordinary democratic mess this has been.

What have we learned? At the very least that our democracies need tender loving care. If so, we must find shared languages in which to conduct our democratic conversation across the many divides that both infuriate and enrich us.

This book is a quest for one such language. It was born a few months after the referendum as my way to tell the story – my 'three screams' as my friend Anne says. It became an illustrated Brexit journal, a collection of vignettes and images, a subtext for the daily sound and fury of the negotiations filtered through the language of myth. Over the last two years, it crystallised as a play in three acts, with protagonists both foreign and familiar: Ulysses and Penelope of course, but also Moses and Pharaoh, Zeus and Artemis, Narcissus, Oedipus, Jocasta, Laius and Antigone, Chrysippus and Pelops, Theseus and the Minotaur, Ariadne, Iphigenia, Clytemnestra and Agamemnon, Arachne, Prometheus, Pandora, Icarus, Sisyphus and Tantalus, Lachesis, Clotho and Atropos. Their contemporary resonance is hinted at but ultimately up to you, dear reader.

A journey through Brexit mythology is bound to frustrate anyone who is only interested in one or the other, Brexit or myths. For the rest of you, recovering Brexit addicts, mythology aficionados, cynics, idealists, pragmatists, welcome to the theatre of recognition. This is my plea for acknowledging each other's stories, with their many variants, ambiguities and contradictions, short of the expectation that we can ever agree, but in the hope that we can at least enter a spirit of mutual recognition as we confront our experiences and visions of the world. And in this spirit, this is a call for a mutually respectful, do-no-harm Brexit – the smartest, kindest, gentlest Brexit possible in our hard-edged epoch of resentment and frustration. Wouldn't a more civilised intercourse befit the peoples of Europe?

Here, the medium is the message. At one point in his journey, Ulysses famously binds himself to his ship's mast in order to experience the divine songs of the Sirens without joining them while the crew ensure safe passage for themselves by putting beeswax in their ears. Once unbound, Ulysses remembers the truths sung by the magical creatures, while no longer being subject to their lure. It seemed fitting for me to embark on the adventure of crowdfunding thanks to Unbound, the intrepid publisher that frees authors from the strictures of more formal publishing. Once upon a time, authors published pamphlets through subscriptions, adding the names of their sponsors at the end of their book. This time around, we have the internet to help us: eighteenth century meets twenty-first century.

The book was fed by conversations with family, friends, colleagues and strangers on all sides of the Brexit saga before and after the referendum. For their enthusiastic and thoughtful responses, I would like to thank the many participants in conferences where I presented some of these ideas, including in Florence, Dublin, Göettingen, Oxford, Miami, Rabat, The Hague and London. I would like to thank, in particular, Anthony Barnett, Rainer Baubock, Richard Bellamy, Leandra Bias, Cyril Bouyeure, Samuel Bruce, Richard Buxton, Luisa Cale, Anne Deighton, Catherine De Vries, Antonio Estella, John Farnell, Adrian Favel, Nora Fisher-Onar, Paul Flather, Danuta Garton Ash, Timothy Garton Ash, Anna Gerbrandy, Ruth Harris, Andrew Hurrell, Tae-Yeoun Keum, Nina Kruglikova, Robert Madelin, Rama Mani, Anand Menon, Iain Pears, Simona Piattoni, Jean-Bernard Tanqueray, Yaacov Yadgar. Special gratitude to Jennifer Welsh for suggesting that I write this story as a book after a first lecture at the European University Institute in Florence in October 2016; to my wonderful assistant Kira Huju; to Nat Copsey and his colleagues for bringing me into their tent; to Ivan Rogers for our countless exchanges; to Brooks Newmark for his indefatigable encouragement and support throughout; to Financial Markets Policy Foundation in memory of Max Watson; and to the review *Standpoint*, its editor Daniel Johnson and assistant editor Boadicea Meath Baker, for publishing an early version in the summer of 2017. I thank the Unbound team, for trusting in the project from the beginning and for their precious support, in particular John Mitchinson and Ella Chappell, as well as Catherine Best, Kwaku Osei-Afrifa, Richard Collins, Hayley Shepherd and Mark Bowsher. Thank you also to Sue Taylor for her photography and to Mel Brigg for his inspiring cover art.

Last but not least, I thank wholeheartedly the trusting 300 (!) without whom this book could never have been published – to my crowd of funders, thank you for your support. You gave me the confidence (and the incentive) to write up the story.

I owe most of all to my family: my father, whose passionate retelling of Greek myths as bedtime stories shaped my imaginary flights from early childhood; my mother, whose Second World War story as a Franco-German girl instilled in me the instinct of Europeanness as survival; my brother Dimitri, who taught me the love of history; and on the British side of the Channel, my daughter Daphne, who faithfully provoked me with her probing questions all the way through; my son Ari, who offered his beautiful artwork and philosophical musings; and my husband Simon, whose

Like Ulysses, we don't always trust our will power. We understand that it may be good to restrict our own freedom in order to be forced to act in our best interest. Europeans chose to tie their hands to a mast of mutual legal commitments to resist the sirens of free riding. When unbound do we gain or lose control? Has Britain chosen unboundness in spite or because it is the most law-abiding EU state? Is it harder to let go of a mast if you have carved it yourself? Once unbound, can you still stay on the ship?
Ulysses and the Sirens, Otto Greiner, *c.* 1900.

uncompromisingly contrary spirit and unrelenting rejection of easy answers have long kept me on my toes.

To all of you and to my new readers, and in the spirit of crowd-sourcing, this book is an invitation to continue or join the conversation and weave other versions together, with new threads and new colours.*

Let the conversation begin!

Oxford, October 2018

*Readers are invited to take part in the conversation at: http://kalypsonicolaidis.com/unbound

Introduction

Brexit Means Brexit

In the beginning was the word, and the word was Brexit. But nobody quite knew what that word meant.

And then the oracle spoke: 'Brexit means Brexit'.

What did it say about Britain's exit from the EU that the word itself – the most googled word in the UK in 2016 – became the preferred contender for its elucidation? No matter that many different messages were received, in Britain or on the continent: 'we will not backtrack', 'no halfway house', 'we are ready to pay the price', versus 'it's your choice', 'it's all over', 'good riddance', 'you will suffer the consequences'.

Since the June 2016 referendum, pundits and ordinary citizens have found countless ways of dealing with the ubiquitous tautology. Glee, despair or remorse on the departing British ship. Hurt, sadness or spite on the abandoned European shores. Elation or anger. Miracle! Debacle! Studied indifference.

But what happened next, *after* plodding through our emotions? We rationalised, gave reason a go. We turned to the past, trying to explain why this happened. We turned to the future, trying to predict what will happen or prescribe what should happen. Explanations and implications. Sociology and policy. Everyone's hopes and fears converged on an EU legal and political process called Article 50. Its trigger gave us two years to take it in: Brexit really does mean Brexit. We promise, you will not be asked to change your mind.

And yet we are left with the original question: what does Brexit actually 'mean'? More specifically, what does 'means' mean in 'Brexit means Brexit'?

Meaning matters beyond the minutiae of negotiations. Whatever happens next, we know that there will always be people, trucks, firms, diplomats, trains, diseases, insults, fads or songs crossing the Channel. A few more or a few less. And yet Brexit is an event whose ultimate historical meaning we have yet to fathom.

Meaning matters, for Brexit has also been a battle of narratives whose protagonists have spared no shortcuts. Which story was to become ascendant through the rough and tumble of Brexit politics would in no small measure determine UK–EU relations and perhaps even the future of the EU itself for years to come.

Meaning matters in this story, for it affects our individual and collective sense of identity and connectedness. Meaning processes feelings, but does not transcend them. Meaning is about making sense together in all senses of the word, making things apparent to our senses by reverting to stories that are familiar to us and pervade our societies. Whether we think of ourselves as religious, humanist, atheist, spiritual or simply human, we are sustained by socially shared stories, amorphous assemblages that form the implicit background to our common norms and expectations. When such hidden narratives rise to the surface, they often borrow from the qualities of past fantastic tales, which help give shape to what we see. They become 'mythology'.

Myth-mania

Let me start with what 'myth' does *not* mean in these pages. In casual language we tend to think of myth as referring to false or disingenuous stories which mask the true reality – whether of power, of hypocrisy or of ideology – which we, the observers, can see. And thus we enter some sort of myth war where I call your beliefs myths and you reply, no, these are truths. This is not what I mean here.

Neither am I commenting on myths as the name we give to history on testosterone, the bits of history which either we or others use to define who we are and who the other is. Historical myths appeal to our collective memory and how it forges our collective identity. These are stories we tell ourselves about ourselves as peoples, whatever this word may mean. Some take historical myths at face value, happy to own them, as it were. They may refrain from calling them myths and instead call them 'proud moments' or 'historical precedents'. Others throw the same stories back in their face as myths or simply smile at their naive propensity to twist the meaning of history to fit an utterly different present. They call this pattern 'anachronism' or such.

It has been clear to any casual observer that the debate between Leavers and Remainers has been powered by different historical mythologies, or at least different readings of British and European history, to do with Westminster, 'mother of all parliaments'; Henry VIII, first Brexiter from the Vatican 500 years ago; Pitt, Wellington and Trafalgar against revolutionary France and continental imperialism; and the twentieth-century wars of course. Oh and let's not forget Queen Boudicca, who defied the Romans by destroying Londinium...

Which bits do we choose from the 'thousand years of history'? Those which British entry into the EU is supposed to have ended, by surrendering to the continent? Or those which Brexit is supposed to have ended, rejecting 950 years of intermingling since the Norman victory at Hastings? Does it make sense to invoke history at all in order to decide, say, on what grounds we trade together, letting dead men tie the hands of the living? Isn't it more dangerous to over-remember than to forget? Beware. Meanings are not neatly contained in historical memory. 'If we open a quarrel between the past and the present,' said Winston Churchill, 'we shall find that we have lost the future.' And yet, as they say, the future is the place where we will pass all the time that we still have to live!

Nevertheless, the lessons we pretend to extract from history hold great sway. Indeed, the dozen or so 'Brexit novels' published in the run-up to the Brexit vote have all, one way or another, purported to draw lessons from history either for the present or for the not-too-distant future, whereby brave British rebels rise against a 'brave new Europe' from which escape seems impossible. These novels may aim to take on the 'myth' of a benign EU, but they are in turn accused of peddling the myth of an omnipotent EU as the latest instance of *translatio imperii* ('transference of empire'), the deadly drive of great unifiers turning the continent into their plaything. The Brexit saga thus features a clash of political myths of origins: the myth powering English nationalism versus the myth of European unity. Each must be put in its proper place.

Admittedly, we humans have long constructed political myths for more benign reasons without acknowledging it. As Harari reminds us, the value of our money or the existence of something called my nation are *Homo sapiens'* clever collective fictions to ensure the species' survival. We are just oblivious to the optical illusion.

But we can try and change our angle. As when mythology is used as a term of art to deconstruct the ways our contemporary societies think and behave, something so-called post-structuralists like to do. Roland Barthes famously sought to expose the many ways modern myths, inspired by older ones, oppress or mask the true reality of political and market power, through the bourgeois images and practices of the 1950s, commercials, fads and the like. Powerful stuff, which inspired Peter Conrad's captivating retelling in *Mythomania*. While I too believe that myths constitute 'a language that does not want to die' and that we must ask *cui bono* (who benefits) and from what stories, this book is not a post-structuralist tract.

Instead we will journey on the other side of the moon...

Brexit Mythology

For behind and beyond collective memory or societal mythology, my aim is more metaphorical. I suggest that we may want to explore and exploit anew great archetypal myths – sacred narratives that can provide a less contested terrain for our conversation, time-immemorial stories that have been there all along to make sense of our confusion, our yearning for redemption, our desire to know that meanings echo through time and space, across societies and the tragi-comedy of human affairs. These stories offer us countless reincarnations and connect to the visceral nature of our history of the present, and yet do not ask us to take sides, at least initially.

Could it help our conversation, then, to explore the meaning of Brexit as ancient mythology? To juxtapose parallel and incommensurable meanings under the shadow of great archetypes, and treat Brexit, like all such archetypes, as a dramatic pivot around a moment, with a before and an after (before and after the parting of the Red Sea, before and after Icarus fell, before and after Oedipus knew)? And in so doing, to somehow connect a feature of *being* – to be or not to be European – with a feature of *doing* – to stay or not to stay in the EU. It is in making this connection between past and future visible that myths acquire meaning, allowing for an infinite retelling in infinite circumstances, and yet serving as metaphorical beacons for our collective imagination.

Brexiters have been accused of making a career out of creating myths around Europe. Is it not time that myths take their revenge and that we reinvent Brexit and Europe out of myths?

In this spirit, I suggest that the meaning of Brexit can be told through the prism of three canonical myths, or mythical themes, each connecting being and doing in a different way: stories of Exodus, stories of Reckoning, and stories of Sacrifice.

- *Exodus* makes Brexit a story about British exceptionalism, the claim that Britain was never truly European, and therefore that this is a British problem and yet also a testimony to the EU's incapacity to accommodate 'it', a renegade.
- *Reckoning* brings the story back to the EU's shores, with Brexit a harbinger of difficult truths uttered by sceptics of the Eurosceptic kind and beyond. Truths contested and rebutted, of course.
- *Sacrifice*, the third story, pervades both the Brexit and EU narrative, either in the classic idiom of heroic Sacrifice of the British by their continental neighbours for the sake of sacred principles or as condition of EU unity and progress. However, we must entertain the more ambiguous story of ironic Sacrifice whereby Brexit demonstrates that it is precisely because you are free to leave that you should not.

As with Oedipus and the Sphinx's riddle, at the heart of every myth is a drama of questioning, the urge to ask, to open closed doors, to mould a space of suspended meanings around unanswerable questions. In this sense, the three mythical archetypes explored in the following pages can help subvert the meanings of the dominant Brexit narratives which they both convey and transcend, those of *exceptionalism*, *Euroscepticism* and *pluralism* – each purporting to supply definitive truths, and each endorsed by different camps.

Whether these mythical stories echo most faithfully the voice of the world itself, as Francis Bacon would have it, or whether they simply constitute a common referent, we feel we have a sense of what Prometheus' hubris, Pandora's box or 'Herculean tasks' mean.

Here I borrow from the Greek, Roman and biblical traditions, leaving open the question as to whether these stories are universal, with variants in all traditions, religions and languages. Indeed, 'classical' mythology plainly signals that Greek and Roman mythology serve as the mythological databank of the Western world. But does this not reflect the Eurocentric character of the Brexit saga itself – 'the rest of the world' watching with a mix of fascination, bafflement and amusement?

That the world is fully disenchanted, free from mythologies, is itself a modern mythology. These myths belong to us all, each of us entitled to appropriate them as we please, as Stephen Fry, for instance, brilliantly demonstrated in his magnificent recent book *Mythos*.

I am not religious, but I remember the stories that enchanted me as a child, told by a Greek father exiled in Paris. Greeks like to say that at home their classical myths are still very much alive. Is this the stuff of tourist guides? Perhaps. But, if so, it is also the stuff of many worlds explored by schoolkids far beyond Greece: which child or adolescent (and their parents) hasn't read or seen mythology-inspired adventures, like the hugely popular Percy Jackson stories by Rick Riordan, telling of a present-day demigod reminiscent of Perseus whose quests and combats among the Olympians are set in today's New York? Who can resist J. R. R. Tolkien, J. K. Rowling or Philip Pullman when they dream up entire new mythological worlds for us? Mythology is everywhere, whether we like it or not, through films, ideas, politics, music, images. Myths help us understand who we are or pretend to be, and where our collective obsessions come from. Each generation reinvents them, fit for its purposes.

By invoking archetypal myths to discuss politics, however, I am open to accusations of ignoring 2,000 years of political philosophy, which developed precisely as anti-myth, the commitment to advancing propositions that can be assessed critically, found to be false and replaced, from Plato's praise of reason, or *logos*, to Karl Popper's urgent post-war appeal to systematic reasoning as the bulwark against barbarity. It is true that some extreme political movements promote an ugly mythologised view of politics having to do with blood, heroes and demonising others. Nevertheless, the rest of us can chart our own course between elevating myths as ancestral wisdom and rejecting them as ancestral naivety.

...A space of suspended meanings... *Mythomania,* Ari Saunders, 2018

Plato may have distinguished between *mythos* and *logos*, fiction and reason, in order to advocate a radical shift from the first to the second, and yet he himself employed myths to help us experience reality, as Tae-Yeoun Keum argues, and as we will see with the myth of Er. It is undeniable that myths pervade any field of enquiry which seeks to connect individuals and collectives, be it in politics, psychology, sociology or anthropology. Myths offer a bulwark against absolutism of all types, philosophical or religious, disciplinary or nationalist. Writing in great despair during the Second World War, the central European philosophers Max Horkheimer and Theodor Adorno argued against the destructive power of myths and yet implied that they could help us recover new forms of human solidarity and save the enlightenment promise from itself by softening the hard edges of modernity. Ulysses may have been the first exemplar of the isolated, alienated subject of the modern world conditioned by instrumental reason, but he nevertheless sought enchantment by the sirens. Crucially, Horkheimer and Adorno's vision was predicated on rejecting a regressive romantic view of the new as a resurgence of the old, thus eschewing a nostalgic search for origins and lost

11

meanings through the jargon of authenticity which had just fuelled the deadliest of European ideologies.

But forget grand philosophical debates. I believe the most important insight we can draw from myth is this. Myths are here to remind us of our fundamental ontological predicament in a multiverse: that what happens in reality is both irremediably inevitable and absolutely surprising. The great characters of the stories told through mythology *freely* collaborate in bringing about their pre-ordained fate; each of their personal acts meant to affirm their individual sovereignty and yet combining in fulfilling a destiny. The freedom they have passed on to us through the ages is about the choices we still have even as we read the writing on the wall.

For myths do not emerge from the collective soul of humankind in order to provide easy answers to our human predicament. They are not keys to unlock the human psyche, but stand in as its distorted fragments. Always ambiguous, they serve as ever-retreating truth mirages to tickle our minds and entrench mystery. This is what both religious and secular exegesis is about, exploring encrypted meanings hidden in the gaps between conscious and unconscious, reason and desire. And beyond that, myths can be subverted to offer the promise of critical disenchantment, as we embrace rather than decipher their contradictions.

And so with Brexit. From an infinite number of narrative branches, we can extract the first elements of a philosophy of separation: is this Exodus a curse or a blessing? The result of destiny or banishment? If Reckoning is the price for a terrible deed, whose deed are we talking about and how collective must the final punishment be? What is the point of Armageddon, if no one stays around to hear fate's 'I told you so'? What is the point of Sacrifice, if the message gets lost in the fumes of the pyre? Does the scapegoat absorb everyone's sins or expose them for all to see? Ultimately, whoever's Sacrifice it is, is it not always in vain?

It is important to the myths and meanings at stake that these questions remain unresolved. To be sure, myths can be manipulated to score points and assert simplistic world views. All the more reason to hang on to the questions they raise.

Most importantly, if myths cannot pretend to give meaning to our predicament, the infinite ambiguities contained in each myth world can at least open up spaces for our democratic conversation, prompts for mutual engagement. Myths can offer us a shared vocabulary (one among many others, of course) to enrich this conversation, one which embraces rather than scorns recurring paradoxes, contingent meanings and ambiguous messages. They don't override but overlay rational reasoning. Their intense symbolic pulse can help us lower ours as we debate politics and agree to disagree. Their grammar may not let us debunk the other side with mere data but nor does it let us get away with simplistic slogans. And their open-endedness allows each of us to reinvent them and creatively engage with the political on our own terms. Let us welcome timeless mythical protagonists, then, as characters in our democratic public sphere.

I exploit archetypal myths in order to better delve into deeply held tribal beliefs about the meaning of Brexit, as these meanings cross or collide in the dark: Leavers versus Remainers, Leavers versus other Leavers, young versus old, cynics versus idealists, Europeans versus non-Europeans, sovereigntists or cosmopolitans, each tribal in their own way. Sometimes, entire categories of people (the French, the working class, xenophobes, Europhiles) may at least be perceived as sharing a given meaning which defines who they are. But most of us find meanings as individuals; and some of us hold several meanings in our heads at once, often mutually incompatible ones, and recognise them as tenuous and fluid, open to constant reinterpretation.

We may not be capable of seeing the world simultaneously through the minds of many different peoples, what Kant called an enlarged perspective, but at least we can try basic empathy for other tribes' stories. Our apparent inconsistency may simply reflect the contradictions of the world itself. (In this spirit, I need to own up to my own ambivalent 'we' in this book, as I move between 'we' as British to 'we' as EU nationals living in Britain, to 'we' as Europeans in general, to 'we' as, well, human.)

In sum, we may be better able to agree to disagree on whether Brexit is good or bad, whether it is about British or European dysfunctionality, or the plight of losers, or the arrogance of winners, if we can engage each other through Brexit mythology.

Don't get me wrong. This is not a Habermasian agenda in which one hopes that irrevocably opposed positions find reasonable agreement through debating around shared stories, although the Brexit saga reminds us how adrift we are from German philosopher Jürgen Habermas's ideal of the public sphere.

Instead, I believe that there is often no rational solution to political conflict; we know this from all the great mythical stories. As Amos Oz famously quipped, tragedy after all is a clash between right and right. Brexit is not only a negotiation between partially conflicting, partially overlapping interests, as liberals would have it. If you believe in agonistic pluralism – that political conflicts can never be overcome, only channelled peacefully – your best hope is to help shape the arena where your differences are confronted, not to erase those differences.

In this book I make a plea that each other's stories be acknowledged, with their many variants, ambiguities and contradictions. In so doing, we may come to understand that if Brexit were to unfold in a true spirit of mutual recognition and respect we would all be the better for it. And in this spirit of recognition, I have from the outset called for a 'do-no-harm Brexit', a kind of Hippocratic oath to be applied to the societies involved. I hope that such an imperative will come to pervade the future relationship between sides which are bound to remain intimate rivals. Brexit 2.0, as they call it.

And so it is with the three meanings of Brexit. None is a simple story, but each offers variants which, when combined, leave our collective future more open than we currently fear. Each offers a space in which to engage strange or alien viewpoints, and to use the narratives kaleidoscopically to shed light on each other. Even as we inevitably hold on to our prejudices (or are they convictions?), a smarter, kinder Brexit should be possible in our hard-edged age of resentment and frustration, if only for the sake of our children.

In short, this book is a polemic against those who see the world in black and white. It contains images because they can perhaps serve as the best mediation between our individual and social imagination, like 'imaginal animals' as philosopher Chiara Bottici put it. Myth may spring from deep human emotions, but the expression of a feeling is not the feeling itself – it is emotion turned into an image. These images can often be liberating, offering clues to the indeterminacy of the stories, but they can also be oppressive, imprisoning us in dominant meanings. It is up to us how we choose to see them.

A final caveat. This book is an invitation to participate in a conversation. It is neither a Kantian, nor a Freudian, nor a Nietzschean, nor an anti-modernist tract. Nor do I claim to present a specific kind of scholarly take on the relevant literature, be it biblical and rabbinical exegesis, modern theological writings on demythologising sacred texts, the ethics of Greek myths à la Bernard Williams, or the great debates in socio-cultural anthropology and ethnography around figures such as Claude Levi-Strauss, Edmund Leach, Eric Dodds, Eduard Fraenkel, Ernst Cassirer, Roland Barthes or René Girard, engaged in structural analysis, post-structuralism or deconstruction. Nor do I offer a speculation on the formative influence of Judaism, Christianity, Islam or ancient Greece on our modern political psyche. Snippets of insights from these traditions may have found their way into the pages that follow, but my fascination and respect for, say, the rabbinical tradition which sees the Bible as the repository of an infinite number of truths does not affect my atheism whatsoever. Avivah Zornberg, one of my true inspirations, calls the Torah a world of evolving revelation. This for me has been true of all the archetypal stories we shall encounter or rediscover together.

...A dramatic pivot around a moment, with a before and an after... *The Flight of Icarus*, Gabriel Picart, 2004

15

Exodus

Brexit Means the UK Will Leave

The most straightforward and widely shared meaning of Brexit, both in the UK and on the European continent, has simply been that it is about Britain – Britain's prerogative and thus Britain's problem – and Britain's fault. *Brexit simply means that the UK will leave the EU*, for better or for worse.

In the Brexiters' version, they have been leading a people enslaved by the shackles of Brussels on a journey of escape, unwittingly echoing the heroic tale of another people escaping slavery in Egypt, served by the stubbornness of prophets bargaining with Pharaoh over terms of departure, and complete with the parting of the seas. Egyptians, Europeans: let the people go!

Leavers disagreed on the ethics of unleashing some kind of modern plague on the wretched Europeans if they tried to stop them. They disagreed on whether forty years of wandering in the wilderness before reaching the Promised Land ought to be part of

...Complete with the parting of the seas... *Exodus*, Mel Brigg, 2010

the package. And they disagreed on whether liberation ought to be pain-free or painful. But they agreed on one thing: the Sea shall part.

Of course, an exodus – a mass departure by a large group to escape a hostile environment – does not have to be the mark of an elected people (after all, it is the 'ordinary' people that want to leave, isn't it?). History has shown that exoduses of all types can be the mark of a curse. Either way, leaving is destiny. Whether or not those embarking on the journey were exceptional to start with, any Exodus story is a story of exceptionalism.

And so the story goes. Brexit is a very British thing, an outcome that can be seen as over-determined by British exceptionalism: by geography (the island nation); by history (the un-invaded nation); by politics (the mother-of-all-parliaments nation); or by class culture (the Euroscepticism-as-identity nation). Brexiters disagree on how far back we need to go to anchor Brexit into a grand historical narrative that defines its special status in Europe: 1,000 years since the last invasion by the Normans; 350 years since a glorious revolution which entrenched parliamentary sovereignty; 200 years since the onset of industrialisation which turned Britain, its industries and finance into the centre of the world *beyond* Europe; seventy years since its continental cousins demanded yet another rescue, demonstrating their repeated folly. Whatever the historical benchmark, British disengagement from the EU is simply a reversion to type, the defence of what Andrew Gamble called 'a world island' with its eternal vaguely antagonistic attitude towards continental Europe.

In this story, the tabloid newspapers did not cook up the British Eurosceptic brew; they simply stirred it. This is the only EU country where more of those polled 'disliked' than 'liked' the EU over the past decades. No wonder that the British uniquely view Europeans in their midst as 'migrants' rather than fellow European citizens – even while arguably more willing to employ them without discrimination than any other member state. No wonder they are the most impatient about the EU's flaws, more ready than others to leave the club altogether rather than simply moan about it like the French, the Italians or the Poles.

So, according to the UK's new prophets leading the Exodus, to defend British sovereignty against EU encroachment is to depart for a Promised Land of non-CAP (Common Agricultural Policy) and non-regulated milk and honey, where we are not governed by others but do the governing ourselves. Forget Rivers of Blood, ours is a Sea of Hope!

> If we strip the Torah's Exodus story to its bare bones, this is what happens: the Israelites had been welcomed to Egypt when led there by Joseph, but were later enslaved for 400 years. Moses, Pharaoh's adoptive son, who might have lived in 1500 BC, flees to Midian after killing a slavemaster. When instructed by his God, Yahweh, to return to Egypt to demand that the new pharaoh free the Israelite slaves, he is fearful of the task, perhaps because of his speech impediment, and resists until Yahweh agrees to send his brother Aaron with him as his spokesman. All the brothers ask of Pharaoh at the beginning of their mission is a three-day break to worship. But Pharaoh and his advisers are unyielding and instead punish the slaves by cutting their supplies of straw while still insisting that they meet their daily quota for the manufacture of bricks. Many slaves complain, but Moses perseveres, performing escalating wonders to convince Pharaoh to play ball, turning his staff into a snake, polluting the Nile with blood, unleashing on the hapless Egyptians plagues of frogs, gnats and flies, sending infestations of boils, hailstorms, locusts and darkness. And yet Pharaoh reneges on every deal he has made following each round of disaster. The final strike: Moses tells him all the firstborn of Egypt will die overnight, including his own son. And yet even as he seems to relent under this terrible threat, Pharaoh pursues the Israelites all the way to the Red Sea, sealing his fate. The Israelites end up wandering for forty years in the wilderness, where Moses will receive the Ten Commandments, before finally reaching the Promised Land where only women and children will enter. There will be wars and lost tribes, and eventually a new Exodus.

Brexit will be our catharsis, a voyage from self-doubt to self-rediscovery. The old Anglosphere will be our new Jerusalem, connecting Great Britain's future with its glorious past, and the English heartland with its British parts. For, in order to draw on the imperial Britain of the past, English nationalism as the hidden cause of Brexit must now define some sort of identity for itself as the offshore 'other' of the European continent, a continent where being multinational means something very different. The more European tongues echo inside its cities' double-deckers, the greater the appeal of Churchill's 'community of English-speaking peoples'. The great escape from the EU allows for a politically correct Englishness which loves 'our' Pakistanis and paints EU-centredness (read favouring EU nationals over Commonwealth nationals) as parochial. Here, it is not Britain that is narrowing its horizons, but its continental counterparts. The whole thing wasn't about the racism or immigrants, it was about freedom. Ah, the particular mix of triumph and drudgery that is a Great Escape! Can it be not only from the EU but from all the memories that continue to weigh us down? Let's move on!

Ironically, images of another kind of Exodus of the non-metaphorical kind were conjured up to motivate Brexit voters: a column of Syrian refugees who had not chosen their Exodus. No country along their route seemed to want anything else than to let

...Where the Europeans are spared the plagues... *Seventh Plague of Egypt*, John Martin, 1823.

these people go. And yet, their Exodus fuelled the metaphorical Exodus which occupies us here.

The Exodus story of liberation of a people is not only a heroic tale sung by Brexiters. Eurofederalists on the continent admit that letting this people go is quite a relief. The British are a people typically cut off from the continent by any trace of 'fog in the Channel', a continent whose aspiration to harmony they never really understood. De Gaulle was right, say the Eurofederalists, even if for the wrong reasons: the Brits are simply 'not European enough' to remain part of this EU. Let them delude themselves in their fantasyland. 'Tired of fog? Try the Frogs!' teased French recruiters with glee in the early Brexit days...

But... Exodus-lite?

But our myths, of course, never quite mean what they seem to mean.

The Exodus of the Israelites as told in the Torah, the second book of the Old Testament, has inspired an infinite retelling in the celebrations of Pesach, an infinite re-enacting by groups fleeing for their freedom throughout history, and countless reinventions by revolutionaries calling for liberation from oppression, all part and parcel of the incessant forward march of humanity as a whole. Exodus stands as both a religious and secular narrative encapsulating them all *and* uniquely each of them, as Thomas Jefferson and Benjamin Franklin thought when they designed the Great Seal for their new nation, the United States (one of them preferring the opening of the seas, the other the subsequent march in the wilderness).

Not all subsequent experiences of deliverance need be seen as pale replicas of the original. They can be simply echoes fit for their own time.

Most of us cannot claim access to the meanderings of the biblical Exodus, access to all the counter-voices implied or silenced in its triumphant master narrative, the alternative subversive readings woven in its Midrashic interpretations, the endless questioning, heretical meanings, allowing the text, the play, the saga, to be read in so many ways. We can only heed the undecidability of it all as Moses, the teacher, stages the process of learning for his people, the original tribes and the generations after them.

Fast forward 2,000 years. There is little hint of the sublime in our story. This Brexit of ours is not an Exodus whose purpose is 'to know that I am God'. No God, no revelation, no virtuoso prophet, no hearing of voices, no smoking mountain, no transcendental space of loneliness. No hint of the spiritual in Brexit.

But neither the writer, the reader nor the protagonist needs to believe in God, in Moses, in the story itself, for Exodus to be invoked. Some may replace the words God or Prophet with *destiny* and *leadership*. But if the original Exodus has left unconscious memory traces in all of us, it can serve a variety of purposes: as grand inspiration, as a cautionary tale, as the other side's deluded referent to be mocked. Some might find our game of mirrors irrelevant; if so, fine. Others might find it irreverent, but only if they take it literally. The sublime can ricochet into triviality and yet still speak of our current predicament.

Perhaps we also remember that we have been there before. As recounted by Chris Coltrin, when John Martin, Francis Danby and David Roberts painted their vision of the Exodus in the 1820s, they reflected a widespread British belief in a coming apocalypse where the country, the modern-day incarnation of the ancient Israelites, would be delivered rather than destroyed, immune from continental turmoil thanks to its more benign form of monarchical government. Their Exodus stood in for British exception too, but one at the service of social reformist ideals.

In our Brexit as mundane Exodus, all the original themes are subdued and subverted, disguised as facetious, diminished as politics. But the messianic tone is there, unquestionably, both sides playing to an audience, acting out their own pedagogy and counter-pedagogy.

We may recognise the superposition between different narratives, a grand narrative of liberation and a darker narrative of panic and confusion, an understanding that authentic freedom is framed by necessity, but that necessity can be a choice even in an interdependent world.

We may recognise the ambivalence of a relationship, the hidden intimacy between Pharaoh and Moses, intimate rivals, antagonist kins, behind the great face-off. Revolutionaries tend to be rebels against the very system that raised them. One intimate step further, we may be reminded of Freud's Moses, an Egyptian noble who, he believed, gave the Israelites the monotheist religion of Ikhnaton that Egypt had disdained, but who ultimately had to renounce his split allegiance and abandon his Egyptian roots. It all fits.

We may recognise that even in the biblical Exodus, liberty does not follow liberation as day follows night; a return to Egypt is always there potentially, ominously. A 'stiff-necked' and stubborn people will not necessarily do what it is told; it is simultaneously eager and unprepared to leave Egypt behind; it never wanted to go so far when it all started.

Then as now, we the reader, the observer, the actor must take in the way every possibility is explored, rejected and resurrected in a catharsis of dreaming, speaking, screaming possible futures.

Most prosaically, the Exodus narrative raises obvious questions. Can you choose to just go in today's world? What happens when you do not have supernatural power on your side? Does Brexit fit into the family of political deliverance if the pharaoh of *this* EU story is in truth a political dwarf, or if no one in the UK has truly experienced slavery, from an EU master or any other master for that matter, until, that is, we surrender to technological shackles? If Exodus became over time the paradigm of revolutionary politics, as recounted by the philosopher Michael Walzer, does it make sense to invoke precedents for Brexit which were precisely about liberation from the British Empire? Whatever the answer, can we not imagine a modern-day Exodus-lite, where the Europeans are spared the plagues and the Brits are spared the endless wandering in the desert?

He Did Not Listen

Persecution and embittered lives: the Exodus saga starts with slavery. In Egypt, we find a world of constriction, a world of hell, a world of formal lifeless images, inescapable for all who live there. We confront a pharaoh whose words are irrevocable, whose heart

...we hear his silent verdict: 'No slave ever escaped from Egypt.' *Joseph Dwelleth in Egypt*, James Tissot, c. 1896–1902

is impenetrable, an amoral autist. Before the Israelites' request for freedom, we meet him defying life itself, ordering a separation of the sexes among them to curb their reproductive energy. We find a man, the power he represents, ominously afflicted with an essential deafness – 'he did not listen' is the leitmotiv of the plague narrative. Here he is, again and again, incapable of knowledge, incapable even of admitting not knowing. He will have submission, not contract. His uncompromising orders allow no room for interpretation, nor can he interpret the other side's requests. Even confronted with the relentless plagues, we hear his silent verdict: 'No slave ever escaped from Egypt.' No wonder Pharaoh will not let the people go.

And yet other meanings open up like trees of probabilities, probable truths and possible imaginaries.

Why does God need to harden Pharaoh's heart as he prepares to hear the last plague threats? To underline his imperviousness to all appeals, either from the other side or from his own, or to actually make him impervious? Is it not problematic that such hardening may bring about a terrible outcome? Why does Moses, benevolent Moses, assume he will not be heard uttering his threats, when being heard would spare innocent people, albeit Egyptians? Does he hope that the warnings will at last have an effect on some of the Egyptians?

Perhaps it only makes sense to stretch the drama of warning followed by resistance, yielding followed by denial, if this is a story that must be told. Here we have it. No pharaonic stubbornness means no epic story.

But how stubborn can you be? What kind of compulsive disorder has possessed the Egyptian king to enact such obstinate refusal? Can we not contemplate the idea that Pharaoh has a higher purpose? Could he be trying to approximate an ideal of power? Deluding himself that impenetrable means invulnerable: the inexpressive catatonic sealed Sphinx...? To hear, of course, is to make oneself vulnerable.

...Perhaps it is simply the fear of vulnerability that lies at the heart of his expressed arrogance... *Pharaoh Notes the Importance of the Jewish People*, James Tissot, c. 1896–1902

In sum, the original Exodus gives us: a pharaonic power who will not yield and whose stubbornness makes the story real, the impression that nothing seems to release his ever-tightening stranglehold on the Israelites, a story requiring just enough resistance, just enough yielding, for it to be the story that it needs to be.

But one can also read an alternative Egyptian narrative at the heart of Exodus, the story of an absurd exercise in gratuitous destruction, sinister and hateful, where damage control is the best we can do.

If so, is this not also a story of pharaonic weakness mirroring a story of omnipotence? Zornberg tells us how, in Midrashic literature, Pharaoh may have become a prototype for the pathology of arrogance, even conceiving of himself as generating his own greatness, but perhaps it is simply the fear of vulnerability that lies at the heart of his expressed arrogance.

Why does Pharaoh not say, we Egyptians would like you to stay, we still have so much to achieve together, please stay! Could there be another reason behind his rigidity? What if Pharaoh is paralysed by fear? Fear that some of the people under his rule might call upon their own imagination to reinterpret worlds which until now have been subject only to his own normative empire?

If so, would it not be easier for the Israelites to assuage the fear, bestow reassurances, thrive for common ground, sweet-talk the grand escape? Have *they* listened carefully enough to what Pharaoh has and has not said?

How Many Tribes?

That would be assuming the rebels are in control of their agenda. But in truth, Egypt is a place where the Israelites themselves have lost their distinctiveness, their sense of purpose, even failing to resist assimilation. During 400 years living in Egypt (forty-six years of EU membership?) they certainly have had time to become natives, part of the complex pharaonic machine, admirers of the Egyptian ways. Integration can be gruesomely literal, as when they find their own babies wedged into the walls they have helped to build. And it is always incomplete. Too fertile, too different, too integrated: the lethal combination feeds the pharaoh's paranoid view that the Hebrews are disloyal, perfidious guests in our midst, and that Trojan horses would be ready at any time to destroy the grand imperial project from within. Let's not forget how, as a toddler, Moses, future overthrower of Egyptian law, had taken Pharaoh's crown and put it on his own head, thus enacting the newcomer's usurpation of power.

And so, aren't the Israelites responsible for their fate in Egypt rather than simply victims? Faced with their apathetic scepticism as he tries to free them, does Moses not fear that they may be better fit for slavery? Does he not fear his own inadequacy? Hence his audacious challenge to God: tell me, are they, how are they, fit for freedom?

In the Exodus story, there is a 'before' when the Hebrews even fail to realise their Egyptian exile and bondage, an apathetic people even in response to God's offer of redemption. Can a people be unredeemable? Indeed, as Pharaoh reacts to his demand for freedom by increasing the pressure on the Israelite slave workers, Moses protests: instead of ending their sufferings, his early requests have only made them worse! You may ask whether it isn't too early for Moses to complain that the promise is unfulfilled...

But you might also recognise the wisdom of a leader who cannot countenance the short-term pain of his people for long-term gain, thus rejecting the hallmark of every pathological ideology. Isn't it right to be concerned about that pain in the here and now, regardless of any grand future? Would it not be wrong to pursue a long-term mission with such perverse short-term effects?

...Why has thou done this to us... *The Exodus*, Horace William Petherick, 1839–1919

This may be the real thread of the Exodus story: how do you learn the language of freedom? What connects personal and collective constructions of meaning? Perhaps you may hear 'I do not wish to go free,' when they are really saying 'If I go I will not be free either,' or 'True freedom is to choose to stay.'

Whatever their meaning, the people's murmurings fill the Exodus narrative with a sense of generalised fearfulness, a feeling that deference never quite succeeds in overcoming diffidence towards our leaders, whoever appointed them.

And so, in spite of the magical tricks conjured up to impress Pharaoh's advisers, and despite the promise that they shall go free, many Israelites do not want to leave at all. There is no unanimity, even as Moses makes it clear to Pharaoh before the last plague that there will be no compromise: he and his people will 'go with our young and with our old, with our sons and with our daughters, with our flocks and with our herds, we will go.'

When later the Israelites complain in despair, 'Thou hast taken us away to die in the wilderness,' 'Why hast thou done this to us, that thou hast led us out of Egypt?', Moses replies: 'The Lord himself will fight for you. Just stay calm.'

‡

'Keep calm and carry on' eerily echoes the exhortation that can be seen on posters, mugs and tea towels in every souvenir shop in Great Britain. After all, like all revolutions, this cannot be a unanimous moment. As an English revolution, Brexit means England minus London, Cambridge or Bristol. As a British revolution, Brexit means the UK minus Scotland, Northern Ireland and Westminster. But it is a peaceful one. More than seventeen million of us used the ballot box, not the barricades, for this declaration of independence. That is good enough, isn't it?

Not really. What if we do not believe in your version of milk and honey, say the Scots, the Northern Irish or other tribes who elected to stay. We would be foolish to imagine a Promised Land on this little island! How do you expect us willingly to get lost in a legal and political no man's land, to leave a Euroland governed in our language, literally as well as ideologically, whose achievements like the single market, enlargement and free-trade deals with the rest of the world stand as blinding markers of British influence? When, even on the global scene, 'British' has become the voice of European diplomacy and Britain's waning power has been magnified for decades by its EU back office? In that land we are masters – masters of the treaties and masters of the agenda, not slaves!

For every Brit who still believes the voyage to be a shortcut to national greatness, there is another who believes Brexit to be a race towards a bleak dead end – the infamous cliff precipitating the country into a tumultuous sea, a sea definitely unlikely to part at our prophet's command. Project suicide, they call it.

What of these non-believers: Remainers split between reversers, clamouring for an exit from Brexit, and returners, hoping for a return to Europe post-Brexit? Among those who did not want to leave some would dislike even more the prospect of their people being seen by Pharaoh as ineffective rebels. But most of the resisting tribes have held to the last, searching for grounds to question the finality of the fateful decision.

And what of all those who refuse to leave Egypt, British citizens living in another European country, and join the Exodus – because they have grown too old for the journey or too attached to the life they have chosen?

What of the EU citizens who happen to live among the departing tribes, slaves of slaves? Will they all some day learn to appreciate that an Exodus is always an exercise in delayed gratification? And if the Exodus has turned us into 'friendly aliens', will we turn the title into a badge of honour or exchange it for British citizenship?

Or will the rebel tribes elect to exit Brexit and embark on their own 'Brexodus'? Confusingly for *our* story of Exodus, this is media speak for those who resist the romantic lure of Exodus by choosing to leave a Britain that is leaving the EU. These are the tribes who refuse to be let go, part of the growing tide of sad, angry, deceived, uprooted EU citizens who no longer feel at home on the British ship, or the businesses that cannot survive outside the EU/Egypt's ambit. While Brexit-as-Exodus embraces the imagination of those who, seeking to be free, do so by claiming their love of place, Brexodus becomes the fate of those whose life has been defined by space, the continental space, of which the island-place is only a small outpost.

‡

Forget the complexities. Moses' Exodus was not a consensual affair. This is a binary story, a tale of two Britains.

Some hear the tale of entrenched ancestral political geography, the Leaver-Remainer divide mirroring the camps of the Civil War when the conservative north and west supported king and court against the merchants and the liberal south, bolstered by the Scottish rebellion and Cromwellian Ireland. Is Brexit another variation on left vs right?

Or is this an utterly contemporary tale? Forget the old divides: region, class, church, party. This is a modern cultural war between the more or less young, schooled or urban, extroverts and introverts, between sides who differ on everything from the death penalty to art – even on sexual fantasies! – with moral and political trench lines drawn inside families across the country. And unsurprisingly, women are more prone to 'stay calm' in this story.

These are not passing opinions. Each side has absorbed its new identity with a passion: I Leaver, I Remainer. *They* are unpatriotic, traitors, cowards, unimaginative, rootless; *we* are patriotic, courageous, honest, irreverent. *They* are uneducated, irrational, insular, bigots, xenophobes, racists, dupes; *we* are open-minded, open-hearted, open *tout court*. My virtue is bigger than yours.

The Exodus version of the Brexit story exudes emotional clarity. Going or staying is believing, whichever side you are on, with oddly physical feelings, involving dead, torn skin, one side 'shackled to a European corpse', the other side 'amputated' from Europe's body politic. We can almost touch Hector's body being dragged behind Achilles' chariot under the walls of Troy, his native city.

Of Bond, the Modern Kind

Perhaps it boils down to the contrasting connotations of one word: bond. Bond as bondage or servitude for some, bond as the ties that bind for others. Shackles versus sharing.

But is it all that simple? 'House of bondage' meant that the Israelites were the toys of arbitrary power, a condition with no end in sight. In contrast, their covenant created a bond among them, freely and repeatedly entered into. Yet even the Exodus story offers degrees of oppression, attachments to Egyptian habits, comforts and protection that can be chosen too. And a free covenant requires a new kind of bondage through obedience to the law. As tools of privatisation these laws may even contribute to loosening the social bond. The same ambivalence prevails when the UK's assumed bond with Commonwealth countries is perceived over there as a call to continuing subservience. And when the EU underwrites the most stringent debt bond in the modern history of creditor conditionality, the Greeks can be forgiven in calling such a brand of European solidarity Euro bondage. Europeans may share a bond with each other symbolised by free movement and still resent the European house of bondage.

Can the shepherds on the road to Exodus imagine more enticing entanglements? Retain a bit of bondage in exchange for some ties? After all, Exodus chimes as much with peaceful coexistence as with violent separation. Democracy may call for losers' consent, but that covenant is predicated on the idea of sharing in a common destiny, however uncertain. Liberty is about a long conversation on a winding road, not a fleeting moment of liberation.

Maybe the tribes can learn to walk together again. Maybe Brexit means one side's fear of 'others' in their midst outdoes the other side's fear of solitude and otherlessness, of becoming bereft of 'others' altogether. And yet surely there was no 'Brexit tide of hate'. Surely, pro-Europeans are not citizens of nowhere – they may have an elsewhere, or even many elsewheres, but they have their village too. And if you say, I like what they dislike, should you dislike them? Does it help to deride Brexiles, Brefugees or Remoaners? Why hast thou done this to us, that thou hast led us out of Egypt?

Is one's instinct simply sovereigntist or cosmopolitan? Can the sovereigntists acknowledge that the EU's job is to manage the inevitable loss of sovereignty in our modern world? And can the cosmopolitans acknowledge that the EU may have gone too far in doing so? Do we not all prefer the Brussels of everyday bonds by twinning cities, universities, festivals and schools to the Brussels of bond yields?

Like an impressionist painting, this Exodus presents decidedly blurred edges; the viewer is offered glimpses she cannot hold onto in an ever-shifting landscape. In the frame, we see lifelong Eurosceptics wishing to remain for the sake of economic caution and lifelong Europhiles opting to leave for the sake of national pride. And we see many continentals continuing to hope until the last minute in the staying power of the ties that bind. Others prefer to let go a people who so mistake their continental embrace for suffocation.

Those who try to make sense of it all from the outside might do well to squint in order to sharpen their vision, blur the hard edges of the debate and tune out the hyperbolic expressions of nativist sentiment heard on John Lennon's island, all the while wondering at how un-British they have become, as if the decision to go meant letting themselves go. 'Where are our familiar neighbours who used to blend together the eccentric and the pragmatic?' you ask. They are still there, promise.

More frustrating still, the Leavers have radically different ways of 'not being European enough' à la de Gaulle. Some want to leave because they find Europe too big, others because they find it too small. For a Promised Land, the parochials dream of the shires, the globalists of the Antipodes. The former want more protection and to pull up the drawbridge, the latter less protectionism and to build bridges. While the former exude resentment about the EU's place in the UK, the latter exude confidence about the UK's place in the world.

It is not clear which version other Europeans dislike more, as both are slightly alienating in their own way. If the Brits have left us because they find Europe too big, we can confine Brexit to all that is pathetic about Little England. If they have left because they find Europe too small, there might be some panache, however delusional, in their story of how Cool Britannia goes global. At least at the beginning, an astute observer may have found grudging admiration in some EU quarters for those bloody-minded Brits – they dared to do it!

Resist, Regret, Respect, Relent, Repent

Who said it would ever be easy to leave Egypt? Where the Torah speaks of extracting one nation from the midst of another, a forceps delivery, we observe the wrenching of a nation from the strictures of its own continent.

Exodus offers variation on a familiar cycle. The imperial centre will resist separation, regret will be expressed more or less genuinely but the decision will be respected, the centre will relent – until it repents for relenting and resists again.

Europeans may say: our EU is no Pharaoh, it has no chariots to pursue the departing tribes. You may say: in fact, there is no 'there' there, no authority, power, relentlessness. Nevertheless, EU fragments become the thing itself. Its leaders. Its citizens. Its shadows. Who speaks in its name?

What if Pharaoh's subjects had resisted the departure en masse? It is sadly too late to say 'we will miss you' when they have already made up their mind, at least in their majority. But at the time of the referendum, a love wave of messages, pictures, petitions and videos was sent by thousands of European women, men, adolescents and children to their British friends, friendship messages in bottles, as it were, across the Channel. Citizens from all walks of life pleading: British friends... Please stay... Don't go... We love you!... We would miss you terribly... Help us repair the EU... Don't abandon us alone with the French/the Germans... This is about friendship between peoples, not about treaties... Our Europe is not about poor cousins to the south, or lesser relatives in the east, only a dysfunctional family all around... however dysfunctional, it is your family... It may be broke, but together we *can* fix it!

But the love wave came too late.

And you Europeans may say: the British were no slaves but masters of the game. This is why the plea was this: don't stay for your sake but for Europe's sake. Don't just ask what Europe can do for you, ask what you can do for Europe. We appeal to your greater collective self, historic Britain, visionary Britain, responsible Britain and common-sense Britain. Your ideals of openness and welfare, your Karl Popper and your John Maynard Keynes, moulded the European project. We need you to continue to make a nuisance of yourself, but around the table, not from the outside.

And so the pre-vote 'Please stay' turned into resistance, 'Please, change your mind', into relenting, 'If that is the way you want it...' into repenting, 'We won't make it easy'.

Regret has many variations on the continent. For every European applauding the departure of these foot-draggers, another knows they will miss their expert footwork. Sadly, more believe in British leadership on the continent than do in Britain itself. For Britain has been everyone's great balancer − of the French on behalf of the Germans, of the Germans on behalf of the French, and of both on behalf of the periphery. A highly sought-after ally in council negotiations, it has managed to champion smaller states while claiming pre-eminence in the core power trio. From Italy to Spain to Poland, every country claims a special relationship with the departing UK, all the while swearing allegiance to the remaining EU twenty-seven. From Latvia, Lithuania, Estonia, Slovenia or Slovakia, constructive ambivalence has become the new normal.

And beyond, Commonwealth citizens may be flattered to have been seen by the UK as less problematic migrants than the Poles next door, but they also regret the closing of their gate to the EU. Those who felt betrayed in 1973 (when Britain joined the European Community) hail the return of the natural order of things: Australia tops Austria. But in the rest of the world, the prospect of an unanchored global Britannia has left puzzled observers wondering why the Brits would want to abandon a continent that still attracts so many nomads. Admittedly, it does not hurt to be desperately courted by former imperialists. Yet in truth – *polling* truth – people around the world seem less worried or enthused about this Exodus than Europeans. After all, who cares what is happening in declining Europe?

Nor does it hurt in some EU capitals to let the rest of the world have the British back. Come to think of it, why don't some of Europe's awkward peripheral members follow suit? Hungarians, Greeks, Romanians... Italians, for that matter. The dream of a return to Charlemagne's core Europe, a not-so-well-kept secret in Brussels and Paris for the last two decades, is back. Why not spare ourselves the ten plagues and all that? Let these other peoples go too!

Eve, or the Lure of Banishment

In the end, Pharaoh, who had resisted so long, finally urges the Israelites to leave. You may be the ones who begged me to go, say the Egyptians, but we will be the ones who drive you out in the end. The Israelites in turn insist on leaving only by day. They will not leave surreptitiously, tails between their legs.

The truth is, ever since the humiliating British snub to the EU, Europeans have yearned to take back control. Hurt? Disappointed? Self-righteous? Spiteful? It does not matter. Britain ought to feel the taste of humiliation too. She may have thought that she knew what 'Brexit means Brexit' means, but the EU knew even better. When the chorus of scorned European leaders kick her out of their conclave, even while Britain is still in the EU, aren't they trying to enact a more self-aggrandising version of the Exodus story, where it is they and they alone who stand at the gate? You may have chosen to bite the apple of paradise and claim back control, but we define the terms of departure. Brexit was your decision, but it will happen on our terms. This story is not about your Promised Land, but our paradise lost; not *your* Exodus, but *our* banishment!

Britain, Eve... Beyond the incongruous juxtaposition, let's ask the obvious questions. What does banishment among humans say about those doing the banishing? If not paranoid, are they at least insecure? What kind of paradise does one get fed up with? A paradise where the powers that be are unwilling to confront or contemplate dissent? Is it too late for Brussels to recognise that it could have given the UK a better deal, to sex up the Remainers' dossier before the vote? Was more freedom *in* paradise really not an option? Or is it too early for a self-critical EU?

...Not about your Promised Land but our Paradise Lost... *Eve*, John Collier, 1911.

Many on the continent are tempted to deny that this was ever a tale of many Britains, and to convince themselves instead that even Remainers only cared about their own bite at the EU apple, never truly buying into the project they are now being asked to abandon. How convenient! How ignorant of all those British who still thought of the EU as a noble project, however flawed.

Conversely, what does banishment truly say about the banished? Perhaps that Eve 'deserved it', that she had fallen for the promise of fake knowledge and post-truth to be found outside paradise. Or conversely, that she was quite pleased to meet Milton's serpent, a republican rebel revolting against the autocratic god-king. 'Some natural tears they drop'd, but wip'd them soon...'

Is banishment a humiliation or a tribute? Why should the rest of Europe pretend that there is nothing to learn outside the EU's normative walls? Unfortunately for banishers, the people tend to side with the banished, *n'en déplaise à Dieu*, (God forbid). It's hard to reassert control in these circumstances. When Pharaoh banishes him and his people from the land, Moses nevertheless leaves boldly in the sight of all Egyptians, in broad daylight. Some of those left behind in paradise feel that they are missing out.

In any case, doesn't banishment usually boil down to self-banishment anyway? Eve's defiance was her very own as she stood for the beginning of it all. The banished one acts before she is enacted by others. Who doubts that knowledge was a price worth paying for Eve and her descendants, despite the wrath of the gods who punish those who steal it? The EU cannot simply twist the story around and transform self-banishment into an act of its own making.

Not so fast! Isn't banishment always on a knife edge, all or nothing but with little separating the two, a foolish gamble, a short moment of gluttony in paradise? Who says that biting the apple was written in Britain's destiny? If Cicero had not been banished, he would have been the leader of Rome; or rather, Cicero was banished because if not, he would have been the leader of Rome. How do we make sense of the very real possibility that the decision could have gone the other way? If only the British had purposefully elected to stay rather than sluggishly decided to remain, if only there had been... (fill in the blanks here: different media coverage, electoral inclusion of the young, or expats...) we would be talking not about British exceptionalism but about implementing Remain's agenda: let us stand tall and lead, not leave, Europe.

It will not do to turn the Brits into the Banished. They have chosen their Exodus, for better or worse.

Escape from Rome?

If it's neither slavery nor paradise, which Europe are the British people escaping?

Since we all make myths mean what we need them to mean, allow me to corral Europe's foundational myth in the guise of the mythical woman *Europa*, who much before her contemporary cartoon career adorned the frescoes of ancient Rome. Anointed Queen of Crete after Zeus-as-bull abducted her from somewhere in the East, we only know her story as one of subterfuge and seduction, as is usually the case with the god-king. An object of conflicting desires. That is little to go on. What you are trying to escape in leaving the EU depends on how you chose to appropriate *Europa*'s story.

If your *Europa* story is itself about escape, the princess's initial eloping from her native land, you may value an EU desperate to leave behind a past of war and bestiality. If so, you will ask, isn't there something morally reprehensible about pretending that this story of origin has gone away or that Britain can forget all about it? Liberation here is abandonment, abandonment of a vast and unprecedented experiment in reconciliation, that most precious of all human currencies.

Or your *Europa* may be about where she finally landed, on an island at the very edge of today's European continent. In this perspective, could it be that the EU's core is actually its periphery that defines not only its limits but its broader horizons? Could it be that the British are escaping precisely their own centrality to the idea of Europe?

...Zeus' inspired appropriation of a foreign woman... *The Rape Of Europa*, Valentin Aleksandrovich Serov, 1910.

© SPUTNIK / Alamy Stock Photo

Or your *Europa* may be about becoming and about movement, a woman torn from her roots by a power much greater than herself, as if motion was the only way to keep her together. Isn't her secret in her many geographical, cultural and political fragments, the woman's breath inspiring the mutual recognition between the peoples of Europe and their zillions of contradictory stories about who she really is? Has Britain failed to see that if *Europa* cannot stand still, it is pointless to fear its dreaded destination? Britain's liberation may be from evanescence itself.

If Cretan Europe is your *Europa*, it leaves little room for 'bullying' in its name! Instead, it speaks to Zeus's truly inspired move, in appropriating a foreign woman hailing far from the slopes of Olympus who will one day come to represent us Europeans. *Europa* was not from our neck of the woods. Her three brothers after all went to look for her in distant lands and believing her lost, founded cities in the Middle East, Anatolia and Thrace. This *Europa* calls for the recognition that we are made of others. If this is how it is, then the Eurocentric idea of European destiny on the apex of progress becomes a betrayal of our origins.

Sadly, even if we have had many beautiful drawings of *Europa* on her bull during the Brexit saga, too many in Britain have never imagined this decentred Cretan *Europa* anyway, let alone as the true inspiration behind the existing EU. But then again, most other Europeans have not either.

As for Leavers, they have no time for her because they believe in a mythical postscript: *Europa* became bored in Crete, she dreamt of a grander destiny. She cajoled and seduced Zeus to take her to the greatest city of them all: Rome. And this is where the trouble started.

For the next thousands of years *Europa* has inhabited Rome and Rome has reigned over *Europa*. Beautiful and fateful Rome, whose imperial and pontifical tentacles have relentlessly sought to suffocate the rest of the continent. There, *Europa* has been repeatedly assaulted by autocrats and nepotists – after all she was abducted and raped by Zeus, the supreme Olympian who manages the affairs of men without their consent. Almost every major war in European history has happened because of someone trying to acquire dominion over her, someone who more often than not hailed from Rome. Why did the EU founding fathers decide to sign their founding treaty in Rome, Eurosceptics sigh, if not because history repeats itself, giving us the EU as the fifth empire. We knew this already when we entered the EC in 1973, but only since then has the mask fallen, cooperation become subordination, contract become enhanced interrogation. Ask the Greeks. These days, Brussels stands in for Rome, even if, ironically, Romans have turned against Brussels.

When Brexiters draw a crude comparison between Brussels and Moscow, they no doubt choose to ignore the essence of the enterprise as an exercise in free choice. But can Europhiles ignore the nagging questions: what is free choice in the face of asymmetrical power? Where does the impulse to dominate others on the part of some EU countries come from anyway? Colonial DNA? Human, too human? Macho, too macho?

Perhaps the mainstream EU narrative of a Greco-Roman-Christian civilisational unity of Europe is unattractively close to the nationalist calls for an exclusively Christian Europe. Should Europe not instead resist all temptations to build itself against others, except perhaps the otherness of its own warring and imperial past? Isn't nationalism best left to nations (hmm, not even them), and Euro-nationalism to be avoided at all costs?

Cretan Europe versus Christian Europe. Will we witness a self-fulfilling Brexit which hastens the advent of the kind of EU that many in the UK imagined and wanted to escape? Better to exorcise our Roman demons and reinvent a union where most Europeans want to stay, inspired all over again by the story of our oldest ancestor, Cretan *Europa*.

Clash of Messianisms

Readers will disagree on whether the EU holds tyrannical pharaonic powers. But they may also disagree with casting it in the part for another reason: if Brexit is a messianic project, so is the EU. What inspires those who make grand speeches from the cliffs of Dover and what has inspired the European project from its foundation is the belief in a sacred mission, and that in the name of the Promised Land we can paper over the here and now. For the European project may be the product of geopolitical and geo-economic realpolitik, but it also stems from the messianic mindset of its vanguard, busy weavers of the ties that bind, motivated from the start by the conviction that theirs was a sacred mission to free Europeans from the shackles of war and nationalism. This is the impulse that has propelled our technocratic founding fathers – ah, if there had been founding mums! The liberation they had in mind might have been from Europe's own past but they followed a teleological credo whereby the end justifies the means and the means may be chosen by the few if need be. There lies the EU's original dream and original sin.

If since Aristotle we have been moving towards a non-teleological understanding of ourselves, this ought to be true for institutions too. Brussels, hear what people think in their vast majority: that the EU is the right place to address their most pressing problems, above all these four: immigration, terrorism, finance, the environment. That what is wrong is not the substance of cooperation but the form it takes. No one would yearn to take back control if the EU was not perceived as a runaway train towards an unknown destination.

Some will argue that we need messianic idealism to fight the dark force. Writing after the last war, the philosopher Ernst Bloch called for the invention of an atheist messianism, a concrete utopia, grounded in a faith in technology and the idea that humanity is capable of immunising itself against the viruses of violence and greed. On this count, the jury is still out. But messianism all too often serves to justify a monopoly of power, unless we can imagine the kind of messianic moments described by another Jewish philosopher born in the twentieth century, Emmanuel Levinas. These are the moments when we ask how best to take responsibility for the lives of others, a form of messianism which would never end the need for discussion and for persistent watchfulness.

Exceptionally Exceptional?

'By God, I do love the Ingles. God dammee, if I don't love them better than the French!' Will Brexit finally free the French from Voltaire's infatuation?

Admittedly, you've got to be quite special, or high, to 'see the sounds' at Mount Sinai ('All the people saw the sounds ... they saw and trembled,' says the Torah). But who in this day and age still believes in 'Chosen People', except as some sort of collective narcissistic disorder?

And yet, British exceptionalism feels like a conspiracy these days. The British identity complex and separation gene scrutinised under the microscope by historians, sociologists, anthropologists, geopoliticians alike, the old Victorian story of the commonalities between the Israelites and the British people no longer needed as a prop.

Is Brexit then not about doing but about being, be-leaving, as

Leavers like to say? Are Leavers an exception to the golden rule of voting behaviour in their vote *against* the status quo, driven as they were by anti-establishment anger? Or could their decision be the truest measure of British exceptionalism, namely a widespread belief that we never truly were part of the EU to begin with: not the euro, Merkel, Brussels, or the other side of the Channel, this ever-remoter Union. To leave is to revert to the status quo ante, the place where we used to be before the exile into Egypt actually took place.

The Brits can argue among themselves as to whether British exceptionalism is about the election of a people or childish delusions. But for most on the continent it can only be indulged if it means one thing: Britain has been and will remain the exception.

We get it, say Britain's continental neighbours. We know: you withstood Spanish, French and German kings, emperors, dictators and armadas. We admire your unique blend of healthy democratic disrespect for authority and necessary deference to government. We understand: your leaving is the price we pay for those nasty continental traits you thankfully do not share with us – memories of occupation, a need for a supranational antibody against nationalism, a yearning for stability after centuries of border swaps. Lucky you! Good luck, Lords of the Churchillian Rings!

No sour grapes, they might add disingenuously; we won't even comment on the parochialism of your globalism, your deluded imperial revisionism and custodianship of great powerlessness. While the colonial gene remains part of Europe's DNA, at least in all its former imperial nations, you alone let it define your future.

Could it be harder for the rest of the continent to admit to the Brits' 'can-do' exceptionalism? That only they do not mind acting as political eccentrics who question received wisdom? With Orwell, the Brits tend to believe that if liberty means anything at all, it means the right to tell people what they do not want to hear. But they are misunderstood by others when they do so in their own cryptic way, 'with the greatest respect' and all...

Can we admit that they are the only ones with not only the mindset but the muscle power to be capable of doing the deed (even if those with the mindset and those with the muscle are not the same people)? That no other EU country could have achieved such an amazing, deluded act of stubborn self-confidence, invoking memories of past noble defeats, Dunkirk spirit and all, along the way.

The drafters of the exit clause knew it: only the British civil service would be capable of revisiting the following in two years: 12,000 European regulations, 7,900 legal implementation instruments and 80,000 pages of so called *acquis communautaires*, the laws passed by the EU in the last seven decades.

'Could the queen stop Brexit?' a student asked me in a Moroccan university adorned with the portrait of King Mohammed VI. 'Hum,' I replied, 'couldn't, wouldn't...' For many around the world, the commitment shown by the British elites to go through with a popular mandate most of them profoundly disagree with has been a political phenomenon truly worthy of admiration. Will the Moroccans ever be allowed to force their own top brass to do their bidding in this way?

But then again, will the Moroccans, or anyone else for that matter, ever experience such a parliamentary melee, with its mindboggling mash of procedures and passions, rippling down through the centuries from its original font, another (glorious) revolution. It may have seemed like democratic chaos. But we could also agree that far from making a fool of itself, the UK has demon-strated to the world what an epic political struggle can look like, where both publics and politicians mobilise absolutely peacefully against the other side while mingling in Westminster square and in Westminster lobbies. Nowhere else in Europe have we been graced with such genuine debates about Europe. Granted, the timing is a bit odd. But better late than never. Ah, the Ingles!

...After all, nothing is less exceptional... *The Passage of the Red Sea*, G.H. Phillips after Francis Danby, 1829.

‡

And yet...

How exceptional can British exceptionalism really be? After all, nothing is less exceptional than exceptionalism, that sense of specialness at the heart of every national identity, starting in Europe. Think of the Portuguese and their oceanic melancholy, the Poles and their own messianic story, the Estonians and their avant-gardism, the French and their grandeur, the Greeks and their worship of resistance, the Spaniards and their buccaneering past, the Italians and their world-class taste, the Belgians and their dark humour wrapped in dark chocolate...

In truth, the claim to exceptionalism may be the most widely shared feeling among EU members, each with its own 'proud tradition' and 'finest hour', each with the unique palimpsest of its language, as Elena Ferrante would say, each with its own fierce debate about the fit between the national and EU projects. We may prefer one exceptionalism over another, of, say, the self-deprecating Belgians over that of more self-satisfied nationals, or of smaller nations over bigger ones, and you may deplore any sense of uniqueness based on self-abasing contempt for others, but we can't deny the ubiquity of exceptionalism.

Perhaps the British are only more exceptional in being most oblivious to the uniqueness of others? Who knows. The British mystery, to take Karl Popper's formulation, may have captured the imagination of many in Europe for a long time, but fascination wears off.

Perhaps the British have always been the most ambivalent of all Europeans about the EU, half in, half out for the last four decades, sometimes in, sometimes out in the last four centuries. But which national public is not ambivalent about the EU these days? And which country has given the project such extremes, from Winston Churchill's original vision and Harold Wilson's entry combat to Clement Attlee's bailing out and Thatcher's turnaround.

Or perhaps the British thrive better than others on inconsistency. How can you be both insecure enough so radically to underestimate your influence in Brussels, and secure enough so blindly to trust that you can go it alone?

Is the separation gene not a matter of degree, a lower capacity for dual allegiances, say, between island and continental European peoples, a greater British unwillingness to admit dependence on neighbours?

Has the never-extinguished imperial urge present among some pathetic oldies not turned into dying embers among younger Brits? Just like, more or less, in Portugal or France?

Or is the whole specialness business a collective prank, a very English one at that, best expressed after the war by Flanders and Swann, that most notable of British comedy duos. 'The English, the English, the English are best/I wouldn't give tuppence for all of the rest,' echoes to this day their 'Song of Patriotic Prejudice.' And piling it on to the audience in their introductory wit: 'Thanks to the English you are not... Spanish.' For every Englishman knows in his heart that invaders became ancestors in each of the age-old battles for Britain, right?

In the end, British citizens understand as well as their continental neighbours the power of cooperation. They just want to do it on their own terms. Annoying! Asked before the vote whether there should be more decision-making at the European level, the result was close to the European average (above 50 per cent) regarding health care and social security, stimulating investments and jobs, securing the energy supply, protecting the environment, promoting the equality of men and women and even dealing with immigration issues. They do get it: no country is an island, or two.

Some of us may have preferred a British conversion to a nearby like-minded exceptionalism, replete with similar talk of unacceptable outside interference and national identity: that of the Danes. And yet, Brexit only encouraged the Danes' EU-ness, at least in its immediate aftermath. Perhaps when your exceptionalism lies with the delights of *hygge*, which elects a cuddly present by the fireplace over a glorious past or future, stepping out alone into the cold is a step too far. Mindfulness versus Exodus.

In fact, all Europeans may be more like the UK than they will admit. Which country in the EU does *not* have a transactional view, asking 'What's in it for me?' Are there examples of a member state willing to override its own interest for the sake of something called EU interest? This is the beauty of an EU game honed over decades to extract positive sums from individual national calculations: the European interest is not some transcendental truth known to the happy few in Brussels. The European interest is the final compromise, the never-ending quest for agreement, the seeming devotion of the many busy bees of European diplomacy to the overall balance of the hive. The Brits are only exceptional in telling it as it is – and in their belief that leaving the table altogether could strengthen their hand.

More prosaically, all this talk of exceptionalisms obscures the reality that there are only better or worse answers to the same sets of globally recurring dilemmas thrown up by our ubiquitous liberal capitalist modernity – control vs cooperation, local vs global, order vs justice... The idea of an exceptional EU as some special *sui generis* project embarking on a reinvention of shared sovereignty may just cloak the banality of it all.

At the very least, isn't the EU's own claim to exceptionalism predicated on its capacity to accommodate the many variations of exceptionalism in its midst? At its best, the EU must serve as a multifaceted mirror in which all exceptionalisms can be reflected and deflected in equal measure, a machinery designed to turn exceptions into rules, and exceptional countries into rule-bound ones. Some will say that British exceptionalism lies in part in its vulnerability to this logic, in its willingness to be law-abiding, its propensity to take the EU too literally when others know how to bow to the rule without enforcing it. Why has the UK not followed the lead of Germany's supreme court and asserted its own constitutional integrity? Could it be that the EU lost the British people because they took it too seriously?

Not so, say the twenty-seven in unison. The Brits are addicted to the special status we have offered them in the last two decades and the conviction that we owe it to them. How else could they be the masters of euro-clearing in spite of their disdain for the euro? Exceptional treatment is a privilege for members. If they become out-almost-in, they cannot get the same treatment they got before Brexit, as in-almost-out! Brexit can only remain an exception if we no longer treat the UK exceptionally as we have over the last decades. Respect by the EU for the constitutional integrity of its member states and by the member states for the EU's integrity is a daunting balancing act best practised from within.

Thankfully, Commonwealth citizens are expected to step right in, all 2.4 billion of them, and demonstrate life's bounty outside the euro-perimeter, still there for the picking. But in the rest of the world, including the Anglosphere, British exceptionalism is an old story that may be past its sell-by date. For all the hope that the empire will strike back, commonwealth countries have moved on, worrying about their globalised youth and localised poor, not the UK's regional woes. And from China to Brazil, South Africa to Japan, those tuning in to the EU saga have asked the same question: if British exceptionalism cannot be soluble in a union which tamed its imperialist undertones, what makes the Brits think that we, the rest of the world, will step in as their new Promised Lands? In spite of the old ties, isn't it more likely that Sudan, Sierra Leone, Kenya, Lesotho, South Africa, India, Myanmar or Sri Lanka will get used to dealing directly with Brussels without a London gateway? When the British prime minister rightly invokes the extraordinary wealth and breadth of the relationships Britain already has, from Mauritius to Madras, from Newfoundland to Swaziland, did she explain what it was about the EU that prevented these relationships from flourishing before Brexit?

Or is it a mark of British exceptional attention deficit disorder that it could not do both at once when in the EU: continental and global politics. Membership of the EU club has never prevented its members from going about their global business. What is true, however, is that without the EU, Britain might well have to creatively reinvent its bilateral relations around the world, a deflated global island for sure, but global nevertheless.

Let's face it. Even if exceptionalism in Europe is no exception, the British brand has long predestined the country to hit the road first and probably alone. Always prone to out-Asterix the French, always the *empêcheur de tourner en rond*, the spoilsport, no matter that this was precisely why others valued its hard-headed intuition that the EU was going around in circles. They were annoying but kept us on our feet, like...

...*una mosca cojonera* (literally a fly with balls), quipped a Spanish friend.

Liminal Fates

This could be an inglorious Exodus for the UK, heralding a reverse change of status: from master to slave.

It could never be otherwise. Not only because this is not a negotiation among equals, but because, regrettably, countries do not actually move. In this story of metaphorical Exodus, a people seeks to move from a space, a space of free movement of stuff and persons, while staying in the same place. And in the process they discover, or, rather, rediscover the orbital pull exercised by the local continental pharaoh. When you are European, is it possible to arrive anywhere else?

History would, of course, have told them. The UK could never ignore continental affairs, even less so with the birth of the EU. The EU may not be a superpower but it has become a regional regulatory hegemon. It does not apologise for it: we have poured so many resources into it, yet this is a public good for all those who want access. Over time, no country anywhere near Europe has been able to escape its orbit. When it comes to trade, economists explain that this is all about the gravity model; that geography matters, even in the modern cyber-age, and that you tend to have more relations with your neighbours. This is said in a tone of the utmost gravity – the other kind of gravity, the one that belongs to those who model our future.

...A reverse change of status from master to slave... *The Departure of the Israelites out of the Land of Egypt*, David Roberts, 1829

As with any story about gravity, the pull will be hugely asymmetrical, a function of the weight of the respective bodies. And if the body is the EU, an empire expanding by invitation, reciprocity may be

abolished altogether, since those on the outside are *our* neighbours, *our* neighbourhood, *our* garage, *our* backyard, the dumping ground of *our* recipes for nations-in-the-making.

In Roman times the *limes* (boundary lines) of the empire were not only its limits but its zones of contact with the outside, zones neither in nor out, where overlapping fears and desires to belong clashed in bloody skirmishes and banquets. Two thousand years later, the EU has perfected the management of liminal fates, the fates of those who live in its orbit, of those who live neither in nor out, by choice, by necessity or both. In this liminal zone, countries never stop negotiating with the EU, as regional partners become regulatory satellites.

The menu of 'models' that have dominated Brexit negotiations simply offer alternative ways of orbiting around the EU. Here are various countries which can negotiate different levels of rights and obligations and where the trade-off between cooperation and control has been resolved slightly differently. But the basic bargain is always the same: you are given a level of access as a function of your level of convergence. And you will not affect what you are accessing and converging to. As *Norway*, you take all the single-market rules and can sometimes deflect one or two. The EU has the final say. As *Switzerland*, yours is a more customised deal but matched with an all-or-nothing guillotine clause. As *Ukraine*, you have less trade access but no free movement obligation. As *Turkey*, in the customs union, you grant other countries all of the access concessions the EU has made, but do not receive concessions in return since you do not take part in the common commercial policy (unless the EU were to mandate parallel negotiations). You are a trade-taker. These are not models, but variations on the same dilemma.

The EU says: you might have preferred to be 'in Europe but not ruled by the EU', but since you want access to our ecosystem, the only option on offer is 'not in the EU but ruled by the EU'. Your choice.

To be or not to be Norway, everyone asked. And so our Norwegian friends confessed: 'distorted sovereignty' works for us because we trust our state to act as a buffer and our whole relationship with the EU has been utterly de-politicised anyway – this is our collective conspiracy to park the membership debates which have so divided us. Hard to imagine that in Britain! And, anyway, we Norwegians have had centuries of bullying by Sweden and Russia. Can Britain, a country with a great tradition of bullying others, follow our humble example?

So, Brexit means neither regulatory independence nor regulatory influence – the worst of all worlds. This is a logic for aspiring, not departing states. Enlargement in reverse cannot mirror enlargement. No wonder both Leavers and Remainers hate the whole idea. Only the urge to leave and the yearning to stay could have made this equation OK.

Britain will be governed at a distance. That is the definition of colonialism. Brussels may live and breathe multilateralism but still wants a relationship that binds the UK unilaterally to EU rules. Call it a vassal state or a dominion, says the EU, we call it a privileged relationship. Call it legal imperialism, we call it normative power. Call it castration Brexit, we say it's your call.

Admittedly, some in Brussels have doubts about the political sustainability of the UK taking trade dictation inside a customs union. President Macron says it most plainly: 'What is going to happen for Britain is not taking back control: it's servitude.' But no one has a better idea. *En bref*: Brexit has exposed the fate of Europe's liminals, its intimate outsiders. The UK's can-do exceptionalism cannot change the logic, simply make it visible.

And in the process produce nice ironies:

- One: Brexit will finally manage to turn the tabloid vision of the EU as Brussels diktat into reality by moving Britain from the best of both worlds – 'in-almost-out' – to the worst of all worlds – 'out-almost-in'.
- Two: Brexit means that we the Brits finally reflect on what it means to be on the receiving end of imperial unilateralism, an old habit we have been all too happy to reinvent as a member of the EU. 'Can you imagine,' exclaims a member of the pro-leave group Lawyers for Britain, 'that if we stayed under the jurisdiction of the European Court of Justice, this would be akin to the kind of extraterritorial law imposed on China during the Opium Wars?' Somehow the author cannot bring himself to write 'extraterritorial law *we* imposed...' Who says analogies cannot be ironic. Brexit means that the old colonial logic has come full circle, and that we get it at last. In the process, we discover that being governed at a distance is no fun at all. We

borrow their victimhood but we cannot suffer what they suffered from us. Decolonising Britain? Good luck...

Leavers argue that Brexit means that you must emulate those who have freed themselves from British imperialism. 'If you want to understand the Repeal Act, think of India's constitution after they declared independence from us,' a Brexiter explains to me in an Oxford hall funded by colonial bounties. The true, pure, genuine Brexit would have involved no talking with the EU at all: a unilateral declaration of independence. A message in a bottle, or on a postcard, the cost of a stamp to Brussels. In the Brexiter's repertoire, betrayal started with the cost of a Eurostar ticket. Unilateralism is not just the prerogative of the Trumpian bully but the ultimate weapon of the freedom fighter.

Alternatively, or actually at the same time, British negotiators desperately insist on mutuality, symmetrical schemes, reciprocal 'due regard' by courts, two-way equivalence determination, gentlemen's agreements. They say: the road to Brexit may be paved with legal compunction but the law should still be a contract. But the EU says: your taking back control cannot mean we lose control of our own affairs. Our extraterritoriality is greater than yours!

To be sure, Britain can choose variants of Canada's deal, a country beyond the orbital pull (even if it would love to join the EU): less access and less convergence. But, well, this will recreate borders that the people of Ireland and businessmen thought had been erased forever.

For the EU does not just break down borders but creates them, too, when it comes to withdrawal as well as enlargement. Even the World Trade Organisation wants it so, courtesy of non-discrimination among outsiders. Ask Ukraine when Poland entered the EU. Fine for the east, but no one wants this between north and south in Ireland, right? Britain's ultimate exceptionalism lies with geography: no other EU countries have worked so bloody hard at abolishing a border only to see it fated to become part of the EU's external wall. With Brexit, the country's two biggest political headaches, the Irish and European questions are conflated into one.

No doubt EU negotiators were sincere about a border-free Ireland, but most in the UK were even more so (you don't forget a bombing era!). Yet in its desperation to draw an external border somewhere Brussels probably overreached in the form of the infamous backstop, unsettling some of its most ardent defenders on the British Isles. Perhaps its idea was to propose checks without borders but it all amounted to partial EU jurisdiction over a part of the UK. Brussels may have long aspired to 3D-print its rules and institutions within its neighbours' borders, but never before has it suggested territorial differentiation of this kind. Are there better ways to alleviate the very real and present concerns of the Irish people? If the backstop was about keeping the island together and protecting it against over-reach by the EU too, let the island-wide institutions created by the Good Friday agreement become the ultimate backstop. Ironically, technocratic mindsets and constitutional politics might collude in stabilising this potentially most volatile of all European boundaries. The missing ingredient: trust!

Bargaining Pedagogy

Exodus: we get it, said the EU, when the time came to strike a bargain. These negotiations too will be about the story that *will* be told. But this time around, there will be no Almighty to tip the scales. Watch our sclerotic bureaucracy turn into a lean, mean bargaining machine. We will teach the British people and the rest of the world what Exit means. This is not patronising but pedagogy. Bargaining pedagogy.

Two years of almighty pedagogy later, what have we learned?

Above all else, we have learned how quickly a relationship sours, how seamless is the move from the same side of the table to facing each other on opposite sides. And how 'Brexit means Brexit' echoing loudly enough from the leaving side can so easily boomerang back from the side being left. What a pity that the UK public had to undergo its EU crash course in such an antagonistic setting, learning about what the EU has done and will do to us rather than what we do in the EU.

We have learned that when negotiations are like no other before, no one can appeal to the rules of the game. But when you are fighting hard for what you had before, the rules tend to be the same as they were before.

We have learned that much of the result has little to do with good or bad negotiating tactics and much to do with structures of power and the harsh geopolitics of regional hegemony. But one should not conduct such strategically critical negotiations with short-term survival governing every step of the way.

We have relearned the classic ways in which negotiations fall hostage to hawks, entrapment, escalation, cycles of attrition, brinkmanship and stonewalling, and that maybe it is better to save the other side from itself than to lose a negotiating partner altogether.

And that the lesson from the Greek debt saga in negotiating with the EU was neither to give in nor to call Brussels' bluff but to more cleverly play the EU game, and remember that in getting to yes the pragmatists are in capitals when negotiations pit tangible costs against abstract rules, but are in Brussels when compromise magic needs a legal wand.

We have learned that if most negotiators on both sides see the game as a damage-control exercise, talk of mutually advantageous agreement becomes a contradiction in terms. Why offer Britain favourable terms, EU negotiators ask. Why? It is not the EU abandoning the UK! They forget that the word favourable is relative when you lose your place around the table. And they forget that they are negotiating mostly with those who did not want to leave.

...Threats of walking are empty in an interdependent world... *Moses Forbids the People to Follow Him*, James Tissot, 1896

We have learned the power of denial, when the EU brands the UK Chequers proposal the end of Europe and yet never tires of explaining that Brexit is the least of its priorities.

We have learned that the summoning-up of the Dunkirk spirit was inevitable but that in the end threats of walking are empty in an interdependent world, on either side. Pharaoh ignored the signs of the Hebrew messengers with his 'Get out of my sight! If I lay eyes on you again, you're dead,' but could not but continue to negotiate. Reality checks are always a good idea, since we tend to overestimate our alternatives to agreement, each believing our own propaganda.

We have learned that you should not offer the other side sticks to beat you and thus present their position as sadly unavoidable. The EU was right: the negotiations were taking place within parameters that the UK had itself narrowed. The UK was right too: they were taking place within parameters that the EU had itself defined as the law. Both were wrong in denying the space for play in the other side's frame. And don't label calls for moderation and respect patronising. Amplify them, or keep the negotiations boring.

We have learned that a successful conversation must be anchored early on in common concerns. Moses began his negotiations with Pharaoh with a moderate demand for three days free from labour for a festival of worship, with only a gentle threat of shared consequences from rebuttal – 'lest our God strike us with either death or disease'. Alas, the risks are not recognised until the actual painful consequences happen, and it is too late to part amicably.

We have learned that there is never 'nothing to negotiate'. Witness Pharaoh's overconfidence after Moses' rather moderate initial demands: 'Why would you suggest the people be exempt from work? Back to work!' Humiliation does not pay, especially when matched with cultural stereotypes – 'You're up to no good – it's written all over your faces'.

We have learned that it helps to demonstrate knowledge of the other side. Not only was Moses an intimate of the pharaoh's court, he also cleverly approached the boss directly early each morning on his stroll by the river. The UK should have known that one-on-one civility and friendliness in the EU does not mean that their red lines will be scrapped. Nor can public speeches stand for a conversation. Beware: message sent is not necessarily message received.

We already knew that the other side's inflexibility graces you with a proper fight – when the inevitable rejection comes, righteous indignation about their intransigence feels good. But you will not escape their rebuttal. You may call us dogmatic, say EU negotiators, but this is our reality check. Our post-offer onset of stubbornness is simply a return to basic principles. You are not being lectured like naughty schoolchildren, simply like the school dunces.

We have learned that you learn about 'what ifs' once it is too late. Recall how Pharaoh, shocked by the plague of flies, says yes to the reason but still no to the demand. 'Go ahead. Sacrifice to your God – but do so within the geographical boundaries of Egypt.' Why does he proceed to renege on the deal? Unwisely, he fails to follow the golden rule: when considering alternatives, choose the one which minimises prospective regret. Like so many before them, the various sides of the Brexit saga may live for a long time with regrets about the early offer they rejected.

But we have also learned that in our world a round of negotiations is never the last one.

We know with Aristotle that the essence of political tragedy is to reject the good for the perfect. Since negotiations are like two parallel games of chess, inside and outside, internal vetoes can strengthen your hand but weaken the prospect of agreement. In the process, we have witnessed how the idea of compromise, our most precious civilisational jewel, can become a dirty word even in the great British democracy. And yet what do you do when two sides want no deal at all – one in order to effectively leave and the other in order to effectively stay? Is it not foolish for the UK's negotiator in chief to threaten each of these sides with the other's desired outcome, thus making such an outcome more credible? What if you don't always get what you want? Especially if what you want depends on others getting nothing of what they want. This is not rocket science. If your first best solution is incompatible with that of others, you ominously risk getting what you want least, your third or fourth or nth best, if you don't compromise. Go instead for your second best, not as a concession to the other side but as a service to your own cause.

We had learned already that it is a bad idea to present the results of a negotiation as a *fait accompli* when you desperately need buy-in. We have to ask why these negotiations were not embedded in a national democratic process to build a modicum of consensus in the UK.

And we have learned that it can be too late when both sides want to call the whole thing off. 'What is it that we have done, releasing Israel from our service?' asks Pharaoh. 'What is it that you have done to us?' ask the Israelites. It makes little sense for Pharaoh to pursue the Israelites, fed up as he is with them, but he does it nevertheless, almost drunk with the drama of it all.

To be sure, much has been lost in translation between London and Brussels.

In London, the world has long enjoyed the unique spectacle of a House of Commons where two sides face each other ready for battle, eager to shout their denial of anything they might accidentally have in common. In contrast, Brussels showcases a stage of rational deliberation, conflict-minimising strategies and Byzantian compromises. As we move from Brexit 1.0 to Brexit 2.0, could they ever both picture themselves in the House of Commons but on the same side of the room, facing a mutual problem called Brexit?

And, of course, we ought to know that when negotiations are over, they are *not* over. There will be hindsight and narrative illusion – Pharaoh and his advisers should have foreseen the escalating consequences of playing hardball. Whose predictions will we castigate? And there will be post-settlement embellishments and post-settlement reinventions, both sides tempted to renege, both sides taken for fools.

In the end, should the British fear Pharaoh's revenge, the blind spot of Exodus, if the Egyptian throne fears that too many of its citizens might sympathise with the Leavers' cramped, crazy hopes? The problem for the moderate observer who yearns for a gentler Brexit is that concessions to the other side's views end up feeding its bloody self-righteousness.

Lost in Transition

But, of course, Moses never makes it to the Promised Land. He only contemplates it from afar.

Taking the people out of Egypt cannot be the same as bringing them into Canaan. In between, they need to learn to fight their own battles and invent their own society.

Exodus is a drama played out over forty years, in perpetual

...In the end, the prophet stares at the horizon, his gaze upon a landscape that he will never inhabit... Wanderer above the Sea of Fog, Caspar David Friedrich, c. 1817

disequilibrium, with many protagonists displaying infinite patience and infinite haste. Much happens during the journey – Mount Sinai, ascent and descent, breaking the tablets of the law, serpents and angels, rebellions. As with all grand projects, it was always about the journey, not the destination. Transition through the wilderness is all Moses got. Did he carry too much baggage, too many doubts on his shoulders? Is it always about leaving the difficult task to the next generation? The climax takes us back to its beginning, Moses' original and continued resistance to carrying out his mission. In the end, the prophet stares at the horizon, his gaze upon a landscape that he will never inhabit.

We have heard some famous Brexiters speak of the many decades before Brexit bears fruit. But in truth, like all mutinies, the Brexit cry was never about what actually happens next. A year before the exit date, the then British foreign secretary Boris Johnson promised, 'Our national journey out of the EU is almost over and a glorious view awaits' – a promise plastered against the white cliffs of Dover on the front page of the *Daily Express*. Was he trying to pre-empt the wilderness test? Revolutionaries always underestimate the importance of transition, but when the time comes to walk from A to Z they suddenly discover a whole alphabet of traps and betrayals.

Transition, the Brexit stage that dares not speak its name. Still-pay-no-say, everything-but-seats, a status quo without dignity. If the Brexit transition is the worst of all worlds – having no voice while still conforming to all existing Union regulatory, budgetary, supervisory, judiciary and enforcement institutions – the irony of such a radical loss of control in the name of taking back control has not been lost on anyone. A UK held hostage to Northern Ireland has to decide who will stay behind an EU tariff-and-rules wall, choosing between an open-ended transition and an infinite backstop, or Russian dolls of backstops designed as an insurance scheme for a seamless border until another solution is found. Did we need a scheme that is not part of the future relations and utterly disliked by all sides? In this story, it may be the British crossing the desert, but it is the Egyptians who decide where the desert ends.

Forget the Irish question. What if transition itself never ends, post-transition transitions rolling down the years. Call it a phased process of implementation, an open-ended alignment period, a preparatory standstill. Clearly a transition with a time limit is ineffective: what if we are not ready? But a transition without a time limit does not work: we will never be ready! After all, Norway's EU relationship via the European Economic Area was designed as a brief transition too. And yet, a journey with no stated end does not have to be endless.

Out in the wilderness, what will be the glue that binds? What wonders and temporary relief will we find? What memory rituals? What agonised reliving of counterfactuals? Will this be the UK's very own Thirty Years War, Dante's ultimate trial in limbo, limbs of an exhausted body politic pulling in opposite directions, faces twisted around looking backwards, bodies of evidence buried face down in the mud?

Of course not! The tribes' time in the wilderness is full of chatter. There will be talk, talk about the future relationship and talk with whoever else the country chooses, talk among us and talk beyond.

What better way to de-dramatise.

Utopia is not an end state but a commitment to permanent reinvention, not about tomorrow but about the here and now, the breach in our present which suddenly allows for myriad possible futures.

Wilderness, Tamed

...Limbs of an exhausted body politics... *Dante's Inferno*, Sandro Botticelli, *c.* 1485

Why did the children of Israel wander aimlessly rather than proceeding directly to their destination? We are told that you cannot liberate yourself from a slavish mindset in one go; revolutionary vanguards always tend to complain of the people they lead as an undeserving lot, not quite ready for their own liberation. We are told that a whole generation died in the wilderness because they doubted, even Moses, who felt compelled to send spies to check on the lie of the land and come back with samples of its produce. 'Surely it flows with milk and honey', they report. But there is a catch. Their sin? To lose heart at the sight of fortified cities and resident giants and thus to succumb to despair about the odds of success. Only a glimpse at life outside the Pharoah's jurisdiction is enough to demoralise them. What if the land of milk and honey has been Egypt all along, they wondered. As payback for their doubt, the forty days' spy-tour turns into forty years in the wilderness. Only the women, and Caleb and Joshua, the two men who had argued against waiting, will eventually make it.

The wilderness speaks of the Israelites' ambivalence about the movement to freedom, even after all that has happened. And yet that ambivalence, that doubt, is also the key to a freedom fully contemplated, the straight path not so obviously preferable to the crooked one, a crooked path stretched to allow the incremental measure of freedom, both as test and testimony. If to rebel against slavery is to adhere to a part of oneself that does not exist (says philosopher Paul Ricoeur), freedom can only be an aftertaste. Perhaps the Hebrew spies were creating room for a change of heart, a return to Egypt to escape the scourge of war in the Promised Land. 'Was it from want of graves in Egypt that you brought us to die in the wilderness?' the people ask, their recurrent desire to return always pulsing just under the surface. Can they never stop 'thinking thoughts' about leaving Egypt, Exodus stretching out like a long argument along the zigzagging road of their sarcastic subversive emotions – at the sea ('let us be and we will serve the Egyptians, for it is better for us to serve the Egyptians than to die in the wilderness'), a month later ('for you have brought us out into the wilderness to starve this congregation to death'), and later ('to kill us and our children and our livestock by thirst'). Ah, the Egypt that protects!

Hence, as Zornberg beautifully writes in *The Particulars of Rapture*, in the indeterminate space of the Exodus we must contend with two very different narratives. It is this juxtaposition which determines the poles of freedom: the narrative of the day, public and demonstrative, and the narrative of the night, a story of panicked hustle, reckless havoc and unconscious yearning. It is this second narrative which opens up to our idiosyncratic questions and desires, and to other future stories. The gold of Exodus is not only a lie. It represents both a blinding and invisible presence, teasing the imagination and yet infinitely changing. Nothing is quite what it seems.

The counter-narrative can be brutal: it is about gods who only offer the delusion of release, the better to destroy people in the desert, a counter-narrative spoken by the sulking people themselves as they live through one punishing hardship after another. We were lured.

In these intertwined narratives, Exodus depicts the agony of all journeying, laden with fear of the unknown and indirection, the grip of anxiety, uncertainty, danger, along with dramatic mood swings from elation to scepticism, ecstasy to bitterness. How can we deny the real and present possibility that once the people see the challenges that arise while wandering in the desert, they might prefer to return to where, although 'enslaved', they can fall back on the familiar routine, the old consistency in their lives. Even when we are promised manna from heaven, aren't we all reluctant to try something new, to veer off into uncharted territory, to stray from our comfort zones? We all hesitate to know what we truly desire and to seek possibilities anew, expectant.

When two roads diverge in a wood, would we not want to be able to say, like Robert Frost, 'I took the one less travelled by, and that has made all the difference.' Or, like the Babylonian Talmud, 'There is a long way which is short and a short way which is long.' The grand narrative – that through their circuitous route in the wilderness from slavery to freedom, the Hebrew tribes become a unified nation, a people of Israel, stronger and more mature through overcoming adversity – becomes paradoxically incidental.

Many questions remain. Is it fair for the privileged among the people to decree that no short-term hardship is too great for the sake of the long term? Why were women the ones, almost the only ones, to make it to the Promised Land, the destruction of a generation in the desert limited to the men only? Are women the resilient ones or simply more capable of shrugging off past humiliations? Is wilderness in the end about learning to banish second thoughts? About burning our bridges one by one, even in exchange for a bridge of indeterminate length to an unknown destination?

‡

'God brought them out of Egypt; he hath as it were the strength of an unicorn,' says the sacred text. Maybe unicorns are the only way? But only if genuinely magical thinking is to take over the whole damn story.

‡

When contemplating the dismal prospect of never reaching the Promised Land, why did one arch-Brexiter complain of how the end of the rainbow, presumably with its pot of gold, seemed unattainable? Those of us who know our science knew this already. A rainbow has no end. And yet science tells us that you could be standing at the end of a rainbow right now in someone else's eyes. They will need to be at exactly the right angle relative to the sun's rays. And that angle is forty-two, the answer to the ultimate question of life, the universe and everything. Maybe it is no coincidence.

Promised Land, Promise?

The new Britain in a post-Brexit world will be the greatest country on earth – that is the Promise! 'A land of wheat and barley, and vines, and fig trees, and pomegranates; a land of oil, olives and honey.'

From the first Exodus to ours, we twenty-first-century folk can truly hope for the best of both worlds: there will be no wars with the locals in *this* Promised Land – protracted class war excepted. There will be no Canaanites and other peoples to dispossess in *this* Promised Land – except for the millennials and their shrinking horizons. There will be no lost tribes in *this* Promised Land – Scots excepted. And no scorched earth either. Only a green and pleasant land, lawful and Mad Max-less.

Hang on! Has the original Exodus not left us a lesson of paramount importance, that one does not enter a Promised Land duty-free? The promise is always going to come with conditions and caveats. Even without the Lord in the picture, you do not get a promise like this without strings attached.

Can a promise best be kept as an ever-receding present?

Whose promise is it anyway? Which moral agent will be accountable? And to whom? Who sets the conditions and who is to fulfil them? How long can a promise be pending? If freedom is not the absence of constraints but the ability to choose the right constraints for your community, what constraints is Britain to choose on this interdependent planet of ours?

...surely it flows with milk and honey... *Moses and the Messengers from Canaan*, Giovanni Lanfranco, 1621–1624

Who will own the promise when there are such radically different ideas of what it should mean?

Digital image courtesy of the Getty's Open Content Program.

Libertarian or statist Brexit advocates? Materialists dreaming of milk and honey, idealists dreaming of a society of pioneers, or those who understand how the two are intertwined? Or will everyone pretend, in a very British way, that the country never voted for *this* Promised Land, a land disowned by all in the end? We have not left enough, we have left too much. Brexit could have been great, could never have been great.

We don't know what a promise means to those who reject its premise. But perhaps the promise itself can lead them to change their mind. 'I admit it,' one hears in the corridors of power, 'I did not want to leave, but it's not every day that a country of our size gets to remake its relation to itself and to the world from scratch.'

But who will have offered the most honest Brexit?

Who cares about electoral promises anyway, short of true commitments and solemn vows? What is a promise worth in the face of radical uncertainty? Should a promise be kept if the world changes?

Many a revolutionary promise has ended up making hardly any difference at all.

Will our grandchildren sigh, fifty years from now: 'They sang "Jerusalem" until they were blue in the face, but nothing happened!' Will they have abandoned 'leave' and 'remain' labels to this moment in time? Or will they remember a Thirty Years War about what country we wanted to be? How much agency is there between doom and glory? Between the land of opportunity and ambition and the no man's land of delusion and destruction?

In fifty years' time our grandchildren will know if the promise was based on illusions or foresight, if homegrown afflictions have finally been tackled once EU obstruction has gone or if they have exploded without EU facilitation.

They will know which side of the political spectrum has tied the hands of the other, whose agenda will be locked out – high or low standards, more or less state aid, nationalisation or deregulation, arch-socialism or arch-capitalism, and if the great patriotic Brexit ended up repatriating or outsourcing work and public contracts.

They will know if this was a promise for some but not for others. Middle Earth's juxtaposition of rolling green uplands and post-apocalyptic wastelands. If the winners turned out to be the traffickers and crooks, or honest traders and workers. They will know if losers were compensated and if the masses have found their calling by producing bad art in a world overtaken by robots.

They will know if Britain has been debilitated by inwardness and reinvigorated by outwardness. If the end of mass immigration from Europe meant a darker-skinned Britain or a thinner, leaner and more self-sufficient Britain, its working-class revolt turned into a working-class nirvana, everyone in high-skill, high-productivity, highly rewarding jobs – except the robots, of course. And if it has been good or bad to bring back home everything, the outsourced governance, politics and car parts.

They will know if Brexit removed or created excuses for their grandparents not to improve their lives. If they ended up blaming all their problems on Brexit, or praising Brexit for all their accomplishments, even if it had little to do with either. Everyone will almost certainly blame the weather.

In short, they will know if the message of Exodus has been heard – that no covenant can be sustained on the back of social injustice, property accumulation and ludicrous inequality, and that even Canaan becomes a prison where the children of Israel end up oppressing one another, condemned to imitate their own past.

And so they will know if Britain has turned out to be poorer but happier, Brexit's great silver lining. A fairer, more egalitarian country, committed to rebalanced growth, responsible capitalism, redistributed risk and the circular economy. They will even have figured out if social democracy, progressive internationalism and socio-ecological transition has been possible in one country or whether that was always going to be a Euro-wide thing.

And they will have learned how changing a covenant in one sphere – Europe – meant changing covenants in all others, between citizens and nations of the UK, and between the UK and each European country. They might even have authored a written constitution to encapsulate their new insights, a new covenant that can only come to be through popular consent, and thus commitment.

They will have had time to reflect on how their forefathers' desire for transformation meant un-transforming themselves too as EU citizens. And they might also have discovered Russian dolls of unfreedom nested inside freedom.

Can the clock be turned back and undoing member statehood

become an exercise in nation-state rebuilding? Will the many repatriated EU powers be brought back all the way down, and devolution transformed into genuine localism? Often, they will have different answers depending on where they sit.

They will know if relationships on these islands that were transformed by togetherness in the EU have been creatively reinvented, or if the Kingdom is no longer United, while Ireland is one and Scotland gone. They will know if England has happily become Little, released at last from the Great in Great Britain that inspired English Leavers in the first place. And they may have discovered 'English European' to be a more comfortable identity than 'British European.'

And they will know if we have stopped plundering poor countries' doctors, cosying up to foreign autocrats, pretending still to rule the waves. And if the former colonies have figured out that Britain has become one of them, struggling to make good on its newly acquired freedom. They will know if New Delhi managed to extract its own price for coloniser atonement: free movement of people and visas for all. And if the Anglosphere has remained an old-fashioned club for well-behaved white men, or become a hip rainbow club for worldly millennials.

...When Albion is awakened at the end of time, what will he see... Visions of the Daughters of Albion, William Blake, 1793

©Yale Center for British Art, Paul Mellon Collection

But they might never know who won the war of counterfactuals. What would have happened if we had stayed? Would we have been less able to do this or that? Was this or that something we could not do before – train apprentices or trade with the world? Run our schools and hospitals better? Was global Britain not possible as part of global Europe?

And they might contemplate anew William Blake's Albion, both man and land, mapped onto Jerusalem, both woman and city, with his twelve sons impersonating the twelve tribes, and with his daughters weeping and yearning for liberty in a monarchy-oppressed Britain. When Albion, whose fall into selfhood even the cathedral cities, Angelomorphic Eternals or wise Erin (Ireland) cannot prevent, is awakened at the end of time... what will he see?

Suburban Life

On the impossibility of arriving elsewhere

When God created the world, He told the angels He was going to create a promised land called the UK. He described the rolling hills and the verdant fields, great cities, wondrous art and amazing science they would enjoy. 'Won't the rest of the world be jealous?' the angels fretted. 'Don't worry,' said God, 'wait until the world sees the neighbours I'm giving them!'

Ah, the neighbours! The Brexit mantra does not bin them, it only relabels them. We are not leaving Europe, just the EU. Is this a promise, a threat or a plea?

Perhaps it was always going to be Exodus-lite. When, early on, Michael Gove tweeted on 'the need to renegotiate a new relationship with the EU, based on free trade and friendly cooperation', the irony was not lost on the twittersphere: 'What a fascinating proposition'; 'One wonders why nobody ever thought of such a genius arrangement before'; 'Great idea! I even thought of a name for it...'

That is the mark of this strange Exodus. It is not about arriving elsewhere. The Israelites were promised that they would be immune from Egyptian diseases in Canaan. But Britain will never be impervious to European tremors.

The future relationship will be a very neighbourly affair. Canaan can be found on the map as 'Europe-not-EU'. We are European, Leavers say. This is not just about geography, but a way of life and values. Confused Remainers must learn to distinguish between Europe – full of lovely, modern, cultured restaurateurs – and the EU – drunk, overpaid, sclerotic, unaccountable grey suits. We remain a proud member of the family of European nations. No EU can take this from us.

For those who see the EU as Europe's contemporary destiny, Europe-not-EU makes little sense. The EU is all we've got, they say. Europeanness is synonymous with support for EU membership. History trumps geography. The point is not just Europe, but *which* Europe: institutional Europe at peace with itself or fragmented Europe at war. The EU may often be a talking shop, but talking shops matter. European peace is continuously reaffirmed around EU tables. In this day and age, the EU *is* Europe. You must own your choice.

Where shall the two sides meet? No one can deny that 'Europe-not-EU' sounds better than 'Us versus Them'. But this still leaves the 'not' in 'not EU' to be defined.

No longer a member, the UK becomes a so-called third country for the EU, a non-EU state. But perhaps in time the guardians of the faith on each side will learn not to see the UK as any old third country, a people that has left the EU for the big wide world, once again the Channel delineating an 'elsewhere'. 'Brexit means Brexit' cannot obscure a fundamental truth: Brexit means inventing a new category of country, a new animal in the international system, namely 'a former EU member state'. 'We will be a third country partner like no other,' say the Brexiters, 'for this will not be an EU-law free land.' EU members, forget your annoyance and ask: can we treat the Brits as if they have never been part of us? As if they have never helped run our markets, built our cities, filled our coffers...

The Hebrews toiled in Egypt for four centuries before they left, by which time they had become indispensable. Even if the UK isn't indispensable, it would be debasing the status of EU membership to hand out worse treatment to the UK than to those who have never been our equals around the table, who do not know our grand strategies and our dirty little secrets. In time, some secrets become obsolete and the old familiarity wanes, but this common past can never be erased.

You may rush to airbrush the UK from EU maps, as happened to Algeria upon independence in 1962 (who has ever found an EC map which includes it?). But this will not be as easy as if the UK was never there. For better or for worse, the UK has left its footprint at the heart of the enterprise. Only the sheer self-righteousness of Brexit ideologues could end up erasing Britain's *acquis* (legal framework) in the EU, testing the goodwill of even its most loyal supporters on the continent.

But these ideologues are not the whole UK. Where else than the UK is the EU defended with such passion, life outside it hailed as a wasteland of uncertainties, young and old marching together against the enforced Exodus?

We know from experts who measure these things that linguistic and colonial ties may help boost trade with the anglosphere, but that geography and culture matter even more. Can future sentimental ties tip the scales? Is it not also up to EU citizens and their leaders to ensure that the cultural costs of Brexit are not greater than the economic ones, and that the ideals of common Europeanness remain?

Many on the continent want to convince themselves that a restrictive future trade deal will affect neither the bigger geopolitical alliance between the two sides nor bilateral relations between, say, France and the UK toiling together in Mali. True. No bargaining linkage has been made. The Brits swore their unconditional security support early on. But politics is not just about deals on paper. Political atmospherics matter. Which UK government will send soldiers to die in Africa alongside the French, if they have helped kill the UK car industry?

Intransigence will continue to be about self-preservation for the EU. It fears a UK in Europe-not-EU freed to undercut its continental competitors. Clearly, we cannot offer absolute frictionlessness, the coveted meaning of membership of the single market, only 'as little friction as possible.' Full access to the EU's single market must be a fair game, on a levelled field, a French obsession from the very beginning in 1957. Fair enough. But how do we agree on what 'fair' means in 'fair competition'?

Inevitably, then, the road to global trade for the UK will no longer run through Rome. It may not be sheer madness to choose more passports for inbound global talent even if this means fewer passports for EU-bound financial services. In time, preferring a European over a Brazilian applicant might come to be seen as betraying the cosmopolitan ideal that so many young Europeans profess to have. A Brexitland of equal global citizens may become as attractive as one of equal Europeans. If we are truly one planet, millennials in power may ask, why should southern or eastern Europeans be privileged over global southerners and easterners?

Or perhaps in time the new generations in Europe will conjure up a new promised land together; reinvent the idea of being

...As if they had never run our markets, built our cities, filled our coffers...
Egyptian hieroglyphs of Hebrew slaves making bricks, collage and elaboration from engravings of Tomb of vizier Rekhmire, c.1450 BC

European as actors in a web of networks, of which the EU is only one. After all, the Jews did leave Egypt but not the Middle East. If the kingdom of Egypt had been a trans-Middle East union, the Exodus would have become a mere walk in the back garden for the Hebrews.

Perhaps the Promised Land was always going to be nearby, a pirouette away. Perhaps it can never be anything but a glorified suburb of the sprawling EU, connected to other suburbs as Europe's *limes* look both inwards and outwards. Would this be so bad? After all, even Leavers might remember Margaret Thatcher's 1975 campaign slogan: 'Support your Local Continent'.

Or perhaps it will not be a matter of goodwill, memory, faithfulness to old ties, but, rather, a matter of realpolitik. Ring-fencing Britain is no less possible today than when Napoleon tried to implement his neutral blockade, only to see it circumvented as soon as it was announced. Instead, Britain could become the EU's indispensable intimate rival, the necessary pragmatic Yin to its hubristic Yang, or vice versa. Perhaps it is in the EU's interest to contribute to the meaning of Europe-not-EU instead of scratching its self-inflicted wounds.

Who can deny that a world of emperors and warlords replete with variations on the Putin–Trump axis will long continue to lay bare the old commonalities and shared interests in Europe, both Europe-as-EU and Europe-not-EU. On the day Brussels agreed to the withdrawal agreement, two sanction threats were issued from Europe: the UK joined the EU in warning the US over trade, and the EU joined the UK in warning Russia over poison.

Perhaps reinventing a new alliance requires separation, and union is only possible between bodies that stand apart in the first place. Might it not be possible for the UK to walk hand in hand with the European Union, rather than joined at the hip? A Brexit cordial can be the new *entente cordiale*, but this time not *against* Germany but *for* Europe and its presence in the world. For a new *Europe cordiale* whose civility starts at home.

The Sea, the Sea

In the long shadow of history, Brexit will not be about Pharaoh, the wilderness or the Promised Land. Whatever the shade of Brexit, it was always about keeping eyes on the prize, a single date: Departure Day. What mattered in the end was only this: the sea, the sea.

Moses' negotiations were a charade; we always knew the ending. In this stubborn affirmation, the Exodus offered Brexiters less a bargaining blueprint than a lesson in revolution. Forget petty calculations. In the end rebels just go for it. Before leaving, Moses challenges Pharaoh: 'As you live, not one hoof shall remain. Then all these courtiers of yours shall come down to me and bow low to me, saying, "Leave, you and all the people who follow you!" After that I will leave.' Oh the sweet frisson of defiance.

Breaking free requires the most dramatic leap of faith. The Red Sea did not become dry land 'until they entered it'. The best Brexit would have meant crashing out in the turbulent waves. Clean. Chaotic. Spectacular. Nothing can derail us. We can just walk away. 'No deal' was not a threat but a goal. The people will go. Not one shall remain. If they had resisted further, the army of EU bureaucrats would have drowned in an Irish Sea of red tape. No matter that at the edge of the sea we have not turned back and fought but continued fighting among ourselves.

Could it be that this one fantastically awesome image gives us a clue to the contradiction at the heart of the Brexit story? The dramatic parting of the seas from the cliffs of Dover justifies yielding to almost any old version of wilderness or Promised Land. The next battle, Brexit 2.0, will be fought another day, by all sides.

At some point in the Exodus story an angel pleads, 'Save the Israelites but don't destroy the Egyptians.' To no avail. The sea shall part and close again. As the continental troops prepare for the next Brexit battle, perhaps our plea will echo: 'Save the EU but don't destroy the British.'

...And Moses stretched forth his hand... And the waters returned, and covered the chariots, and the horsemen, and all the host of the pharaoh that came into the sea after them; there remained not so much as one of them... (Exodus, 14:27) *The Egyptians Drowned in the Red Sea*, Gustave Doré, 1866

You may ask: if there are no slaves and no tyrants in this story, why should we bother with the sea at all? Or you may pause to witness this moment, in the spring of 2019, as the unreconciled British tribes watch the sea close behind them while contemplating the impossibility of arriving elsewhere, and as their European neighbours, undrowned on the shore, sigh 'what about us?' while contemplating the departing tribes' dreams and fears.

© PRISMA ARCHIVO / Alamy Stock Photo

And did those feet in ancient time
Walk upon England's mountains green:
And was the holy Lamb of God
On England's pleasant pastures seen!

And did the Countenance Divine
Shine forth upon our clouded hills?
And was Jerusalem builded here
Among these dark Satanic Mills?

Bring me my Bow of burning gold!
Bring me my Arrows of desire!
Bring me my Spear! O clouds, unfold!
Bring me my Chariot of fire!

I will not cease from Mental Fight,
Nor shall my Sword sleep in my hand,
Till we have built Jerusalem
In England's green and pleasant Land.

'Jerusalem', William Blake, 1804

Reckoning

Brexit Means Everyone Should Leave

Which brings us to our second story – for Brexit is not just about Britain, of course.

As we shift our gaze from the little island retreating within its shores to the continent as a whole, itself the small tip of the Asian landmass, we find countries submerged by one seismic wave after another, each stronger than the one before, with no time to absorb the preceding aftershock. Europe is drowning. Europe is burning. Chaos is upon us and the shockwave threatens to engulf our very foundations.

Brexit no longer just means the plain fact that Britain will leave,

©Tate, London 2019

…One seismic wave after another… *The Deluge,* Francis Danby, *c.* 1837

but instead suggests an injunction: *Brexit means that everyone should leave* before we all drown and fall into the abyss.

As meaning drifts towards stories of Reckoning, we read Brexit as a revealer of uncomfortable truths. The Brits only dared to make them visible. There are certainly bigger problems in the world than Brexit, but Brexit served as the canary in the coal mine. Now starts the descent into darkness.

The uncomfortable truths? Brexit may have been a bombshell in the European landscape, but the landscape was already devastated by the policies and mindsets that betrayed its people, overdosing on capitalist destruction and neo-liberal hypocrisy.

Stories of Reckoning tell us that this was not a tsunami of crisis coming from nowhere, or from Wall Street or Palmyra, but one of our own making, we Europeans, a chastisement for past deeds, our very first War of Interdependence. They tell us that the EU's commanding spheres are being punished for their hubris, for engineering collisions between worlds in pursuit of frictionlessness, and for ignoring the rolling waves of popular protest and democratic revolt across Europe.

And they tell us that the EU is punished less for what it has done than for what it has failed to do: deal with unfair globalisation, uncontrolled migration, the unfettered enrichment of the few.

From the eurozone's multiple debt wounds to the tragic moral tale of refugees dying to be with us, this is a union whose open-society values are mocked from within by leaders who prefer to look to Putin rather than to the spirit of Mandela, against the backdrop of terror in our cities inflicted by our own children, kids from the suburbs who, in another universe, could have been the friends of their lifeless victims.

Brexit's message to the world – that the EU is no longer a space you should want to belong to – rings like the harbinger of things to come. Brexit is about the fate that is awaiting an ever-older union that has given up on attractiveness better to lock itself up in its contradictions.

‡

Denial is the only reason for EU leaders to hang on to the first exceptionalism story and pretend that British Leavers are the only ones to feel left behind by economic growth, left out of politics and left aghast by societal change.

Denial blinds us to the lethal work of the wicked sisters, contempt and humiliation: contempt for the other side that does not sound or act like me, and humiliation of all the victims of power, the power to make invisible, to belittle, deny or crush whoever is in the way.

Denial of what happens next when economic integration begets social disintegration, and when a fair-weather construct fails to prepare for the great floods of political climate change.

Denial of our deepest ambivalence, that of an old and shrinking continent sitting naked on a demographic time bomb, yet bent on keeping out the only ones who could possibly defuse it.

Denial helps us pretend that there were no Italians, Greeks, or Poles after the British vote who, feeling trapped in a loveless EU marriage, sighed with desperate envy.

In this story, Exodus's forty years in the wilderness becomes perpetual purgatory for all sides, a limbo Europe whose internal squabbles have blinded its sinners to the greater ills they have countenanced. A Narcissus Europe eternally gazing at its own image but never able to grasp it, lonelier than ever.

There may be no other spectacular exits in the near future, but the spectre of European disintegration became real and institutionalised with Brexit, spelled out in procedures, article numbers and summit agendas. Euroscepticism is now not only in power in some EU capitals but also able to command the very boundaries of Europe, a core marker of our collective identity – if there is such a thing. And it has transformed every domestic theatre into a localised battle for the survival of Europe. Ironically, Brexit voters may have been early messengers, but the political characters of the UK theatre are not cut from the same populist cloth.

As a story of Reckoning, Brexit is the first small step in the triumphant march of those who are able to capture the public imagination across member states and beyond in the new politics of anger, popular insurrection and tribal eruptions. It will not do to dismiss the prophecy as self-fulfilling. The Eurosphere will ignore it at its peril. Europeans must reckon with their demons.

Oedipus was destined to die as a baby. His parents, the king and queen of Thebes, had been told the prophecy that he would kill his father, Laius, and marry his mother, Jocasta. He had to be 'exposed', abandoned to die. As the story unfolds, the shepherd tasked with the deed hangs Oedipus upside down from a tree, hence his name (*odein*, swollen, *pous*, foot), but then he sees some men take the baby away – perhaps he even talks to them... Twenty years later, we find Oedipus, an accomplished young prince who has been raised as their own son by King Polybus and Queen Merope of Corinth. Alas, one day, Oedipus, teased about having been adopted, runs to the Pythia (the high priestess) in Delphi to hear the truth. Instead he is only told about the terrible prophecy. Devastated, he runs away from the parents he still thinks are his own. He encounters another chariot at a crossroad and kills the men driving it, who do not want to give way. A few days later, entering the city of Thebes, in mourning for its king, he defeats the Sphinx, a lion-bodied female with eagle wings and serpent's tail, who is preying on Theban youths and devouring all who fail to solve her riddle. The riddle? Who walks with four legs in the morning, two on midday, three in the evening? The answer is Man. Oedipus is rewarded for solving the riddle with the hand of the widowed queen Jocasta. Twenty years later, as Thebes is engulfed by a terrible plague, Oedipus is advised by the same old Pythia in Delphi that salvation can only come through finding King Laius's killer. The old sage Tiresias warns him that hearing the truth will mean his downfall. But Oedipus does not give up and ends up extracting his story from the shepherd. Jocasta hangs herself. Oedipus puts out his own eyes. He will wander the earth for another twenty years with his daughter Antigone, who finally brings him to die in the sacred woods of Erinyes with Theseus as their witness.

But...Whose Judgement?

Of course, stories of Reckoning are no more straightforward than those of Exodus. They come in different shapes and forms. Reckoning has to do with both realising that something happened because of what I did or failed to do, and dealing with it. It is not asking Louis XVI to erase his famous scribble in his diary on 14 July 1789 as the Bastille was being stormed: *Rien.* Instead, it is wishing he had lived to make up for it.

For whom does the bell toll in our Brexit Reckoning? Which variant shall we heed? Which apocalypse shall we fear? Who is to blame and who will be saved? We know that after hubris comes nemesis, the goddess from whom there is no escape – but where does redemption lie?

Some believe in indiscriminate judgement and others that it is all in the sorting of the worthy from the sinners, the glorification of some and the chastisement of others. Others remember that before becoming the implacable punishment for hubris, nemesis was simply justice's twin, ensuring one's deserved fair share.

Some believe that the last judgement will never happen, that Brexit means that the EU now lives in its shadow in a state of permanent ontological insecurity, a Reckoning forever postponed, forever possible. But for the faithful, God's grace in delaying Judgement Day does not mean it will never take place. Doomsday is only deferred.

...Who is to blame and who will be saved... *The Last Judgment*, Hieronymus Bosch, *c.* 1482

In this godless world, who or what will decide on payment for our collective mistakes? Who will be our judges ruling on the meaning of consequences?

If it were true that, as Dominic Johnson argues in *God is Watching You*, most humans have only walked the righteous walk because they believe in God's eye in the sky, we are in trouble. To replace this intimate conviction, we have created institutions in the forms

77

of norms and procedures – but are these adequate substitutes? Probably, at least if they are manned by humans humble enough to recognise that they are not blessed with a God's-eye viewpoint and that they are fallible. Power-holders of all stripes, beware of your hubristic demons!

And who will be saved from the flood? Who will be accountable for all this economic violence if we cannot agree on what has failed to deliver on the promise: markets, capitalism, modernity, which of their variants?

To be sure, if Brexit is a story of popular wrath, it seems that everyone does agree on one thing: financial elites must be punished for the twin sins of gluttony and contempt, the happy few who revelled in their favourite game of casino capitalism, playing Russian roulette with the welfare of hundreds of millions of people, keeping all the gains for themselves and robbing the masses of both their wealth and their dignity. But, of course, we know better. In the real world, it is these very sins that have enabled roulette addicts to escape the blame net. After all, who among the powerful does not believe that they are the ones who belong on Noah's Ark?

In truth, causes and consequences tend to be impervious to the eye in the sky, to ideals of just punishment and reward. Every Greek tragedy offers scores of collateral damage – the Chorus whispering to us across the ages that, as always, the most vulnerable will pay inside and outside the UK: the periphery, the south, the east, the (still) left-behind.

What Truths?

Everyone these days seems to speak of simple truths. Yet the uncomfortable truths that must be faced tend to be very elusive.

Oedipus was always going to kill his father, Laius, and marry his mother, Jocasta. The fates decreed it when he was born. But for what reason? Who failed to heed the prophecy? His parents, who wavered at his birth and instead of killing him left him to die on the mountain? The shepherd, who took pity? Oedipus himself, who failed to read the signs? Or does the whole affair go back to the foundation, an old forgotten story about his father before Oedipus was even born? Funny how we tend to accept that Oedipus' terrible fate originates in a prophecy, an old wives' tale. What if it was instead a father's punishable deed? Would this not change our sense of the origins of just blame?

Once we raise doubts about who started it all we must give up the idea of Greek tragedies as stories of inexorable destinies, against which humans can do nothing as puppets of the gods, luck or the butterfly effect. In truth, the Greek tragedy may offer impossible choices, but it is after something else: the quest for agency, a person, a moment, an act, when we can decide to play out a 'consequence' in a particular way. How could King Oedipus, who gave us the answer to the most befuddling riddle of all time, not be in charge! As the paradigmatic seeker *and* avoider of truths, Oedipus both very deliberately solves the Sphinx's riddle, and very accidentally fulfils the prophecy. Duelling with a stranger on the road who happens to be his father, falling in love with a queen who happens to be his mother – who would have known! When much later the old prophet Tiresias reluctantly tells him, 'You killed the man whose killer you now hunt,' and later again, 'He'll soon be shown father and brother to his own children,' we, the audience, understand with a gasp what has happened, but Oedipus at first refuses to, blinded by what he thinks he knows of the world and of his own life. Can Freud's 'What have I done?' (if you happen to have sex with a member of your own family) ever be redeemed by acknowledging that the truth is blindingly obvious? On realising what he has brought about, Oedipus stabs out the eyes which could not see, and in this very stabbing sees for the first time.

...Everyone these days seems to speak of simple truths... *Oedipus*, Elysium Conservatory Theatre, Los Angeles, 2014

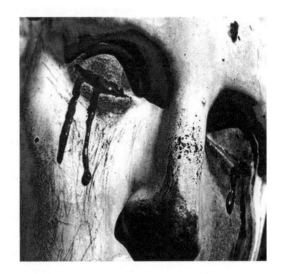

Ah, truth tends to be so complicated. Can we ask, as we watch the unfolding Brexit saga, what riddles have we failed to solve and who are the ones who should be taking their own eyes out?

Endisms Galore!

When the status quo is challenged, stories of Reckoning come like ritual incantations, especially from the great and the good who have most to lose. We hear different pitches and different vocabularies, but a common language of foretold destruction, with everyone hoping that optional salvation is part of their personal package. In leaving the EU for an unknown destination, the Brits will create their own apocalyptic ricochets in the unsettled sea of human twenty-first-century civilisation.

For Brexit has spelled the return of an endism fad which pervaded the turn of this millennium some years earlier. We were told then of the end of history, the end of geography, the end of territory, the end of the state. Endisms galore! But endism ended too. History, geography, territory, the state, they are all here to stay. Still, there is a vast gap between hyperbolic and cautionary endism.

End-of-Days stories of indiscriminate Reckoning have existed since the dawn of mankind. This is where the rationalist reader acquaints herself with the esoteric yet widespread belief in the Mark of the Beast, $\chi\iota\varsigma$, which inspired artists as diverse as El Greco, William Blake and Andy Warhol. Accordingly, the fifth seal of the apocalypse, when broken, will let free the righteous souls awaiting their revenge for having been persecuted unfairly, since they had refused to submit to a certain logic inspired by Satan. A logic now exposed. The reader may discover that some people on earth today bear the mark for acquiescing to what is done in the name of global economics and profit-across-borders gone mad, a mark manifesting itself in the form of a microchip implant as required by frictionless trade, that very same condition desired by most Leavers and Remainers.

If not this exact version, does Brexit bring some version of the apocalypse closer? In the immediate aftermath of the vote, some commentators contemplated the Archduke Ferdinand scenario, whereby Brexit would unleash an inevitable chain of events: the continent profoundly damaged as its biggest financial centre is cut adrift... a few more states decide to leave... having lost the prospect of membership, south-eastern Europe slides back into conflict...

Russia opportunistically seizes the moment... the EU remains divided and paralysed... no conventional deterrent can be found... nuclear Armageddon.

Not quite.

But even if global peace is not at stake, even with EU disintegration nowhere near, the Brexit earthquake and its aftershocks can spell a more mundane Reckoning short of End-of-Days variations.

For one thing, the British vote of no confidence in the EU has simply accelerated a geopolitical sorting-out on the global stage. With less commercial might, less of an English accent and less institutional credibility, the EU will have to move one more echelon down the power ladder after the US and China. We already knew of Europe's relative decline, have long provincialized it in our mind, says the rest of the world, but we thought the EU was there to help bring about elegant decline, to help its member-states punch above their individual weight. With Brexit, that image is shattered. Even when baffled at the UK's decision, the rising powers, each with their own entrenched balance-of-power prism, are no longer impressed.

Add Donald Trump to the Brexit mix and this is the beginning of the destruction not only of the EU but also of Western political civilisation in its entirety (so said Donald Tusk, head of the European Council, shortly after he was elected), the great unravelling of the liberal international order and of a global capitalist economy built on a volcano of debt and volatility stocked by J. K. Galbraith's predatory class feasting on decaying systems originally built for the middle class. As with the 1900s, once the major powers overlook their own rules, the rest is up for grabs. Not only can the West no longer lay claim to the status of global rule-maker, but it is the very idea of a rules-based multilateral order that is being jettisoned by the British go-it-alone decision. That we need a dose of liberal self-reflection is a British understatement.

Anyway, says the West's 'rest', your ambition of global rule-making was not sustainable, a problematic residue of your colonial mindset, a white man's burden we are happy to relieve you of. Revisionist powers of the earth unite! In the far reaches of the globe, one hears the echoes of post-imperial *Schadenfreude*. If the very nation which invented the 'standards of civilisation' for its empire

Image courtesy of The Rosenbach Museum and Library

...A microchip implant as required by frictionless trade... *The Mark of the Beast is 666*, William Blake, c.1810

of yesteryear cannot accept the most advanced 'standards of cooperation' on earth from its neighbours and allies, how can the EU expect to remain a normative gatekeeper for the rest of the world?

More *sotto voce*, we hear the sigh of peace builders from East Asia to the Middle East who had been inspired by the EU story of reconciliation, a story of enemies turned into neighbours, and neighbours turned into friends. If the EU is rejected by one of its own, and one which has made such good use of its peace tools in Northern Ireland, where does the hope of peacemakers around the world lie, they ask.

Our post-Western age has begun.

Popular Wraths, Plural

We should stop speaking as if Brexit is either an inevitable end of an era or an accident.

Brexit means Reckoning: the price paid by Europeans, British and continentals alike, for endlessly delaying the need to acknowledge blindingly obvious truths. Brexit means stabbing ourselves in the eyes so that we can see again. Oedipus did not seek someone else to blame. Reckoning is about acknowledging that your own actions may have helped to precipitate events – even if you never intended to marry your mum.

Where has the EU gone wrong? What kind of chastisement awaits? Who is on the stand? Who in charge of the sorting out?

This judgement is neither the first nor the last of its kind. For we recognise here the historically recurrent pattern whereby the health of societies – or dare we say civilisations? – has fallen prey, again and again, to the autistic disconnection of predatory ruling elites, the privileged few who will not be chastened by civil societies, civil servants, civility *tout court*. Is this the moment when the EU reckons with the cyclical, history-old process of elite replacement from which there is no escape?

As a story of popular wrath, Brexit is but the bluntest expression of the Eurosceptic verdict on the EU, a Euroscepticism which may feed today's populist challengers but which pre-dates and transcends it. It would be a mistake to dismiss Eurosceptics as unredeemable enemies of the Union or to wish them away. For they belong to a clan of political shape-shifters: existential or reformist, closed or open, right or left, kneejerk or thoughtful. The breadth of ideas and ideologies coloured by Euroscepticism is remarkable.

To simplify: the damning popular verdict oscillates between two magnetic poles, in Britain and across Europe. There are those who vote or demonstrate *against* Brussels *for* London, Budapest or Athens. And there are those who vote or demonstrate *against* London, Budapest or Athens *through* their NO to Brussels. Both tend to mobilise around the amorphous idea of sovereignty.

For the first cohort, those against Brussels for London, national sovereignty is at stake. The EU's sin is its very *raison d'être* – its mission of taming nationalism through transnationally agreed constraints, by sharing sovereignty among states.

For the second cohort, revolting against London through rejecting Brussels, popular sovereignty is at stake. The true target of a 'people's Brexit' or Grexit or Frexit is the insurgents' own national establishment, the system nurtured by their own elites. NO to Brussels is a shortcut, not the main message, which is: sovereignty will no longer be kept out of the hands of the people. EU Exit is the only change on offer.

The two cohorts may overlap but each has asked for its own stage. Show trials? Glorious democratic soul-searching? Enter the courtroom. Meet the Chorus.

Sovereignty Angst

Scene: the courtroom

Questioner: What is your relationship with... national sovereignty?

EU: I have tried to tame her, to reassure her that my member states remain sovereign entities, able in the last resort to decide their own futures, but that she needs to be shared, pooled, conditioned, regulated, nudged, monitored, in order to make togetherness possible.

Q: But isn't it black or white in the end? You have it or you don't like virginity. And if you share it, nobody knows where it's gone!

EU: It has not gone anywhere! It's still with the countries of Europe, of course. But I am here to convince them that their precious sovereign prerogatives come with all the trappings of relationships.

Q: Ah, taming with a strong leash! Unsurprising that she might yearn to 'take back control'...

EU: Ideological crap...

Q: ...or our most basic animal instinct. Don't we all want to take responsibility for our own lives and be empowered to do so? Don't we all hate to be told what to do? Personal intuitions trump political abstractions. Control is paramount. Any parent of a teenage rebel understands this, right?

EU: For sure, I have plenty of those around my table. And they get it: I am actually the one who gives them back control. If you play by my rules, or in fact the rules they all make up together, you control all the others around the table. And, the icing on my cake, they all take back control together from Washington, Moscow and Apple.

Q: I'm not sure calling this game 'European sovereignty' clarifies your relationship with the national kind. More of one, less of the other.

EU: Silly thought! The two should be best friends. When a state volunteers to share sovereignty with its neighbours for the sake of greater influence in the world, it does not abandon but proves its independence. European sovereignty is about empowering Europeans not disempowering European states.

Q: *This is all very abstract. Cool Britannia, Global Britain, British outreach beyond its borders does not require EU blessing.*

EU: Why choose? Cool Britannia was about ruling Europe, not ruling itself out of Europe, and the road to Global Britain is through Global Europe.

Q: *Britons won't know until they are free to cooperate with whom they like, will they?*

EU: OK, I admit it. There is a trade-off, a trade-off as old as human attempts to live together. More cooperation means less control. We need to find the right balance.

Q: *Talk about balance! You are totally biased in favour of all those exporters, students, patients and idealists, who value cooperation over control, and against all those import-competing, migrant-competing, identity-sensitive souls who value control over cooperation. No wonder the clamour for taking back control has long been heard in the streets of Paris, Amsterdam, Dublin and Athens.*

EU: National sovereignty will not help these folks I am afraid. It does not make sense for a nation to try to retain exclusive control over her 'own' affairs given that what is her 'own' is up for grabs in an interdependent world. You know, Gaia's space, air, seas... And remember that markets, rights and duties tend to come as a package. Integration opens markets, requires rights for movers and duties to help losers.

Q: *True. But in the end, peace is not built on quick sand but rests on sustainable national orders and viable states...*

EU: ...but not in isolation.

Q: Sure, sometimes a little help from our foreign friends is indeed welcome. National sovereignty can be a lonely thing. When they showed a dramatization of the Gunpowder Plot on the BBC, it seems that British viewers really hoped for the king of Spain not to abandon Kit Harington's Catesby and Guy Fawkes to their sorry fate. But then they remembered: Guy Fawkes is our bloody bastard, not yours.

EU: Actually, British history is European history.

Q: Nevertheless, British, hum, English nationalism is unfamiliar, perhaps because it's not the same as the continental kind. They may be provincial but not xenophobes. They have taken in more Poles than all of you lot combined in the last ten years. They mostly love their neighbours down the street but simply could not cope with building the equivalent of a new city of public services every year.

EU: Maybe. But sovereignty won't serve their beers at the pub.

Q: But it will mean they decide who does. Don't be surprised if across Europe, fingers pointed resentfully at the 'other-within' rotate inexorably towards you, because you are committed to chipping away communities' most fundamental collective instinct: the capacity to exclude...

EU: Indeed! Inclusiveness is my greatest achievement...

Q: ...or dictate. Even with your grand lofty ideals you are starting to regret your one-sidedness in the eternal war between settlers and nomads, those anchored to a place and those who move within a bigger space. Your raison-d'être is to erase national borders.

EU: True. But free movement should not mean free for all. I am the one who decides what it means.

Q: Which brings us back to national sovereignty. Refusing to be governed at a distance does not mean she is xenophobic. A people's aspiration to self-determination can be an inclusive nationalism, can't it?

EU: If we were talking at the time of Garibaldi perhaps, a

nineteenth century when nationalism tended to be based on shared principles rather than race, ethnicity or religion, the cradle of nascent democracy. But after all that has happened since, nationalism has lost its lustre. Today, legitimate calls for more self-government unavoidably become laments about victimhood and ethnocentric grievances.

Q: Not so fast! What if national myths came with a grain of salt and refrained from coalescing populations against the ethnic other?

EU: Sure, there's nothing wrong with feeling pride and even love for one's country. But it's not OK to turn identity from a comfort blanket into a weapon: nationalism, ethnocentricism, racism, sexism... I don't want to be pedantic, but these are pathologies.

Q: What about Eurocentrism? Isn't that your pathology?

EU: Alas... or rather, thankfully, we are done with world dominion. Good luck to the Brits with their Empire 2.0!

Q: The fact is, Brexiters seem to be more concerned with Empire 1.0, you know, universal domination on the old continent itself... Rome will be Rome. Better to go it alone than stay in an ever-tightening continental embrace.

EU: I know what you have in mind. I loved *Darkest Hour* too. In fact, I exist so that our hours shall never be dark again – hey, I have just brought back daylight saving time forever! But seriously, my *raison d'être* is anti-hegemony, binding mighty nations to mutual rules in order to prevent the rise of any single one of them and protect the smaller ones against their big neighbours.

Q: In truth, beyond all the lip service you pay to equality, you never abolished the currency of power per se. Just made it invisible.

EU: I prefer to think I circulated it, from Prague to Paris, Madrid to Amsterdam, to Zagreb, Sofia, Tallinn, Berlin, Oslo, Bucharest, Nicosia, Luxembourg, Lisbon, Copenhagen, Warsaw, Dublin, Helsinki, Athens, Riga, Ljubljana, Vilnius, Bratislava, Stockholm,

...At the heart of every myth
is a drama of questioning...
Oedipus and the Sphinx,
Jean-Auguste-Dominique
Ingres, 1808–27

Vienna, Budapest still, Rome of course, and yes, London, the City *par excellence*. Oops, let's not forget Brussels.

Q: Indeed, Brussels! It has got more than its fair share. If you are so fond of your national capitals, why did you transfer all summits to Brussels? Why are you so obsessed with oneness, one voice, one president, one parliament for yourself? You were not built to transcend the nation state but to transform it. Why would you want to look just like it?

EU: Because I am envious? They've got the budgets, the armies, the state apparatus to do everything they want. All I can do is shiver naked or borrow their clothes.

Q: Cut the European queen some cloth! We wouldn't want her to succumb to pneumonia. Maybe you should let state sovereignty dress herself with new clothes that you could borrow from time to time. Call her progressive, emancipatory, open sovereignty exercising her prerogatives, mindful of others, taking back control to hand back control, serving at the European table more of her favourite dishes, autonomy, plurality, polyphony, polycentricity...

EU: Sounds fashionably attractive. But I am afraid her instincts cannot be trusted. In too many capitals, she falls for kleptocrats, oligarchs and nepotistic clans.

Q: Less so in the UK...

EU: No comment. I would love to be able to rely on solid national social contracts, a living rule of law culture everywhere constructed from within. Warsaw, Budapest, Athens, Bucharest can do worse than read *Magna Carta*.

Q: We agree! Except that it won't do for you to create debt colonies in the meantime, sacrificing the young generations in the south on the altar of the common currency. Greece's lost sovereignty has been the salt on other countries' symbolic wounds. Ask the Brexit campaign...

EU: ...or remind them that the keys to Greece's freedom are still held in Athens.

Q: Not if the north can help it. Admit it. The game in your town has been to let loose prejudices and clichés: Greek squanderers and swindlers, mean and miserly Germans, decadent Italians, unreconstructed easterners. You've only encouraged Europeans to push each other's national buttons.

EU: How can I help what happens between such different peoples? When I give them the euro to create some healthy entanglement between our economies and our destinies, southern Europeans hear suffocating embrace and northerners hear dangerous entrapment. Silly billies! The euro is our new global launch pad.

Q: Granted, your mission is not easy. But how clumsy of you to look and feel like a power grab when you are just a boring functional response to interdependence. How silly of you to blindly embrace the power of the market. How hypocritical of you to claim to tame sovereignty but stay furiously committed to the sovereignty of your members' debt!

EU: Clumsy, silly, hypocritical, to reject the Brexit story? Sovereignty cannot be only about control. It is about responsibility. Responsibility is about relationships. Relationships are negotiated. Negotiations are about compromises. But compromises are still your sovereign decisions. The circle is complete.

Q: Well, it has not always felt like that to the British public even when Her Majesty's government affirms that Parliament has remained sovereign throughout membership. Sovereignty is a sovereign impression.

EU: Indeed, we are acting together in the theatre of sovereignty: you pretend to ask for it, we pretend to give it back. What happens when impressions come up against facts? When Britons discover what they owe to their cherished sovereignty? Say... that it was Thatcher, not the EU, who decided not to tie fishing quotas to ports so they could be sold to a few companies and foreigners... And so on...

Q: You are admitting that it matters who wields it. Can we agree that we need to reclaim sovereignty from all those who abuse it, wherever they sit?

EU: Indeed. Our demanding gaze must rest firmly on states not only because they are the privileged place where democracy and solidarity can be deployed but also because they are the main institution that accumulates, uses and therefore potentially abuses power.

Q: I could not have put it better myself! We will reconvene another day. In the meantime, please do me a favour. Continue engaging with national sovereignty. Admit its mysterious hybridity as a useful and dangerous fiction, a force for exclusion and inclusion, a shield and a weapon for coercion, the road and the obstacle to imperialism, the cause of war and the pillar of peace. I don't care if you think she is a particle or a wave, divisible or indivisible, attractive or ugly, just face up to your relationship.

‡

The audience in the courtroom is getting impatient. With their feet on the ground, they stand up. They voted less against Brussels than against London through Brussels, against the sovereignty monopolisers, starting with the devil they know. London, Oxford, Cambridge: it's your bloody sovereignty, not mine.

They move to another stage nearby.

Naming the Beast

Chorus:

Brexit means the naming of the beast: us. We are the
people but no protagonist in this play can speak in our name.
We are the *masses* and no one can know us. We are the *mob*
and no one can stop us. We are the *plebians* and no one can
outfox us. We are the *citizenry* and no one can patronise us.
We are the *public* who watch attentively. We are the *crowd* and
we are wise. We are the *multitude* and not one among us can
claim to know our mind. The naming does not make us real,
or one. But we have imagined ourselves into being to bask in
our popularity. We are the sum of all the struggles that have
come before us which we have no right to undo.We the people
have no enemies except ourselves, no friends, only
courtiers.

All want to honour and serve us. The EU pays homage to our
cause: popular sovereignty, they say, the very core of European
heritage. Remainers lament that we have been duped. Brexit is a
populist con, not a popular revolt, they say. Leavers rejoice that
we have spoken. Brexit is the people's will, not an ignorant whim,
they say.

No longer can we be ignored or ordered to change our minds. Nor
should our say be God-equivalent – we do change our minds, you
know! Our status is not morally supreme but politically superior.
We will not let politicians appropriate our anger, even if our MPs
must interpret it. We say: with Brexit we have reminded everyone
that democracy is always incomplete and unpredictable, the shaker-
upper of all Leviathans.

Remainers say: the EU was just unlucky. Brexit is collateral damage,
our national democracies the targets. The EU is democracy's
friend. In the south and in the east, in Europe and out, it has given
us, the *demoi*, an anchor. It helps shame our nepotistic oppressors
and moderate extremists. It empowers us in every guise: activists,

consumers, women, fighters against corporate greed and privacy theft. Brexit will weaken us...

Leavers say: Brexit will strengthen us. It will demonstrate the EU's complicity in our fate. Brussels has enabled our elites to collude across borders, escape political constraints at home and hide behind its laws against our wishes. Call them plutocrats, technocrats, bureaucrats, eurocrats, elitocrats or epistocrats, their creed is to reassure the markets, not the masses. They advance, votes-what-may. When they do not like our say, they re-elect us. National and supranational elites unite! Brexit is our payback for ganging up against us.

It started at the foundation, the plan to replace us, unruly warmongering mobs, with a grand European scheme. We might have deserved it. We had eaten our democratic child and happily killed each other in an endless war. The well-intentioned founders, humanist technocrats, former resistants and fathers without mothers, enshrined their views in a cathedral of limitation. Ulysses in dark suits, they tied their hands to the supranational mast better to resist our people's sirens, every time political battles would have been lost at home.

Shielded by Brussels, our European establishment sacrificed us to unmitigated market competition and austerity fetishism. Shielded by their privilege, they let us bear all the risks. Shielded by Weber's iron cage of bureaucracy in a Euro-bubble, they achieved the impossible: an iron cage in a bubble! A bubble to keep us riffraff out... A bubble we can neither enter nor poke. So don't be surprised if we put our lips together and blow.

James Madison, the great American founding father, was wrong to doubt us. We the people have read him with fickleness and passion. We have nothing against his fences to constrain power, checks and balances and all. We know with Montesquieu that the stuff we can't do is best done at the top, by a cadre of competent administrators devoted to serving the general interest and the rule of law. But we wonder about their post-sell-by-date credentials. We wonder what makes Madisonians think that those at the top are less self-interested, emotional and fallible than us. There can be madness in technocratic reason.

We know that the Olympians who preside over our destinies in our capitals and in Brussels want to protect us against predatory forces, corporate elites or obscure interests. Many of them are nice, educated, tolerant, environment-friendly, moral enthusiasts. And when they are nepotistic and corrupt, we ask the EU to help us rein them in. But we remember our (Greek?) ancestors and how the lives of the true Olympian gods, from Zeus downwards, were best enmeshed with humans. We have a soft spot for Machiavelli's advice to the prince, to use his skills against grandees and for the populii, to entrust the people with defending their city.

We know that the best among the elite can manufacture our consent without inventing enemies or denying the difficult choices we must make. Against the extractive elite, we trust the defiant elite who do not monopolise power but seek to empower others. But, still, we can't blindly trust them over ourselves. Let's face it, democracy today is a fiction to cover up the ways the wealthy continue to squeeze us. Only rule by the poor would be true democracy...

We are told that the EU may override our domestic politics for progressive ends. But that does not make the means any less anti-democratic. We are not localists against globalists, nationalists against internationalists, communitarians against cosmopolitans. We are on all sides, just as elites can be tribal.

We can be expert publics if you let us. The problem with our transnational elites is not that they lead, that's what they are paid for, but that they don't feel the need to be followed. After our insurgent vote, we were not surprised to learn that the more ruling-class elites felt we distrusted them, the more they tended to trust their European counterparts. Huddled in their lifeboat, they drift in the belief that Reckoning is simply part of the false consciousness that has beset us, hoi polloi, an ungrateful lot who fail to acknowledge what they have done for us. We the people do not seem to grasp that their Brussels conspiracy is truly for our own good, there to deliver public goods, precisely because these are 'public' and thus cannot be left to the public's whims.

What is subordination to the common good worth anyway,
if the common good has been privatised, captured, twisted
and monopolised?

The intelligentsia doubts our sound judgement. Do we appreciate the ways in which populist politicians and the technocratic sphere feed each other's conceit, as they collude in proclaiming that we are one and only one true people, national or European, a single expression of the general interest, and that they alone can know and enact it, in truth responsive only to the requirements of their staying power? Do we agree that majoritarian politics are a convenient shortcut, but only if winners are conjured up from a genuinely democratic process, and only if they do not monopolise the public space but respect oppositions and minorities? Do we appreciate that losers' consent is predicated on winners' respect for them? And that the people have no enemies but only disagreements? Do we take it upon ourselves to change the rules of mutual political engagement in Europe and absorb each other's concerns across borders? Yes on all counts.

In an ideal world, we European citizens stubbornly remain a multitude, unamenable to attempts to pervert our cherished popular sovereignty as if we were one. But the elites in that ideal world refrain from dismissing as 'populist' the kind of politics which channels our pent-up frustration, admittedly short of the nasty nativist kind. In that world, we all know that democracy is not just about elections but is a way of life. We reclaim our right to politics and to disagree intensely but with civility in the public sphere within and across our countries. And we proclaim that a decision can only be democratic in a moral sense if it is attuned to the dignity of all the peoples affected. In such an ideal world, our squabbling European politicians refrain from pitting us against each other, peoples against peoples. Instead, they park their egos to respect the most basic power imperative: thou shalt do no harm.

We, the sleeping sovereign, have awakened to the eerie silence of

democratic corruption, our muffled voices echoing in the distance…
Out of reach of electoral cycles, the EU may be a beautiful idea but
most among us have not been allowed to make it our own when
it comes to decide. So it must reckon with all the other ways we
express how we feel, in squares, on the web or in the ballot box…

As we clamour for the EU's democratic atonement, Leavers or not,
British or not, we the peoples of Europe will let no one speak in our
name.

Blame Games

Fine, the people have spoken. And thus the people can be blamed.

'It's not the EU punishing the UK for leaving,' cries the EU. 'It is the
consequences of Brexit that are punishing.' For Brexit has consequences.
They are unavoidable, as night follows day, as a volcano from
which we must protect our hapless people on the continent, says
a representative of the French president. This is what your 'Brexit
means Brexit' means to us.

To be sure, the idea of Brexit-as-Reckoning for the EU's travails
did not survive very long after the initial tremors of the vote. Instead,
the Brits were writing their own punishing scripts, attracting the
lion's share of blame while the EU was drawing inferences. The
inevitable ordeal would be ring-fenced. When the EU's intransigence
was invoked by Brexiters as a form of cruel and unusual punishment,
leaders shrugged their shoulders. Should Eurocrats have shuddered
when accused of nastily twisting the lion's tail? Should the UK's
soon-to-be-former EU partners have bowed to the constant flow of
insults? 'What country, by the nature of your error, should give you
safe harbour? Go you to France or Flanders, any German province,
Spain or Portugal? Nay…' Listen to your great Bard: Brexit means
your reckoning not ours.

And yet, as Aristotle said, 'Anyone can become angry – that is
easy… but to be angry with the right person, to the right degree,
at the right time, for the right purpose, and in the right way – this
is not easy.' Have EU leaders measured their anger wisely? Does

the EU landscape genuinely justify one-sided blame? Perhaps they should address too the vast array of British citizens who did not want it all. Has the EU not invited the invocation, even by the most moderate British observers, of the 'dictated peace' imposed on the Germans at Versailles at the end of the First World War? A century later, can the EU afford to have a resentful nation on its doorstep? It may not be wise to cut loose an economy equal in size to nineteen of its members simply to make a point: Brexit has consequences. Britain will not be Weimar, but if Weimar goes global on the cusp of migration waves and machine invasions, globalised blame games will not be the answer.

As we swim in the river of time, upstream to the causes of these infamous consequences of Brexit, downstream to the consequences of the consequences, blame dissipates in a thousand shreds. Yet, the blame cycle will continue. Leavers will blame the government for its betrayal, the government will blame the EU for its inflexibility and will blame Remainers for their defeatism, and the EU and Remainers will blame Leavers for their fantastical designs. All so that the wheels may turn and yet be forever still.

But what if no one was really to blame? What if the force field was simply too powerful for anyone to reckon with? Is it possible to observe that your own epoch is an interregnum, between one world and another, a change of era devoid of familiar signposts? Why is Gramsci's infamous catastrophic equilibrium of political forces in everyone's mind these days, everyone quoting his warning that we live 'when the old is dying and the new struggles to be born'. Does this have to be 'the moment when monsters arise'?

Edmund Burke blamed the French Revolution, claiming that you cannot simply eradicate institutions that have survived across the ages, and replace them with arbitrary constructs predicated on abstract considerations. Of course, you may ask which of the EU or Brexit is the most arbitrary construct. But you may also side with Tocqueville's version of 'the new struggling to be born'. As he saw it, Burke was wrong. The French Revolution did not replace anything that was not already dead, his old world of provincial and estate assemblies, orders, classes, professions, magistrates and nobles who had given up their duties and burden first, their privileges last. 'When the life-giving flame is extinguished,' he sighed, 'though the organs seem to act as before, the whole languishes at once and dies.' There is no choice but to move with the times but the times seem to move in countless directions. The EU is going through its Tocquevillian moment; old certitudes shattered, new designs only intuited, Brexit just one of its fragments, pregnant with false prophets and real meanings yet to be deciphered.

The Price of Hubris

Some believe the EU is at its best when it is most boring. Its dark-suited conclaves do not tolerate kindly excessive pride and defiance. Repeat: we infer consequences, do not call them punishment, we just say that Brexit cannot be painless, that we can't reward the one who is leaving.

This is an old story. For sure the old Olympians of the Greek pantheon could never tolerate hubris, man's propensity to transgress the order of things. Hubris was to be punished, the gods' revenge to match the deed: creative and demonstrative. Yet, is it possible even for Greek gods to truly punish on a par with the deed when we cannot be sure what the deed truly means?

Take Prometheus.

It can't be much fun to be chained to a rock in the Caucasus Mountains and have an eagle visit day after day to eat your liver, the seat of your soul and intelligence (actually every other day in full conformity with today's science of regeneration). But the world will surely always remember how glorious the cause! After all, the old Titan, older than Zeus himself, had created lovely human creatures by giving life to some carefully crafted God-like images.

...The old Olympians of the Greek pantheon could never tolerate hubris... *Prometheus*, Nicolas-Sébastien Adam, 1737

97

And in his great commitment, he had endowed them with the greatest gift of all: fire stolen from the gods (don't worry about how; the story has many variants). For their sake, he had defied his best friend Zeus who by then was planning to obliterate the human race. Lucky humans. He had offered them the sparks of intelligence; not just knowledge, but more importantly the yearning for it.

How we glorify Prometheus' Sacrifice in the name of progress and defiance!

To be sure, he may have borne his torture stoically because he knew that he would be saved, by no less than a son of Zeus, Hercules, who set him free thirteen generations down the road by killing the eagle (or vultures, depending on how vindictive you believe Zeus to be). Maybe Prometheus foresaw further, the impending fall of the Olympians in the mind of man. Did he reflect that Zeus might have been right to be doubtful about humankind's goodness, that he deserved his punishment after all? Did Zeus ever regret punishing his old friend? Or realise that he got the wrong guy, the humans being solely responsible for their destructive ascent?

Was he tempted to blame beautiful and brilliant Pandora, the gods' poisoned gift to Prometheus' brother Epimetheus, who released all evils on the world and left hope entrapped in her box? Since then, we humans have never stopped wondering whether Pandora's feat meant that hope was kept for us, or from us. Which of the two would be worse? Is hope the only way to keep going, stuck on your rock forever, gazing at a future that will never come?

Hoping to beat the gods at their own game, Kafka suggested other ways for punishment to end. Imagine for instance Prometheus disappearing 'deeper and deeper into the rock until he became one with it'. Or an alternative ending where 'his treachery was forgotten in the course of thousands of years, forgotten by the gods, the eagles, forgotten by himself'. Or yet another where everyone grows weary of the meaningless affair. 'The gods grew weary, the eagles grew weary, the wound closed wearily.'

Destruction. Indifference. Irrelevance. Hubris can lead down very different paths.

And what about the rock, asks Kafka, the 'inescapable mass of rock', support and cage at the same time, which escapes the dichotomy of punisher and punished, forever in between, mysterious and enduring. 'As it comes out of the substratum of truth it has in turn to end in the inexplicable.' Shall we ask, you and I, what is our in-between?

‡

Unlike Prometheus, King Sisyphus was never saved. He will continue to roll his boulder up the hill every day forever, a boulder enchanted by Zeus to roll back down before reaching the top, consigning him to an eternity of pointless effort.

Does anyone deserve such a terrible punishment? Certainly this avaricious and deceitful (shall we call him perfidious?) king had

...And the audacity of it all... *Sisyphus*, Franz von Stuck, 1920

enriched himself through commercial dealings overseas while violating the most basic rules of hospitality, rules protected by no less than Zeus himself (hmm, sound familiar?). The story has many versions. Were Zeus' informers the ghosts of travellers, guests slaughtered by Sisyphus under his own roof? Or the ghosts of his children slaughtered by their mother Tyro when she learned of Sisyphus' plan to dethrone her father? Probably even these terrible deeds would not have sufficed but for his great cunning in blackmailing the gods by trading on their secrets. Or for his hubristic belief that his cleverness surpassed that of Zeus himself, capable as he was of tricking the gods into letting him live forever. Who does he think he is! The audacity of it all left the Olympians speechless.

Nevertheless, even Sisyphus' punishment is not all that it seems...

'I leave Sisyphus at the foot of the mountain,' confides the French author Albert Camus at the end of his *The Myth of Sisyphus*. 'One always finds one's burden again. But Sisyphus teaches the higher fidelity that negates the gods and raises rocks. He too concludes that all is well. This universe henceforth without a master seems to him neither sterile nor futile. Each atom of that stone, each mineral flake of that night-filled mountain, in itself, forms a world. The struggle towards the heights is enough to fill a man's heart. One must imagine Sisyphus happy'.

In truth, Camus tells us, there is no answer to life, the universe and everything. Not even forty-two at the end of a rainbow. Human life, our collective and individual aspirations, *is* truly absurd, the world unintelligible, deprived of truth and devoid of purpose. We must free ourselves of hope and keep going with grim lucidity. But we can live with that – no need to commit suicide. What matters is to come to terms with the ultimate contradiction between the yearning to understand which we owe Prometheus and a world that cannot be reasoned. We can rebel without believing in a better future. The point of it all is the struggle itself. Sigh.

What is Camus' Sisyphus thinking as he walks down the mountain, knowing that he will instantly start his exhausting labour all over again? Perhaps it is the very realisation of the futility of his task and the certainty of his miserable condition that sets him free, free to truly make peace with it all. So what if our trivial boulders fall down again. However meaningless, the endless struggle becomes a *raison d'être*. Not to quit simply because it makes no sense, doing your best, stiff upper lip, whistling up the hill. What matters is not to *choose* but to *own* your faith.

Is this not true for Europe too? Can we assert with Aristotle that all that matters at the end of the day is to give stuff a happiness score? So let us ask: does the EU make us happy? And how broad should our circle of happiness be? And let us say: *Il faut imaginer Brexit heureux, pour imaginer l'Europe heureuse.*

‡

In our two stories of Prometheus and Sisyphus, the Olympians' vindictiveness is at best pointless and at worse unjust. Punishment for hubris is mitigated by original intent, Promethean altruism, Sisyphean ambition. Punishment does not do the job, at least not the job intended. There is always a twist. Prometheus is redeemed by Hercules' might and Sisyphus by Camus' mind. The morality of the stories escapes moralising.

When is hubris OK? Hubris presents many shades, from grandiose to pompous, from admirable to despicable. What colour do you see? It is up to you, the reader, to answer the question on the back of ancient stories.

Do you countenance sins à la *Star Trek*, guilt for daring to go where no one has gone before? Was it fair for Icarus to be punished for flying too close to the sun with his puny wings of wax-bound feathers? After all, he was trying to escape captivity for his father's crime of invention, a confinement to protect Daedalus' secret design of a mind-blowing maze (which we will encounter again later in this book). Perhaps Icarus should have wisely heeded his father's advice not to fly too high or too low, to die an old man in the contemplation of 'what if'... When is it wrong to take existential risks on behalf of humanity? Can our crazy dreams of flying ever further in space save us from ourselves?

And what about the prime candidate for the opprobrium of hubris in human history, the countless anonymous women, guilty for questioning the order of things? We remember Arachne, a mere mortal who boasted that she could weave more beautifully than Athena. In the story, when the irate goddess challenges her to a weaving contest, Arachne weaves scenes of sexual misconduct, exposing for all to see the gods' accumulated misdeeds

...The countless anonymous women, guilty for questioning the order of things... *Arachne*, Otto Henry, 1884

of seduction and abuse of beasts and girls. Transformed into a spider for her transgression, isn't Arachne, the ancient godmother of all those who have marched with indignation, from suffragettes to #MeToo, wrapping us all in her timeless web of resistance and celebrating the power of making visible?

There are however some stories of hubris without silver linings. Who could redeem the 'tantalised' one, a mortal who not only terribly annoyed the gods like every other hubristic hero, abusing their hospitality and stealing their nectar and ambrosia, but one who, most abominably, tried secretly to feed them his boiled son Pelops. Note that the ultimate Reckoning will come through our friend, his great-

great-nephew Oedipus, who pays for everyone else. But Tantalus' own fate is no less gruesome, forever to stand in a pool of water beneath a tree with low-hanging fruits, both receding just in time to elude his thirst and grasp. We would be forgiven to ask if this is not simply our inescapable human condition as we strive for the never quite achievable, our recurring needs and temptations ever there and never satisfied, hubris or no hubris, Brexit or no Brexit.

‡

But who says hubris was only on one side? Did the EU too not overreach in this story when it elected to play hardball? Can we move beyond the clash of hubris?

'Before you embark on a journey of revenge, dig two graves,' said Confucius. Europe must be about leaving graves behind, not digging new ones. Whatever role hubris plays in our story, the time has come to imagine Sisyphus happy.

Where do we start?

Youth as Redeemer

In his journey escaping Thebes, blind and defeated, Oedipus' tragic figure is guided by his daughter, Antigone, to seek life's true meaning anew. He now knows all. His suffering from his self-inflicted blindness and lonely wandering will be his punishment. Yet not only will he be redeemed in death but he is already redeemed in Antigone's eyes; Antigone, whose sense of right and wrong will echo for us throughout the ages when later, after her father's death, she comes back to the world and insists on a proper burial for her brother in spite of *raison d'état*. In these stories about Reckoning and redemption we need to listen to the clear-eyed, those whose future is at stake. Youth as redeemer.

Could Brexit-as-Reckoning ride on a youthquake? Today's pampered, angry, anxious generation, in Britain and elsewhere energised by Brexit's tremors? Will they forget and forgive? Will they fight? The future must be their choice.

Some say that Brexit is 'an old people's home'. Why should this be an insult! Some of us oldies remember a time when we were young too, fifty years ago, demonstrating across borders and political cages our desire for radical emancipation from *our* inherited order, from Tito's Yugoslavia to De Gaulle's France, from Dubček's Czechoslovakia to Franco's Spain. Our call to let subversion range free and subject all dogma to hesitation, contradiction, reinterpretation.

...With Antigone, to seek anew... *Oedipus and Antigone*, Charles Jalabert, 1842

All of you twenty-first-century Antigones and Oresteses, what do you say? You are the first truly global generation, aren't you? You are already reinventing everything. If it is up to you, it will not be a shared past that brings the diverse peoples of Europe together but *your* vision of *our* future.

Brexit advocates call for the democratic liberation of a whole continent. Of course. But how? Democratic choices are only democratic if made knowingly. And in Europe, we live under a strange new era of democratic interdependence: your democratic whims affect me directly. So it is imperative to know each other, each other's funny habits and each other's quirky politics. Everything can help and you will do it better, faster, funnier – creative transnational political debating between schools, fun fact-checking across national media, and – why not? – organising a mega Agora Europe, a mega assemblage of citizens' assemblies embedded in a pop festival, the Woodstock of European politics, once a year, on Mediterranean beaches. Forget Brussels' call for, hum, standardised democratic participation... This will not be about harmony, but engaged and respectful disagreement across borders. Physical and virtual transnational agonistics.

Digital natives, you are already ahead of the game. If Brexit is part of a broader yearning for taking back control of our day-to-day lives, can you honour the message even if you were not the messengers? Will you reinvest the democracy of everyday life and make sure that technological innovation is matched by social reinvention? Can you figure out ways to better harness the amazing wisdom of the crowds while weeding out group-think? Will you reshape the rules that govern our togetherness to embrace a pollinated block-chained smart-networked transnational metropolis? Will you master chaotic pluralism and its network effects, distributed intelligence, heterogeneity, non-linearity and high interconnectivity? This stuff will make your interwoven communities more unpredictable but also more creative than the original architects of pluralist worlds ever imagined. In the process, can you cut through the bureaucratic fog and make the EU radically more open through your myriad ways to check and infiltrate power?

Thankfully, you do not believe in a new institutional magic bullet but in the power of mindsets and the technologies of sharing, sharing secrets and sharing power. In your democratic landscape, rules and institutions are a means of bridging *ethos* and *praxis*, not ends in themselves set in calcified stone.

Can you narrow the gap between power and politics, create diverse polycentric institutions to bring out the best in humans and their capacity to innovate, learn, adapt, trust? Can you reinvent a creative, tech-savvy bureaucracy to control those who take all the important decisions, international financial markets, corporate oligarchies and the like?

You know that democracy ultimately is measured by its emancipatory effect. This means pushing back against our very asymmetrical relationship to rules designed by experts. And this in turn does not just mean constraining the strong but empowering the weak to interpret, appropriate and remake existing rules.

You are rightly terribly impatient with the attitude of EU institutions in response to the myriad European citizen initiatives which have percolated through in the last few years. Here are thousands of people who have volunteered their time and enthusiasm for all sorts of causes, some more appealing than others. Why not say: whoa! How lucky we are, we bureaucrats, to be the addressees of committed young people who know how to harness the power of the internet! How can we learn from them? Why castigate direct democracy and referenda, why deny their transformative potential, when we should create the conditions for them to work?

Democracy is only real when truly indeterminate.

Teenagers, the EU could do worse than harness your democratic effervescence. To be sure, effervescence needs to be channelled effectively, as when champagne connoisseurs adopted the saucer-glass in 1848 – their desire for heightened sensation was no accident in an age of revolutions. In the alternative world of pluralist effervescence where struggles, arguments, compromise and agreement to disagree reign supreme, in conversation with others around the globe, you will explore a kaleidoscope of options, a hundred shades of meaning, and tame the dark side of modernity. You will rediscover the ethos of dissidence, the great gift from Eastern Europe, and the ethos of empathy, friendship and hospitality, humanity's saving grace. Like the 'imaginal cells' dormant in the body of the European caterpillar, you will awaken our societies again.

The Myth of Er, Enlightened Scepticism

The last judgement is not inescapable. The EU is not doomed. Reform is still possible. For Reckoning always links a prediction and an injunction: 'you will pay *because* you must pay', but in this space in-between, in the slim potential for escaping the court's admonition, lie all of humanity's hopes, fears and gambles.

Why does Plato, at the end of *The Republic*, resort to storytelling in order to explore the space between choices and consequences, instead of the rigorously reasoned style of philosophical method he has hitherto championed? Is it that Reckoning is too elusive to be contemplated otherwise?

Meet Er, a Greek soldier killed in battle who returns from the dead and recounts what he has seen of the afterlife and the workings of the cosmos. He tells of four great chasms, two in and out of the earth, and two in and out of the sky, through which celestial judges order the souls of the dead to pass. The souls of the unjust descend into the earth while the souls of the just enter into the sky. Er watches as the unjust re-emerge dirty and haggard, leaving behind

...Plato's wondrous Spindle of Necessity... *The Empyrean*, Gustave Doré, 1868

the irredeemably wicked, having paid a tenfold penalty for their life's deeds, while the just float back pure and awed. After comparing notes, Er's soul-companions journey to a place where they see the stars and planets revolving around a 'shaft of light stretching from above straight through earth and heaven, like a pillar, closely resembling a rainbow, only brighter and clearer'. There, they catch a glimpse of the structure of the universe, Plato's wondrous Spindle of Necessity, 'which causes all the orbits to revolve' as they turn in the lap of said Necessity. The three Fates, the daughters of Necessity,

Lachesis, Clotho and Atropos, sing to music played by sirens: Lachesis sings of things past, Clotho of things present, Atropos of things to come. Each of them from time to time takes hold of some of the rims of the spindle to help turn them, Clotho the outermost, Atropos the innermost, and Lachesis both... what a sight it must have been.

What happens as the souls stand mesmerised by the Spindle of Necessity? Do they understand that fate can be moulded by character, one's becoming chosen by one's way of being? How will they choose their next mortal incarnation, and will the righteous and the unjust tend to choose a different new life? Why is it that even the gods have a hard time distinguishing one from the other? Is the true character of men's deeds bound to be revealed at one point or another? How do we knowingly make good choices when given a second chance?

In the story, chance and choice mingle as the souls, ranked through lottery tokens, each choose their next life. Er observes how souls tend to go for a life on the opposite end of their past lives' spectrum of righteousness. And humans tend to choose the apparently easier lives of animals, and vice versa. Afterwards, the souls are made to drink from Lethe, the river of forgetfulness, and are lifted up for rebirth on the surface of the earth. Er finds himself alive on the funeral pyre, able to recount his journey through the afterlife.

With the myth of Er, Plato tells us that we might or might not learn from our past lives when choosing future ones, but that either way it is not an easy thing. Even the gods can be tricked by the pious but false 'man of the people' (sic), who pretends to be righteous but, given who he really is, is destined to eat his own children in the next life. In this tale of equal-opportunity afterlife, only love of wisdom, justice, courage and moderation, not the pretence of these virtues, can break the cycle of reward and punishment.

Can the EU and its custodians become wise and be saved? Perhaps Plato would suggest that only systematic self-reflectiveness can break the current cycle, that like his master Socrates every thinking person should embrace benign scepticism, that there is no truth of the matter but only the quest, committed to the critical virtues of suspended judgement and systematic doubt.

Brexit-as-Reckoning starts with fighting the eternal temptation of messianism in European affairs, the sense of so many involved in the making of it that it is their sacred destiny to sacrifice the means for the end, that it is they who know and appreciate what the mission entails. Plato's story of Er echoes as a warning. Messianism makes it harder to learn from the past lives of the Union.

Here, it might help to distinguish between existential and transformative Euroscepticism, scepticism about the EU's very being and scepticism about its ways of being. While the first type of scepticism makes this moment the last judgement, the second type criticizes the EU but doesn't want to destroy it. Instead, it takes us through Plato's Spindle of Necessity where we learn both that our actions have consequences even after our souls have drunk from the river of forgetfulness, and yet that we still always have a choice. If the EU is both a project and a polity, existential Eurosceptics are after the former while transformative Eurosceptics question how the latter works.

For the EU to truly ward off the minority of existential Eurosceptics, it could dare embrace the transformative Eurosceptics who can best counteract the politics of salvation wielded by xenophobes or demagogues. Choosing a better new life cannot be decreed, says Er; it is only made possible by the cultivation of virtues in this one. Respect, Recognition, Reckoning. Will these virtues be cultivated in our Union of Others?

Elites may doubt whether enlightened scepticism is really for ordinary citizens who cannot live happily while constantly putting into question the basic structure of the order under which they live. This asks the question back to front. We ought instead to ask whether democracy can survive without a generalised attitude of questioning, contestation and reinvention.

Reckoning as Re-knowing

Although Europe has never ceased to reinvent itself, we the peoples of Europe love to announce to the world that peace, like diamonds, is forever. That is a nice thought. But peace is never a done deal. Its foundations need to be reinvented by every generation, every polity, every era. Deep peace is not an inheritance but a way of life. It is not about harmony but struggle. It needs armies of defenders, with all sorts of clever strategies, all sorts of ingenious weapons, all sorts of parochial accents.

Journeys of Reckoning often have to do with re-knowing something that we had almost forgotten. Can we know peace anew?

We can do so through many different paths. One such path is this: a European pivot from space to time. The EU and its critics have focused on the politics of space, a space made single by markets, regulators and judges, a space where free movement reigns supreme and from which we can choose who and how to exclude. What if the EU were to refocus on the politics of time, time when we reflect back and look ahead, time that can be slowed down better to engage with the needs of the next generation, time to allow for a hundred indecisions, and for a hundred visions and revisions...

Would it not be OK to renationalise space a little if we could radically Europeanise time? Inspired by Er's journey can we shape our present life to serve future lives through the virtues we abide by?

This is not an easy proposition, the myth of Er would have warned us. In the European psyche, Lachesis of the past and Atropos of the future seem to have switched places. European citizens used to be moved by the fear of their past and trust in the future, but are now nostalgic for the past and fear the future most. They have witnessed the rise of emergency politics as the new normal, with states desperately trying to match the pace of markets. Traditional politics, that of electoral rhythms and opinion polls in between, remains a relentlessly short-term affair. Tocqueville in his time was already bemoaning the popular obsession with the present. He saw how the *longue durée* stood as a luxury, a pastime for those who don't have to worry about a roof over their heads and food for the

...We must give time to time... The Last Judgement, Michelangelo, Sistine Chapel, 1536–41

109

kids. And yet we now know that it is urgent to act long term. Our planetary future is at stake.

In Europe, incomplete integration is not the problem; unsustainable integration is. Arguably, the European Central Bank stemmed the euro crisis in 2012 by reasserting political time in a fateful utterance about 'whatever it will take'. We require a quantum leap. Today the EU as a whole must stand in as the guardian of the long term, whatever it takes.

Perhaps this is the silver lining of the EU's democratic deficiencies. If mistrust in the people was part of its DNA, the long term can be the EU's democratic redemption. An EU that is democratically challenged for short-term accountability can be democratically enhanced for long-term responsibility.

Let us dare to think of this moment as the third democratic transformation. Robert Dahl, the foremost analyst of democracy after the Second World War, described two great historical transformations: the birth of democratic city states in ancient Greece and Rome, and the emergence of large-scale representative democracies in the eighteenth century. It seems as though the evolution of representation towards increased inclusiveness may have reached its limits. After the *polis* and the nation, the third democratic transformation will be transnational, as the only way to secure our planetary future. And it will be so inclusive as to stretch democratic time much beyond the voters of today. We will invent a transnational democracy with foresight, to match the long-term planners and autocrats of the Far East and elsewhere who threaten to beat us in the mastery of time.

We will stop trying to transform closed and self-centred democracies through vertical restructuring beyond the state. Instead we will practise the art of managing democratic interdependence through horizontal connections and reciprocal vulnerabilities between local spheres, smart towns, cities, regions and states. We can be committed to perfecting our national democracies and at the very same time to a cosmopolitan regard for the welfare and autonomy of others, including those others yet to be born.

We live in a world of second chances, not last judgements. Let us not trivialise this opportunity with serial last-chance summits. Let us instead turn our public spaces, our schools, our screens, our parliaments into the time vessels that our children deserve.

What if Brexit in the end gave humanity its motto for the rest of this century? We must take back control of our future, prevent a man-made catastrophe that will dwarf the oxygen apocalypse of two billion years ago. Only because it is fragile is our universe creative. The Anthropocene, or age of man, will only last (at least for a while) if we recover our humility in a world formed and reformed gloriously in our absence by comets and bacteria. How will this happen on a planet of predatory super-states governed by manic supermen? Can we still affect today the mindboggling technologies and man-made life forms which may one day erase this very particular stardust aggregate that is the human? How trivial it will seem hundreds of years from now to have focused so passionately on our human entanglements, still blind to the life-world entanglements that were to determine our survival.

Authors of Our Destiny

Which brings us back to Oedipus' ultimate question: can we 'unfate' the world? Admit that no consequence is written in stone, either in ballot boxes or in EU treaties? Just as countless consequences could be inferred from the British referendum, so countless consequences could be inferred from EU law. As with most significant moments, there are no precedents.

...We come to understand that what matters most is intent when we ascertain guilt... Oedipus and His Daughters, Henry Fuseli, 1784, inv.833.1.30

It is wrong to reduce Oedipus' fate to a psycho-analytical metaphor, as if the story centred on a timeless message about sexual urges. Rather, let's follow the likes of Bernard Williams in *Shame and Necessity*, or Jean-Pierre Vernant in *Oedipe sans Complexe*, who scrutinised the

© Musée des Beaux-Arts de Troyes

Greeks' musings on human responsibility in this crucial democratic dawn of the fifth and sixth centuries BC. This is the moment when man becomes a citizen, an agent, autonomous from the gods, gauging his control over his personal and political destiny. The moment when citizens, prompted by their playwrights and street philosophers, ask about the source of their actions, and come to see their own will and the bigger context intertwined in a tragic embrace. Even if Aristotle's rational typology of human acts and degrees of freedom closes this epoch, the tragic question, where does my fate come from, continues to nag at our collective soul.

How often do humans actually deserve the disasters that befall them? Why should invisible forces, antique gods or otherwise, dictate our destiny? Neither Oedipus nor the inhabitants of Thebes are guilty in the usual sense of the word.

After all, the brilliant Oedipus is a justice-loving man, passionately committed to seeking his father's killer. He has not intentionally done anything wrong. Why then such a tragic punishment? Perhaps because the gods, or society, cannot withstand a crime unpunished even if the deed was committed upstream, as it were. This is the price of social order. Who remembers that Laius, Oedipus' father, is himself the originator of the curse? A curse from Pelops, his adoptive father who had brought him up like his own son Chrysippus, only to see ungrateful Laius fall in love with Chrysippus, kidnap and rape him and lead him to commit suicide. This is where the curse originates: if Laius ever has a son, let this son kill him and Thebes be destroyed – Thebes, founded by one of *Europa's* three brothers (brothers encountered in the previous chapter) when he abandoned the vain search for his sister. There is always an upstream in the river of time.

And a downstream, too. The ultimate consequences are not foretold. Oedipus in fact will be redeemed and the place where he dies twenty years later will be blessed. As Antigone leads him to that place, we come to understand that what matters most is intent when we ascertain guilt. If Oedipus is rationally innocent since he sinned unknowingly, perhaps his sufferings are sufficient expiation for his sins.

Some believe that we have travelled well on the road of progress since Sophocles' time, including replacing shame with guilt. Shame happens to you, guilt you do to yourself. Enlightenment heralded human agency and moral autonomy. In a modern court, Oedipus, who did not know, would certainly be acquitted on account of extenuating circumstances. We may think that ancients and moderns think differently, but our moral compasses blur into one another. We want to claim authorship of our destinies. Yet who can deny that what your family or your group or your country has done in the past will undeniably affect you for better or worse. You can only accept the inheritance whole, even if unaware of the streams of sweat and blood that have fed it.

Myths touch a nerve because they offer motives that are deeply hidden in modern consciousness. We think of Homer's *Odyssey* as a voyage through random and unforeseeable trials, testing his vow to return home. And yet what if the whole point of his odyssey is that he and his companions in the Trojan War were moral agents, responsible for their actions and their consequences? Would we be fascinated by *The Iliad*'s heroes if they were only puppets of godly designs? How can we explain the terrible fate which befalls each and every one of them after they leave Troy in ruins, if not as a story of guilt and redemption? After all, the Greeks didn't rest content with simply taking the city they had coveted for ten

...Would we be fascinated by *The Iliad*'s heroes if they were only puppets of godly designs... *The Deluge*, Gustave Doré, 1866

years. Instead, they descended upon it like mad dogs, despoiling temples, killing all men in their path and even women and children, taking inhabitants as slaves, setting houses on fire, thus demonstrating that even the most supposedly civilised of men can lose it under the grip of revenge, branding others as enemies, incapable of seeing others as human first.

The stories told in *The Odyssey* of the Greek warriors' respective returns home through nightmares of poison, jealousy and monstrous beings is simply one of retribution handed down by their own conscience, played out through their imagined gods.

Even Ulysses, who has not participated in the sacking of Troy, leaves the shores of Asia Minor with a heavy conscience, contaminated by the deeds of his fellow warriors. It takes him ten years and unimaginable hardship to reach Ithaca and his ever-patient wife Penelope. Along the way, he battles with how much leeway to give to his own agency, how much to trust his own willpower in the presence of sirens and other beings. Yet if *The Iliad* remains the great book of betrayed hospitality, *The Odyssey* stands as hospitality recovered, as Ulysses accepts that he will be changed by all the encounters along the way.

Perhaps you will remark that at least in our time and place not everything is permitted; that we do sign treaties in a calm and civilised manner. But not so long ago we Europeans inflicted on faraway colonised lands and on each other fates far worse than the Greeks, all in the name of civilisation. Brexit is but a bleep on this deafening score. Which European has lost a limb through being called enemy by excited Brexiters? Which Brit has been wounded by a trade weapon? And yet wounds from this strange skirmish may take a while to heal.

Sadly, the deeper wound will probably fester much longer where it concerns that most sacred of all duties, as Plato would have it, hospitality. If we still feel the long shadows of Zeus, god of hospitality, and Athena, protector of the hosts whose forms she takes, we should also know that nothing was simple with the Greeks either: the ambivalent *hostis* meant both host and enemy, opportunity and threat. Even Kant's cosmopolitan project set limits on the duties of hospitality inspired by the earth's spherical form. But at least the Greeks feared, or pretended to fear, the wrath of Zeus if they failed to welcome the stranger into their home. Whose wrath do we fear, we *Homo Deus*, as we unlearn so quickly the meaning of sitting together around a table to talk about our differences?

If only beauty could redeem the world.

Turning and turning in the widening gyre
The falcon cannot hear the falconer;
Things fall apart; the centre cannot hold;
Mere anarchy is loosed upon the world,
The blood-dimmed tide is loosed, and everywhere
The ceremony of innocence is drowned;
The best lack all conviction, while the worst
Are full of passionate intensity.

Surely some revelation is at hand;
Surely the Second Coming is at hand.
The Second Coming! Hardly are those words out
When a vast image out of *Spiritus Mundi*
Troubles my sight: somewhere in sands of the desert
A shape with lion body and the head of a man,
A gaze blank and pitiless as the sun,
Is moving its slow thighs, while all about it
Reel shadows of the indignant desert birds.
The darkness drops again; but now I know
That twenty centuries of stony sleep
Were vexed to nightmare by a rocking cradle,
And what rough beast, its hour come round at last,
Slouches towards Bethlehem to be born?

W. B. Yeats, 'The Second Coming'

Sacrifice

Brexit Means a New Beginning

And so we come to our third story.

What if Brexit was not the problem – Britain's problem in the Exodus story, everyone's problem in the story of Reckoning – but the solution! What if we told the Brexit story not as a warning about things that will come or ought to come, but rather as an event that in itself changes the world?

...A sacrifice to save Europe... *The Sacrifice of Iphigenia*, François Perrier, 1632.

© Musée des Beaux-Arts de Dijon/Hugo Martens

Perhaps, then, Brexit means 'Bereishit' – the Torah's first word for 'in the beginning'. And along with this story of new beginning, Brexit becomes a story of Sacrifice on the altar of the greater good, from which beneficial developments begin to flow. In this mythical variant, Britain takes the form of Iphigenia, 'the strong-born', who is offered to the gods so that the winds will rise and the Greek flotilla can sail off to Troy. It is her father Agamemnon, the commander-in-chief of all the Greek armies, who takes her to the altar with a heavy heart. She resists, changes her mind, acquiesces for love of her father and of patria. Her Sacrifice is pregnant with meaning and promise.

Thus, Brexit can be told as a great new

beginning, and, as with all sacrifices, this meaning is existential: *Brexit means that Britain leaves the EU in order to save it.*

> In Greek mythology and tragedies, Iphigenia is sacrificed on the reluctant order of her father King Agamemnon of Mycenae. It is the only way to summon the winds that will allow the Greek troops who have assembled in Aulis to sail off to Troy and free the Greek woman Helen, who has been taken away by Prince Paris. This is the doing of the goddess Artemis to punish Agamemnon for offending her. Iphigenia and her mother Clytemnestra have been brought to Aulis under the pretence of marriage to Achilles. In some versions of the story, she figures it out, while in others she believes she is led to the altar to be married and remains unaware of her imminent sacrifice until the last moment. In some versions of the story Iphigenia is saved, while in others she isn't. Much will follow. Homer's *Iliad* tells the tale of ten years of war, ending in the pillage of Troy, while the *Odyssey* tells of the return voyages, including Agamemnon's murder upon arriving home by his wife Clytemnestra as (*inter alia*) payback for the sacrifice of their daughter. In some versions of the story Iphigenia's brother Orestes kills their mother and her lover in revenge and the two are reunited in Tauris, where as Artemis's grand priestess she is meant to sacrifice him. Meanwhile, Ulysses alone survives the voyage back home.

This is the simple – dare I say macho – version of the Sacrifice story, which we can call *heroic* Sacrifice, a story which pre-dates the referendum itself. 'Have the courage to vote Leave, not for your sake, but for Europe's sake,' implored a columnist in the French paper *Libération* a few days before the British public went to the polls, 'to bring us together.' Make Brexit 'a sacrifice to save Europe.' God forbid a victory for Remain where Britain would become the only democratically enshrined EU member, its government finding itself at the helm of European games, extracting more and more concessions from its European counterparts and burying forever the federalist dream of the founding fathers. A French nightmare, in other words. Accordingly, only with the Leave vote will 'the sting of fear of an EU collapse' lead other governments to risk new transfers of sovereignty. Please, the French journalist implored, 'create a salutary crisis of the kind that will lead our heroic leaders (*les dirigeants les plus visionnaires*) to act against the mortal risk of crumbling into nothingness'.

A few months after these prophetic words, a visionary leader rose and obliged, heeding the call for more integration and therefore less Britain. Emmanuel Macron became the new president of France at the very same time as Britain triggered the infamous Article 50. Whether or not he was happy to remove the recalcitrant Brits from the European equation, he would use Brexit as an opportunity to cajole the Germans into potentially underwriting his *grand projet* for the EU.

Crucially, these calculations would depend not only on the fact of Brexit but on the manner of leaving itself. The withdrawal would need to be negotiated as one, as if unity 'against' the UK could replace unity against the likes of Recep Tayyip Erdoğan, Vladimir Putin or Xi Jinping. Ah, the tyranny of small differences!

Most importantly, the withdrawal would need to protect the value of membership and thus prevent a Brexit contagion. If Britain needed to be 'sacrificed to save Europe', so be it. No Frenchman was more often quoted during the Brexit saga than Voltaire for his quip about Admiral Byng's execution after 'failing to do his utmost' to protect Majorca at the head of the British Navy against the French in 1756: '*Dans ce pays-ci, il est bon de tuer de temps en temps un amiral pour encourager les autres*' (in this country, it is wise to kill an admiral from time to time to encourage the others). The French and others around Europe would protest loudly against this reading of course.

But sacrifices are always about cloaking exemplarity as protection. Who could fault the EU for seeking self-preservation!

As with the Exodus story, the heroic version of Brexit-as-Sacrifice on the altar of European integration serves Eurofederalists and Brexiters alike. During the campaign, Boris Johnson and his allies went out of their way to reassure their continental counterparts that they should not worry. Brexit would be good for them – with us out of the way you can fulfil your federalist dream, do the stuff we were always reluctant to agree on, give Brussels real competencies in defence or social policies, increase the EU budget to bail out poorer regions, and embrace the goal of 'ever closer union'. Let new projects

Three Archetypal Myths

As with Oedipus and the Sphinx's riddle, at the heart of every myth is a drama of questioning, the urge to ask, to open closed doors, to mould a space of suspended meanings around unanswerable questions.
Mythomania, Ari Saunders, 2018

Exodus

Can we not imagine a modern-day Exodus-lite, where the Europeans are spared the plagues and
the Brits are spared the endless wandering in the desert?
Seventh Plague of Egypt, John Martin, 1823

This could be an inglorious Exodus for the UK, heralding a reverse change of status: from master to slave.
The Departure of the Israelites out of the Land of Egypt, David Roberts, 1829

When the Israelites complain in despair, 'Thou hast taken us away to die in the wilderness. Why hast thou done this to us, that thou hast led us out of Egypt?' Moses replies: 'The Lord himself will fight for you. Just stay calm.'
The Exodus, Horace William Petherick, 1839–1919

You may have chosen to bite the apple of paradise and claim back control, but we define the terms of departure. This story is not about your Promised Land, but our paradise lost; not *your* Exodus, but *our* banishment!
Eve, John Collier, 1911

Or your *Europa* may be about becoming and about movement, as if motion was the only way to keep her together... Has Britain failed to see that if *Europa* cannot stand still, it is pointless to fear its dreaded destination? Britain's liberation may be from evanescence itself.
The Rape of Europa, Valentin Aleksandrovich Serov, 1910

When Albion, whose fall into selfhood even the cathedral cities, Angelmorphic Eternals or wise Erin (Ireland) cannot prevent, is awakened at the end of time... what will he see?
Frontispiece to *Visions of the Daughters of Albion*, William Blake, *c.* 1795

Oh the sweet frisson of defiance. What mattered in the end is only this: the sea, the sea.
The Delivery of Israel out of Egypt – Pharaoh and his Hosts overwhelmed in the Red Sea, Francis Danby, 1825

If they had resisted further, the army of EU bureaucrats would have drowned in an Irish Sea of red tape.
Pharaoh's Army Engulfed by the Red Sea, Frederick Arthur Bridgman, 1900

Reckoning

For whom does the bell toll in our Brexit Reckoning? Which variant shall we heed? Which apocalypse shall we fear? Who is to blame and who will be saved? We know that after hubris comes nemesis, the goddess from whom there is no escape – but where does redemption lie?
The Last Judgment, School of Hieronymus Bosch, *c.* 1482–1516

In these stories about Reckoning and redemption we need to listen to the clear-eyed, those whose future is at stake. Youth as redeemer.
The Death of Oedipus, Henry Fuseli, 1784

As the paradigmatic seeker *and* avoider of truths, Oedipus both very deliberately solves the Sphinx's riddle,
and very accidentally fulfils the prophecy.
Oedipus and the Sphinx, Jean-Auguste-Dominique Ingres, 1827

Can Freud's 'What have I done?' (if you happen to have sex with a member of your own family) ever
be redeemed by acknowledging that the truth is blindingly obvious?
Oedipus, poster, courtesy of Elysium Conservatory Theatre, California, 2014

be announced, new hats be crafted, new positions conjured up. We will not be around to stop your ambitious schemes. It is wrong for us to be there, he said, 'always trying to make things different, always getting in the way, always moaning'. And the ordinary French citizen echoed, in unison, '*Les anglais* never liked Europe anyway, everything will be easier when they leave.'

Indeed, both Brexiters and Eurofederalists relentlessly conjured up a ubiquitous 'veto *anglais*' to bolster their troops and paint Britain as the only obstacle on the road to the dreaded or desired EUtopia. But of course! The British veto needs to be imagined as ubiquitous in order to turn Brexit into a necessary Sacrifice. If Britain was not only the reluctant partner, but also powerful enough to make its reluctance count, its departure would save the European project.

And indeed, as the Brexit saga unfolded, the story of Sacrifice gained ascendancy on the continent as the most dramatic exemplar that crisis is the midwife of European integration. 'Brexit will demonstrate how much more attractive it is to be a member of our union...' 'it will whip Europeans out of their inertia...' 'fully on the move again...' 'it will be a different union from now on...' 'there is a new game in town...' 'we may deeply regret Brexit but we are excited too...' Perhaps in the near future, whether the sacrificial victim will be let off the hook will depend on how well other European countries are faring, or are perceived to be faring. But not before it has served its sacrificial purpose. Alleluia!

But... Heroic or Ironic Sacrifice

In this version of the Brexit story, we remain haunted by Iphigenia's fate: should our sacrificial victim truly suffer or be seen to suffer? Why? What is the point of Sacrifice anyway? To demonstrate to ourselves and to the world the real and tangible strategic advantage of an EU status that our victim has scornfully rejected? Or would it not be enough for Britain to retreat from our shores, serving the EU cause by virtue of its absence?

As with stories of Exodus and of Reckoning, stories of Sacrifice are not easily malleable to serve one or the other camp's specific purpose. Because Sacrifice has played such a prominent role in human history as the glue of social order, stories and theories of Sacrifice offer a multitude of variants, from the penumbra of Greek myths to Christian theories of atonement.

Who can tell the true importance of Sacrifice? Who is truly sacrificed and for what purpose? What is a Sacrifice supposed to buy us? How do we know whether a Sacrifice is worthy? And what makes it real?

'Sacrifice' is a word pregnant with tragic, historical meaning, not as an allegory for a whole country as in the Brexit story, but as the real thing for human beings. In the version of the story of Brexit as a heroic Sacrifice, both Brexiters and Federalists remind us, sometimes subliminally, sometimes explicitly, of the truly heroic Sacrifice of generations of young British soldiers on the battlefields of the European continent. Indeed, it felt like a strange collapse of historical time to hear as a backdrop to the Brexit negotiations the haunting voices of First World War survivors coming to us 100 years later.

But wait. Can this past Sacrifice of human flesh really be considered the underlying motive for Brexit, buried in the French countryside? The Battle of the Somme as evidence of the virtues of Britain's future absence from the continent? Are you kidding?

Unless, of course, we understand the Sacrifice narrative in a way which preserves its genuinely ambiguous nature, a Sacrifice which we can live with (literally): an *ironic Sacrifice*. Cheer up, Britain, 'Keep 'em laughing as you go. Just remember that the last laugh is on you! And always look on the bright side of life...'

Perhaps this was the hidden meaning of Boris Johnson's early Brexit quip proclaiming from the beginning that 'we are going to make a titanic success of it!' Be of good cheer. Sing stoically in the sinking ship.

In this epic collapse of perspective, past and present Sacrifices for the sake of freedom merge in a grand narrative of national pride, the human yearning to be part of something greater than oneself. Isn't this the tragic irony of it all? The irony of invoking the great Sacrifices of two World Wars, still seared in the hearts of many European citizens, as proof that, with Brexit, the world is better off when Britain retreats from the continent's affairs. Let's liberate ourselves from liberation duties, sing our British Leavers, let's abandon attempts at saving an ungrateful continent we once proudly helped to free from fascism. Fascism, let us recall, was founded on a terrible sacrificial creed, the belief that the willingness to sacrifice one's ego and eventually one's life for the group, and above all a nation or 'the totality', lies at the heart of civilisation.

In this modern tragedy of ours, the Chorus retorts: is that the lesson to be drawn from your repeated rescues of the divided European tribes throughout modern history? Rescues from their bouts of imperial overreach, rescues from their mutual domination itches? Isn't it slightly inconsistent to celebrate Britain's current retreat to the white cliffs of Dover as an echo of its past heroic landing on the shores of Normandy? Does it not make more sense for Britain to prevent the need for its own repeated human Sacrifice in the first place? Isn't Europe better off when the British stay involved in its affairs, mission never accomplished? And isn't Britain better off when Europe is better off?

© HandMade Films/Python Pictures/Warner Bros/Ronald Grant Archive/Mary Evans

...Always look on the bright side of life... *Monty Python's Life of Brian,* 1979

But the Leavers' reply will not be silenced: they gave their lives so we could be free.

Surely, both sides can agree: the story of Brexit-as-Sacrifice, however tragic for some, however glorious for others, cannot mirror the British human Sacrifices of yesteryear. Heroic Sacrifice requires heroic personalities. Simply calling the Brexit cabinet a 'war cabinet' might not suffice to elevate the narrative.

But if Brexit rings like an ironic Sacrifice, then the message reclaims the past in a different way. And perhaps you, the reader, can better understand this irony than the protagonists themselves, just like the audiences of Greek tragedies who colluded with the Chorus in witnessing the real twists which the characters could not see.

Things Are Not Always What They Seem

Not only are things not always what they seem, they are not even what they are called. To start with, isn't Sacrifice always a kind of clever trick? There needs to be an optical illusion in the story, for we know that Eurofederalists and Brexiters cannot truly have the same sacrificial version in mind. Surely in the Brexiters' version the sacrificial victim does not die and the executioner does not triumph?

So...

What of the sacrificial victim... ?

Of course, Iphigenia in Aulis was sacrificed for the most worthy of causes: the honour of a Greek woman, Helen, taken hostage by the Trojans, the honour of the Greeks, therefore, who had no choice but to rescue a Greek turned into a slave, and the honour of the house of Agamemnon, who had managed to conjure up the first ever alliance of all the Greek tribes. She would become the ultimate 'benefactor of Hellas'. But did she really need to be?

Various versions of Iphigenia's story having come to us through the ages convey this ambivalence, a function of the storytellers' morality tale and the listeners' active reimagining. The Greeks quarrel passionately over the deed while Iphigenia has to be tricked by a promise of marriage with Achilles (by no other than Ulysses, not such a shameless man after all) into showing up at Aulis. Achilles promises Clytemnestra that he will defend her daughter against all and die for her if need be.

Crucially, Euripides' version is so full of twists and turns that we can hardly keep track, as his characters, even the Chorus, keep on changing their mind. Above all, Iphigenia changes her mind. One moment she wishes to stay alive at any cost, revolting with all her being against the unholy sacrifice, the next she consents to it with equal passion.

Does she change her mind in order to choose her fate, to embrace her future patriotic glory or for love of her father? Does she yearn to annul Achilles' sacrifice or to partake in the soldiers' selflessness in tomorrow's battles? Or does she prefer to be bride and victim at the same time, both fates under the jurisdiction of the goddess Artemis? Does turning the Greeks' half-hearted contemplation of sacrifice into a passionate self-sacrifice change the meaning of the affair? And why do the Greeks need strangers, the women from Chalkis, to witness and support her fate? Are we, the audience, supposed to witness her transformation with a mix of admiration and pity, or to appreciate the irony of it all?

For in at least some versions, this grand Sacrifice rests on an equally grand conjuring trick, as Artemis replaces Iphigenia at the last minute with a deer – the scapedeer version of an (e)scapegoat – thus allowing her to rise from the altar like a phoenix ready to roam the world with her brother Orestes. True, only a goddess of the stature of Artemis could pull off such a stunt in the presence of the assembled Greeks, but remember, she is the one who had asked for the Sacrifice in the first place of 'the fairest thing the year brought forth.' Remember too that she is not only the goddess of the hunt and the wilderness, but also of childbirth, new beginnings.

Myths of Sacrifice often give us a quantum superposition, alive and dead at the same time like the famous physicist Schrödinger's infamous cat. Christ, after all, came back to life and got to hang out with his father for eternity. And as Abraham's faith is put to the test by God's command to sacrifice his adored only son Isaac, another (e)scapegoat saves the day too, just as with Iphigenia (what is it with these lovely animals that they are the ones to bear the brunt?). From these near-death experiences, or perhaps in spite of them, the almost-sacrificed never quite seem to fully come back.

And so, dear reader, who is playing the part of Artemis in the Brexit saga? What godly forces have ordered Britain's Sacrifice in the first place, only to rescue her in the nick of time? Of course, Leavers believe that a post-Brexit UK will be alive and well, thank you very much, free to

...The tragic irony of invoking the great sacrifices of two world wars... Paul Cummins and Tom Piper's *Poppies: Wave and Weeping Window*, Tower of London, 2014

roam the world like Iphigenia. Artemis will see to this. Granted, Theresa and Donald can no longer be seen holding hands, but there are plenty of characters in the wide wild world who will be all too happy to be cast in the role of brother Orestes.

Remainers, for their part, do not see the point of going through the Sacrifice ordeal in the first place. But since it seems indeed to be happening, are they not a bit suspicious of Artemis' magnanimity? Are they not even hoping to be proved right by their country's Sacrifice to the elusive god of sovereignty that has animated the Leavers? Or, conversely, in the discomfort of witnessing their country cast in the sacrificial role, will they progressively turn against the executioner who has forgotten the many Remainers who had pledged allegiance?

...And what of the executioners?

On the other side, wishful-thinking Europeans have wanted to believe in what Christian theologians refer to as the *ransom Sacrifice*, where the Sacrifice annuls bad consequences for the rest of us. Par for the course, you may say, since Leavers vowed to hold the EU to ransom till Britain is truly gone. Here, the 'consequences' for Britain annul the consequences for Europe, which were central to our story of Reckoning.

Indeed, Brexit-as-Sacrifice sounds good to EU members precisely because they hope that through this act of amputation their own sins will be forgiven and forgotten. After all, a ransom is the price paid to release someone or something, a price that approximates the value of release. According to ransom theory, the first major theory of atonement, early Christians believed that if no human could pay for Adam and Eve's selling out of humanity to Satan, Satan had no choice but to accept Christ's death as a ransom. In St Augustine's words, 'By shedding the blood of One who was not his debtor, he was forced to release his debtors.' Perhaps this is about a transfer, a substitution. Or perhaps both the ransom and the released are ultimately one. How could Satan have any just claims against humans in the first place anyway? Is the Sacrifice not a story of collective emancipation rather than a kind of business transaction?

Whatever obscure Christian exegesis we might or might not believe in, the point here is that someone in this story redeems – 'buys back' – something that is precious to all. Is it then some version of the European project that is redeemed by the British sacrifice? But which version? That which Europeans could have aspired to if Britain had never taken part, or that which can only have existed given that Britain did take part?

The ransom paid by Britain will be quite literally a price paid, most obviously payment to the EU's budget, most ubiquitously access to its markets, most importantly the loss of a say around the table. Britain is substituted for bigger offenders to the European cause, since everyone knows that its mainstream political class was not Eurosceptic – at least before the last act of this saga.

But sacrifices have a way of coming back to haunt the executioners.

For, ultimately, Sacrifice is probably always in vain. Yes, the wind did rise to carry Agamemnon's ships to Troy after Iphigenia's Sacrifice, and, yes, our Greek heroes did win the battle in the end, but what about winning the war? As we saw, there are precious few triumphant 'welcome homes' in *The Odyssey* for the Greek soldiers who had originally sailed, thanks to Iphigenia's apparent Sacrifice. Clytemnestra saw to it that her husband Agamemnon would pay for sacrificing their daughter, just as in a parallel universe *Game of Thrones'* Stannis Baratheon is executed for sacrificing his daughter by no other than Lady Brienne of Tarth (whose fantasies are they, these strong women with daggers!).

Is the EU truly freed by Britain's Sacrifice to its cause? Or will the play feature the victim's resurrection and the cursed hangman?

The Great Experiment

It is said that the Enlightenment's greatest legacy is not our commitment to reason, but our propensity to doubt, to ask questions and trust experiments to provide answers through trial and error. Humility in our design and ambition in our achievements. The EU is at its best in such an experimental mode: trial and error, although more on the error side these days.

What will Brexit-as-Sacrifice do for you, EU? Could Brexit, like all sacrifices, come to be viewed as a great experiment? Perhaps all sides one day will come to question their original assumptions, revisit their hypotheses, revise their inferences.

An experiment of this size does not come up every day. Experiments can carry great risks and great rewards, can hurt some and serve others, can baffle and enlighten. The same results can be interpreted differently: a grand success for some, an abject failure for others.

All the same, ultimately we experiment to explore new beginnings.

Sacrifice for Control

There is no denying the irresistible power of 'taking back control'. For hasn't this always been the ultimate goal of sacrificial rituals since the dawn of humanity – taking back control of the winds, rain and thunder. Agamemnon shall sail. The wheat shall grow. Whatever it is that we can control, our kids, our fields or our gardens, our bits of flesh, our bits of earth, isn't it all we have in the end?

In one version of the Sacrifice story, Brexit is a Sacrifice by Brits, of Brits, for Brits, in the name of control. Control of borders, money, democratic decisions, laws, trade policy, Britain's manifest destiny. Sacrifice of short-term order for long-term freedom. Sacrifice of some by others – Scotland by England, the City by northern cities, the young by the old. The Leavers' doctrine: pain for gain. Whose pain? Whose gain? Who decides who and what is expendable – the Sacrifice of a generation; losing Northern Ireland; selling out on shared achievements with EU partners; significant damage to the economy; personal hardship? Or the sacrifice of British citizens living in EU countries who feel abandoned in their hope to retain their free movement rights across continental borders. These are all a 'price worth paying', according to the polls. A tweet asks: 'When we eventually resort to cannibalism, will Leavers volunteer to be eaten first? They seem so eager to sacrifice for the cause.'

How much will be paid or earned for control? All this accounting still lies ahead.

Was it not an ironic Sacrifice to pursue a clean Brexit predicated on a Great Retain Exercise cloaked as a Great Repeal Act, one of the largest legislative projects ever undertaken in the UK, which will keep everything as it is, the EU rules on the books and the EU citizens in their bunks?

No wonder Brexit's greatest leitmotiv has been a version of Lampedusa's quip about his beloved Sicily during the Italian revolution: we in Britain have changed everything so that everything could remain the same. The Italians call this state of affairs after his novel '*gattopardesco*', that is 'leopardesque'. With the Brexit legislation, Britain will have become at least for a time, and probably for a long time, the most EU-compatible country in the world, EU rules and standards fully internalised in the national legal corpus, fully debated, contested – making them our own, at last!

You could retort, how about control of our borders, there's nothing ironic in that. Indeed, that is the true Sacrifice of the story for those ready to sacrifice hard-earned income for its sake. Does middle-class Sacrifice genuinely extend that far? How much are the much-spoken-of losers of globalisation ready to pay in solid British sterling for each EU alien kept out?

In this war of words, control is about process more than outcome. Most Leavers want to keep the rights that came from the EU. Three in four British voters support free movement, at least if it is perceived as a right that they and EU citizens reciprocally enjoy, not as an anti-democratic imposition by foreign bureaucrats. They will probably acquiesce when, one day, controlling immigration will come to mean keeping foreigners from leaving or begging them to come in the first place. It is about who does the asking.

If control matters, isn't there irony in the stance of some English Tories who, as they contemplate their less and less United Kingdom, have made their preference plain: leaving Brussels' Union is a bigger deal than keeping ours together. Brexit, the grand return to the country's true destiny, may as well be Engxit, as England withdraws from the arrangements that have kept Scotland, Wales and Northern Ireland willing participants in its Kingdom United. Perhaps the point of it all is to bring back 'England' to its true size, no longer Great Britain, unencumbered by the weight of its imperial past.

Meanwhile, everyone takes part in the great debate: which will be sacrificed – the promise to leave the single market; the promise of no border in the Irish Sea; or the promise of no border on the island of Ireland. Sometimes one has to engage with a control trilemma.

Some will point out that control was always there, and ask what is so wrong with EU rules you have mostly designed yourselves? And whose rules shall apply anyway when you still want to play the EU single-market game?

Wasn't there some irony too in asking Westminster and Whitehall, the two most pro-European bodies in the country, to conduct and sanction the deed themselves, while in their view sacrificing the national interest? As the most prominent scapegoats of the story, British MPs and civil servants in their majority have ended up damned as unpatriotic if they try to escape their fate, or damned by their conscience if they carry it out. Here is the old British aristocratic oath of obedience at its best, the Sacrifice of their own views to the will of the people. It should be hard for their friends on the continent not to truly admire a whole political class and civil service mobilising to produce an outcome which so many of them deplore.

Does the sacrificial victim not have some agency, they ask? Can it not decide what bits of EU parchment are thrown onto a bonfire that could consume us all? It is hard to deny the sense of humour of voters who instructed Whitehall to restore UK authority on UK matters, reassert the supremacy of common law only to brand as 'enemies of the people' the very judges meant to uphold this law.

Perhaps most ironically of all, Britain's governing elites may yet find more opportunity for centralising power than Brussels ever gave them. And, in time, Whitehall's civil servants will come to appreciate the new opportunities to reinvent themselves in the post-Brexit era, whether as champions of free trade with developing countries or in reweaving bilateral ties. Will the (still) not-in-control citizens of the north-east come to appreciate the dedication of their overworked government?

What about Britain's pretensions to 'great power' status? Will they be sacrificed for the sake of going it alone? What does it mean to take back control of our relationships with the rest of the world? To sacrifice collective clout for a part of one's own, however small, on the world stage? When, after her escape/Sacrifice, Iphigenia plots a comeback with her brother Orestes, they cannot find allies to carry out the revenge plans which ultimately engulf them. Why did they so overplay their hand?

After unabashedly trying to embrace the Donald on behalf of British citizens in the early days, Theresa has since learned who the most reliable partners are likely to be in the post-Brexit era. After all, even his early gifts came with a sting: for a people who have made the art of civilised queueing a national badge of honour, it was certainly disconcerting to be so publicly offered a chance to jump that queue from last place to first, for the sake of a reverse-Obama moment.

Who can deny that Trump's antics emphasise Britain's fundamental Europeanness. But alas, other Europeans didn't seem to appreciate the sweet irony of a prime minister's offer to serve as a bridge for a bunch of transatlantic pirates bent on sinking a Euro-ship, with which she had been burning her own bridges.

Heed the irony that leaving the EU will require importing from it the joys of identity control, a condition familiar to most citizens on the continent. Sadly, ten years from now, British citizens will probably be subject to ever more state surveillance mechanisms to keep track of their comings and goings, not only at the border, but once inside too. The British state will try to hold on to its liberal DNA, letting EU citizens show their footprint in whatever way they want. And EU citizens will discover how precious it has been all along not to be asked whether they had the right to be here or to access the wondrous NHS. Even the natives will be caught in the net. In order to make a country feel free again, the freedom of millions of individuals will have been curtailed.

But then Britain will still need nurses, builders and drivers. Perhaps this will mean more irregular migrants, more exploitation, more inequality, more nastiness – the US-on-Thames. Liberal Britain will be lost. But the borders and all else will be controlled.

A great irony will also be visited upon those of us EU nationals living in the UK who decide to become British citizens precisely when no longer encouraged to call home the country where we chose to raise our children. In the process, we will gain a new colour on our nationality rainbow, a blue British nationality restored as the superior order within these shores, even if devalued on the other side of the Channel.

We need to allow for the thought that the British prime minister truly understood all along the irony of the tragic choices she has been asked to engineer. When she warned of her readiness to put on her jogging shoes in a race to the bottom on taxes and standards, she must have seen the paradox in presenting self-mutilation as a threat, on the part of a country so proud of its standards. Has she been speaking the language of ironic Sacrifice all along? Has she been wearing the mask of sovereign control better to minimise the sacrifice of free trade? If so, has the EU denied the UK the smoke and mirrors necessary to make Sacrifice bearable for all involved: the backstop for Northern Ireland disguised as technical; free movement disguised as mobility; jurisdiction disguised as interpretation; the old customs partnership disguised as new.

Brexit will become a lesson in both the promise and the delusions of control in an ever more interdependent world. In truth, the fight for control in a post-Brexit world must take place where it really matters: in the arenas of everyday life. A lesson I learned a long time ago from veteran politician Shirley Williams is that we all have to learn to let go in life. But not before we have first been in charge.

On the Altar of Principles

Why was anyone surprised with the EU's answer to 'Brexit means Brexit': 'Brexit means Brexit', and its two corollaries: 'Membership means membership'; 'Out means Out'.

If Brexit was going to be an EU experiment, it would have to demonstrate a basic and incontrovertible truth: the EU matters! Being a member makes a difference; call it the strategic advantage of membership. In this war of tautologies, the winner is fated to be the one whose 'means' is the most consequential to the other side. My no-deal is bigger than your no-deal. My integrity (of the EU single market) is bigger than your integrity (of the UK constitutional order). Welcome to macho politics.

And so, if need be, the EU would offer a no-deal (or bad-deal) Brexit as a Sacrifice on the altar of EU principles. This was not a

Eurocracy conspiracy: two-thirds of EU citizens expressed the desire for the EU to try to maintain a good relationship with the UK, but said that it should 'not make any compromise on its core principles.'

You ask, what on earth does this mean? Listen in to the following recurrent dialogue between London and Brussels.

Brussels: Deluded Cakeism Meets Didactic Binarism

UK: Here is the deal: the will of our people is to take back control, but it is in the interests of both sides to maintain frictionless trade and cooperate even better than before. We've made pretty plain what we want. Outside the single market but with access. Outside the customs union but with a customs agreement. You get our drift.

EU: Won't do! You want to change everything you dislike and to keep everything you like, to eat cake and have it too, and have it à la carte to boot. But the EU is a package, and we all have to swallow stuff we don't like. We can offer you our standard menu, that's it.

UK: Why be so inflexible? What you call à la carte Brexit is simply what we call a pragmatic Brexit in the interest of all parties.

EU: What are you talking about? We are flexible! All along we have given you choices, offered to extend your notice or to withdraw it, given you the option to be or not to be a member of our customs union, or to copy whatever third country you like.

UK: We are talking about the freedom to invent a new model, not some false choices between inadequate alternatives.

EU: I'm afraid you have had your go at your own model. In the past, you were always stretching the EU's flexibility as in-almost-out; now you want to do the same as out-almost-in. Today you are asking to keep what you already have, frictionless trade, without what you dislike, legal and political constraints. (*Sighs patiently.*) Let me explain: if you truly want to be almost in, forget your red lines and stay with us, or at least be Norwegian and join our economic area. Alternatively, take on the mantle of any old third country, like, say, Canada or New Zealand, or even Ukraine, and we can agree on a free trade agreement. You cannot be half pregnant. It is one or the other, our PowerPoint slides could not be clearer!

UK: Can you please stop this didactic binarism? You can lecture us like naughty schoolchildren, use this either/or to teach us bad Brits a lesson. But you know full well that we will both benefit from a bespoke deal; we are too big for the Norway model but too European for the Canada model.

EU: Bespoke – well, we can certainly adapt to your circumstances, but the deal between us needs to fit in one of the two treaty categories: European Economic Area vs Free Trade Agreements. The only deals on offer are off-the-shelf with amendments. This is EU law. Repeat: we will not allow cherry-picking, having cakes and eating them, ordering from an à la carte menu, inventing unicorns in a fantasy world...

UK: ...except when you are the pickers and eaters. You are the ones who want to cherry-pick our financial services. And agreements with the Swiss, Ukrainians, Georgians, Turks and Moldavians are all special anyway.

EU: True. Each relationship with each neighbour, or indeed partner from further afield, is special. But all of them are third countries, treated like third countries, expected to deal with us as third countries.

UK: You are being rigidly dogmatic! We have become the victim of punitive legalistic behaviour!

EU: Legalistic fragilistic! How disingenuous of you to poke fun at EU law which you yourself have written over the last forty years. Legal reality is not narrow-minded legalism but the be-all and end-all of the EU. And you know it!

UK: Thanks for admitting that we are familiar with the rule of law – we invented the damn thing after all, we should know. And what we know is that good law is a means not an end, and international law is only sustainable if it serves everyone's interests.

EU: Brexit is in no one's interests. But at least EU law dictates its incontrovertible consequences. The single market is the soul of the EU. What will remain if we give it up?

UK: Don't be melodramatic. We are not asking you to give it up. It is our baby too! But since when are there clear written rules and consequences on how to withdraw? You and we have to make it up as we go along.

EU: Perhaps. But we all need to follow the most relevant EU rules. The EU is a web of asymmetrical deals resulting in losers as well as winners in each and every case. It only holds together because of its rules. No rules, no EU.

UK: We were all for EU rules, remember! Has any other state been as EU law-abiding as us? Even if our common law and spontaneous constitutional evolution is not easily soluble in a rule-based codified setting like the EU, we recognised this was the only glue that could bind our voluntary commitments to each other. But since when did we say yes to superglued principles?

(Enter core principles, stage left.)

EU: Sorry, but these principles are our *raison d'être*. Do we need to spell them out? Start with sustaining the *integrity* of the single market. This principle is our economic foundation. You know full well that the single market operates as an ecosystem which predicates access on taking part in the design, implementation, monitoring and enforcement of rules. Whether we harmonise or mutually recognise our national standards, this is a process. If you leave our common regulatory area, you leave the process. You can't unilaterally decree that you are EU-compatible.

UK: So in the name of the integrity of the single market you are going to reject our pro-free-trade proposals and instead erect protectionist non-tariff barriers?

EU: We are not erecting new barriers, but simply asserting that if we have no way to be sure that you are EU-compatible, we cannot give you unconditional access. This applies to exporters from anywhere in the world.

UK: We are not asking for unconditional access, but for the conditions to be reciprocal – we recognise your rules, you recognise our rules.

EU: OK, let's run with this for just a minute. In finance let's say we need all the safeguards necessary to ensure financial stability, protect investors, secure market integrity and fair competition. Our way or the highway. No third-country supervisors, even yours, can provide such guarantees.

UK: So you say no country in the world would accept such a loss of sovereignty, but this is what you are asking of us!

EU: Well, not only you.

UK: How ironic – while you are constantly trying to persuade other countries to liberalise trade with you...

EU: Ah, they are different. They are not leaving states but aspiring members.

UK: Not all trade partners are aspiring members... and there are no precedents for a leaving state!

EU: True, we have never done this before. That is why we have to invent a method that reflects who we are, guardians of the integrity of our market and its rules.

UK: We valued you for decades as a political machine honed over time in order to craft delicate compromises through creative fudging and subtle horse-trading. And you will put up barriers against us simply to make a point?

EU: Yes, but a good point!

UK: A good point by using a vague term that none of our citizens understand? Integrity has become a mantra that allows your NO to sound principled.

EU: Ours is not a vague proposal: respect the *acquis communautaire*; stay in the EU ecosystem, under our jurisdiction; join Norway!

UK: ...except for free movement?

EU: Sorry, no! Integrity of our market includes another principle: the doctrine known as the 'indivisibility of the four freedoms' (for goods, services, capital and labour). No free movement of goods if services are outside our net. No free movement of people, no free movement of the rest.

UK: Yes, like the holy trinity: an unmovable dogma constructed to reject our reasonable requests after taking in so many EU citizens over the last fifteen years. This does not appear anywhere in the treaty we signed up to. In fact the movement of people comes under three bits, not one bit, of the treaty (workers, establishment, services).

EU: OK, we admit that the indivisibility doctrine is not based on solid legal or economic grounds. But it has served us all well, you included, as a way of making political agreement between us easier. And we have enshrined it with Norway and Switzerland... unless, that is, they backtrack...

UK: Actually, Liechtenstein wriggled its way out of it, and the EEA allows for safeguard measures. The Swiss have also played with labour market rules. All we asked before the referendum was an emergency break for the same reasons. As for actual EU members, you have all found all sorts of ways to circumvent it. We haven't, because we are too liberal to keep track of who is inside our borders. How does one find common cause with fundamentalist principles which do not take in what has happened on the ground?

EU: You know very well that our principles are sacred even if we can all turn a blind eye to their enforcement on the ground.

UK: The problem is that you will not allow us to be as creative as Liechtenstein because the UK is too big. We should just have invoked a public interest clause when we were members. Now that we are leaving, you don't have to apply EU member rules to us.

EU: We understand your special pleading for a *sui generis* privileged third-country status. But why should we be so lenient and cool about it? After all, you are the ones who decided to leave, remember, not us!

UK: Ah, there you have it. The only reason for your inflexibility is vindictiveness. Your position is not about seeking a good outcome, but punishing us for getting out.

EU: If you call punishment seeking a highly logical outcome that gives more rights to members than non-members, so be it. This principle is called 'balance of rights and obligations'.

UK: We understand that we should lose rights, but you tend to forget that we lose the biggest right of all, the right that makes membership special and valuable in the first place: a seat at the table!

EU: Hmm, true... But, hey, that goes without saying.

UK: As a result we understand that we will trade on the basis of product standards we no longer help shape. But we have got to have some discretion in the future for the rest of our policies and rules, including in services.

EU: This is what we fear. A big country like you, on our very doorstep, gaining an unfair advantage in trade goods thanks to unregulated services input...

UK: But we took out frictionless trade in services from our proposals precisely as a concession, to demonstrate we were giving up the most precious advantage: a single passport for financial services.

EU: That does not look like a concession to us, only more cherry-picking! Besides, you will also try to undercut our high standards in labour or environmental law or our state aid rules, in the name of your beloved competitive spirit. Have you already forgotten that fighting unfair competition is what the EU is all about, you know, destroying the cartels that brought Hitler to power? We call this the 'level playing field' principle.

UK: But you cannot expect us blindly to apply all the standards you come up with when we have not participated in designing them!

EU: We can and we will. In fact, we may want to make these commitments even more binding than when you were a member. Once out, you will be too tempted to do what you like.

UK: Isn't this an abuse of your own dominant power as a regional club?

EU: That is what we do with our trading partners! You loved it when you were the ones doing it to them. Welcome to their club.

UK: A club we should not belong to. The best and the brightest in Westminster engaged in this grand exercise in translation, from internal to external EU law. But even they are baffled by your unwillingness to grant us a side table where we can continue to negotiate mutually agreeable standards for trade.

EU: Why would we want to recreate the EU's single market from outside? How wasteful of resources.

UK: Why not, since that is where we will be.

EU: And from there, you will cheat and race us to the regulatory bottom.

UK: Why would we want to run to the bottom? We prefer racing to the top. Our treasury wrote many of the EU's banking regulations, while France and Germany tried to water them down, and then we proceeded to gold-plate them on top! Why not avail yourself of our regulatory expertise?

EU: Sorry, old friends. We respect the UK's wish to take back sovereignty over its laws, but you don't have a monopoly for caring about control. We care about sovereignty, too, even if it is shared among twenty-seven. Our legislators, regulators and court make or interpret EU law, not you. Don't ask us to give up our most hard-earned principle, the 'autonomy' of EU law, its legal order and decision-making. Our legal and institutional set-up is complicated enough as it is without requests from outsiders to take part!

UK: And yet, we all believe in multilateralism, mutuality, equality...

EU: Don't try to blur the principles for inners and outers. The EU can match the UK's stubbornness and bloody-mindedness, you know! If you reclaim your sovereignty against us we reclaim ours against you.

UK: The truth is that this is not about principles but rivalry. Since London prospered at the expense of Paris under the single market, what a golden opportunity Brexit offers to attract back some of its industries. Politically irresistible, even if geo-strategically unwise.

EU: Let's leave geopolitics out of this!

(Enter security, furtively, stage right)

UK: You are deluding yourselves if you think the price of conflict will be confined to economics. What about our shared security?

EU: What about it? On this front we want full cooperation, you said it yourself: the two should not be linked; the UK has unilaterally and unconditionally committed to serving European-wide security.

UK: Of course, in principle. But that we commit to no bargaining linkage between security and the terms of our trade deal does not mean that economics and security are not connected in a broader political way. Call it atmospherics. Yes, we are committed to working together as before on everything from intelligence to Macron's new intervention initiative. But do you expect a smooth security cooperation, either with the EU or bilaterally, if our economic

relations are acrimonious? You can't say, heads you give me your
Chinook helicopters, tails I take your bankers.

EU: True, the UK–EU security relationship will be radically different
after Brexit. Take intelligence, for example. We know you have 007
and all. We love him too! But we have not forgotten that even as an
EU member you shut us out of your Five Eyes anglophone club of
intelligence-sharing and spying data with your chums from the US,
Australia, Canada and New Zealand. Now that you are leaving, why
should you remain part of European Union information-sharing
schemes to track criminals and terrorists through fingerprints, DNA
databases and the like that help identify foreign criminals, or for that
matter the encrypted part of the Galileo system that helps us build
our own independent GPS?

UK: That is a no-brainer. Pooling our resources and capabilities in
law enforcement and intelligence will save lives. And besides, we are
integral to the success of Galileo, in resources and expertise. It is also
our creature. Why kick us out?

EU: Because we will need to protect our essential security interests.
Your warning sounds like a threat to us.

UK: Really? We are going to be treated like a potentially 'hostile state'
by Brussels?

EU: Hostile no, third country yes. Our strategic autonomy dictates
that we never share sensitive information with third countries.

UK: This is putting ideology over security. You will have citizens'
blood on your hands. At least Brexit has taught us that it is always
about trade-offs. For the real security world, strategic autonomy is
the ability of the EU to defend itself or others, but all you mean is the
ability to take decisions all by itself.

(A pause. The parties seem ready to close the meeting.)

EU: You can repeat until you are red, white and blue in the face that
we ought to be more flexible and creative, meet you halfway, but

the bottom line is simple. You have decided to leave the EU and its suburb the EEA, so we will even sacrifice some of our shared prosperity and security on the altar of our principles.

UK: Are you truly ready to sacrifice the wellbeing of Europeans for the sake of ideological purity? This is precisely the intransigence that we so disliked about the EU and that made so many of us want to leave in the first place – and sadly we will never escape it.

EU: You complain about *our* ideological purity obscuring rationality! But your own rhetoric and your polling data demonstrates it abundantly: your Brexit project is pure ideology, ready to sacrifice prosperity for its own sake!

UK: We could collude in minimising these costs…

EU: I'm afraid you are not the centre of the world any more; we do not have a duty to appease your whims and tantrums. You are going to have to swallow your pride. We are the powerful ones, anyway.

UK: How can you try to bully us when we will remain your most important trading partner and military ally!

EU: We are not exploiting our power in order to punish but to defend what is right. Brexit is your decision, not ours – live with the consequences! Don't beg us to save you from yourselves.

(End of scene)

We all relish the story of the rabbi who, when asked to adjudicate in a dispute, listens to Avi and says, 'You are right'; then listens to Shlomo and says, 'You are right'; and then, when their third companion protests, 'Rabbi, you said Avi was right and then you said Shlomo was right, but they cannot both be right!' replies, 'You are right.'

Each side is right, of course, from its own standpoint. And if disputes about doctrine are irreconcilable, negotiations thankfully occur on a different plane. Many deals have actually been struck. But mutual suspicion remains high.

Both sides misconstrue linkages in mirroring ways: the UK by thinking that you can withdraw partially and somehow leave much of the relationship untouched; Brussels and Paris by thinking that you can exclude the UK partially and somehow leave much of the relationship untouched. The UK, with its unwritten constitution, was saying: 'We are trying to make it work, can't you do the same?' The EU, with its painfully agreed constitutionalised order and its Germano-Gallic mindset, was saying: 'These are the rules, can't *you* understand?' What a Brexiter minister calls the theological obsession of the unelected bureaucrat, his European elected counterpart sees as the commitment of its politicians and civil servants alike. Britain fears the black hole of EU dogma; Brussels fears the legal void that will suck in the whole edifice. It does not help to point to the costs. As with Abraham, the more costly the test, the more proof that the EU's faith in itself and the Leavers' faith in their project is warranted. Different planets, incompatible truths.

Pity the Little Children

It can be very personal. Once upon a time in the 1970s, the first and only European school in Britain opened in Culham near Oxford to service the families of thousands of scientists, British or not, working to crack the secret of nuclear fusion and with it offer the hope that we could one day stop global warming. Thanks to the British government the school survived the end of the nuclear site, and even the prospect of Brexit. But the EU may now forbid it to continue to offer a European baccalaureate, a narrow interpretation of member states' prerogatives. Why? Because the Brits deserve it? Why treat these kids as pawns in a game of legal chess? How can European institutions be indifferent to children who are the very incarnation of its supposed ideals of multicultural and multilingual education? Has the bureaucratic logic irredeemably taken over an EU blind to the lives of its citizens? The Brits don't deserve it; Europeans don't deserve it.

Cherry, My Precious

'L' Angleterre, je la veux nue!' When asked in 1967 after his second *'non'* to UK membership if he had actually said this in 1963, General de Gaulle replied: 'Nudity for a beautiful creature is quite natural, and quite satisfying for those around her.' Adding with a wry smile, 'But whatever attraction I feel for England, I never said such a thing.'

The play takes place in a cherry orchard. The old owners are having their last picnic on the grass, leaving cakes uneaten on an immaculate cloth. You may not pick the cherries, the child is told.

To no avail. The child starts climbing the tree of unbalancing, and picks two cherries labelled 'benefits' and 'no costs'. She is promptly told off. She throws them away, and runs to the tree of indivisibility to pick 'goods' and 'not services'. She selects cherries from different sectors of the orchard along the way. That will not do either.

Accusations fly. The kid is now double cherry-picking! The best cherries from the EU members' grove before running to Norwegian Wood, pausing en route near some Canadian Red Cedars.

Fed up with this cherry-picking galore, the adults in the garden snatch back the whole basket.

This is unfair, the child cries, I carefully avoided the green ones. My cherries are perfectly ripe. Beautifully frictionless, although missing their kernel of rights. They are all I have now that I am not sitting around the tablecloth with you.

She watches, standing to one side, as the rest of the party starts eating cake, now that they have them too, immortalised inside Manet's frame.

Shaded by the tree of indivisibility they explain

...Leaving cakes uneaten...
Le Dejeuner sur l'Herbe,
Édouard Manet, 1863, Musée d'Orsay, Paris

© photo musée d'Orsay / rmn

142

patiently that if she gives up her free movements, the only cakes she can have are those imported from a third country, typically adorned with their own exotic cherries; but they will take off the cherries on her share. Our home-made cake does not have cherries, they say, so why should yours? Because I am not comfortably sitting on the tablecloth to eat it? she ventures.

They try to reassure her. We can still stand together under our imported security umbrella, even if we keep your economic cherry basket. She is not sure that this makes sense.

After a few last mouthfuls of cake, the picnic party is ready to leave. They can see that their futile attempt to keep the orchard intact, with its cherries picked by the anointed few, has failed. They couldn't see the wood for the trees. It was the green cherries that gave the orchard its true value.

The child has left. Chekhov sighs. The cherry orchard will be auctioned off on the global market and the trees cut down, sacrificed to the mores of a new era.

Filioque, Freemoque

As an atheist baptised Greek Orthodox, here is a story I was raised with. In the fourth century AD, the Christian theologian Gregory of Nazianzus described his emotion when contemplating the indivisible Three in One: the Father, the Son and the Holy Spirit. 'No sooner do I conceive of the One than I am illumined by the splendour of the Three; no sooner do I distinguish Three than I am carried back into the One. When I think of any of the Three, I think of Him as the whole, and my eyes are filled, and the greater part of what I am thinking escapes me...' No pretence of rationality there. Yet over the centuries that followed, the guardians of the Christian faith would tear themselves apart over the meaning of indivisibility. What does consubstantial mean? Does the Holy Spirit proceed from the Father alone, or from the Son too – *filioque* – thus emanating from both without ever being separated from either?

By the turn of the millennium, the first great schism was consummated, with Rome championing the *filioque* and the Eastern churches opposing it. With religious doctrinal battles cloaking power conflicts in the Roman Empire, the real split had been about the desirability of imperial unity. Doctrinal purity prevailed on both sides and thus unity was lost between East and West. Safeguarding unity would have meant heeding advocates for coexistence through a plurality of theologies, or decreeing both sides to be right if the word 'proceeds' actually takes on different meanings...

A thousand years later, the first great schism of the European Union has fallen prey to a new doctrinal war about indivisibility. This time a holy quartet involving goods, services, capital, free-movement-*que*, constructed incrementally at the turn of the millennium, has become 'as untouchable as the queen of England', to quote an EU politician. Does indivisibility mean that when one freedom is missing the others are distorted? Or that they all four proceed from a singular cause? That to divide them might deny them all? That they are distinct but at the same time one?

Much in the Brexit saga will continue to rest on the resilience of the indivisibility doctrine. After all, if Rome, aka the EU, had not insisted on it, Cameron would have got his emergency brake for free movement of people in 2016 and thus probably won the referendum. Even after the vote, the EU might have prevented the triggering of Article 50 if it had offered that option. And in a post-Brexit world some control over EU citizens in the UK could take place *within* the single market. After all, no unfair competition is acquired with such self-harm. And exceptions can be temporary. Every sacred text invites discretion in interpretation and contestation of such discretion.

Indeed, I have heard much Byzantian grumbling in various EU countries that divisibility can be a lesser evil than giving up frictionless trade for the sake of a doctrine. I have heard that the doctrine is not spelled out in our sacred texts, the Treaties, which contain various aspirations that have been pursued inconsistently and separately. I have heard that enshrining the term itself was dreamed up at a Malta summit or elsewhere; no one seems to know. After all, is indivisibility not the obligation and privilege reserved for members only, rather than for the Turkeys and Ukraines of this world? Why treat the UK as a member in this one way only? And if the reason given is access to the single market, does it make sense to shrink it in pursuit of doctrinal purity?

Of Minotaurs and Scapegoats

Let's face it, talk of Sacrifice is a bit uncomfortable to our modern ear. The age-old practice of doing something terrible (killing your child, as Agamemnon did to Iphigenia) for the sake of a higher purpose is supposed to be the mark of our superior species. No other animal does such a thing.

And then, 800 years ago, Maimonides argued in his great wisdom that God's decision to allow sacrifices was a concession to the psychological limitations of humanity. Striving to overcome these limitations must mean getting rid of the sacrificial mindset. Many Jewish and Muslim commentators see Abraham and Isaac's story as a tirade against human Sacrifice. Fine: myths may tell us how humans were replaced with animals on the sacrificial stand, but why should we continue to stand for sacrifices at all? Should we not ban Sacrifice altogether, from our minds as well as our mores?

...Thus ridding the Antique world of the sacrificial plague... *The Awful Fight between Theseus and The Minotaur*, George Wharton Edwards, 1912

Young Theseus may have been pondering this very question many more centuries before Maimonides when approaching the Cretan coast and the terrible Minotaur guarding the maze of the Cretan king in Knossos. Remember how years earlier Athens had been forced to provide the beast with ritual offerings to commemorate its defeat against Knossos – seven young women and seven young men sacrificed every seven years. Remember how Theseus, the Athenian hero of the story, revolted against the practice, mingled with the young victims, managed to slay the Minotaur and find a way out of the labyrinth, thus ridding the ancient world of the sacrificial

© UniversalImagesGroup/Getty Images

plague altogether. But remember also that the king's daughter Ariadne, none other than *Europa*'s granddaughter, provided Theseus with a thread to retrace his route, a thread of meaning that would write the end of all sacrifices to come.

How do EU actors, from policy-makers to civil society, find their way out of the labyrinth so as to banish the sacrificial urge? How do they resist the temptation to sacrifice Britain and its irritating gang of anti-Euro populists on the altar of European unity? What will they do when they are no longer able to blame Brexit for their troubles? In spite of Maimonides and Theseus, this is no easy proposition.

For alas we do need scapegoats. All great ancient texts, from the Aegean to the Middle East to China, place Sacrifice at the very core of social order.

Why is this? The French philosopher René Girard explains how all societies are driven by 'mimetic desire', a powerful force pitting people against one another, as each one desires what the other has, be it their wealth, their security or their mate. In this whirlwind, collective relief can only be had by expelling or killing a person or a group in the hope of restoring social order. The unassailable violence which always lurks beneath our civilising schemes can thus be channelled through victims of substitution. The fear which drives us to conjure up scapegoats is that of contagious animosity, even if we cannot identify the initial microbe that started it. For Girard, it is the wilful ignorance of this phenomenon that is the secret of our survival as a species. We would be unable to live with the knowledge of our past and endemic violence if we could not expel it onto a uniquely guilty body. Anathema, shunning and excommunication serve to this day to ensure that we forget or at least remain indifferent to the performative function of our collective violence.

The scapegoat theme is familiar to EU affairs; having served as a mainstay of the Europhile narrative; the unpopularity of the EU, we often hear, is down to its use by unscrupulous national politicians as a scapegoat for their own ineptitude. The EU is always unfairly blamed for everything wrong in Europe. Populists everywhere use it as a scapegoat for very national problems due to something having gone too far: neoliberalism, market logic, globalisation, corporate greed. Europeanised failure and nationalised success as the foolproof recipe for EU scapegoating.

The Brexit story would then arrive absolutely apropos, featuring as it does the alternative scapegoat, serving to deflect the mutual animosity that has re-erupted between European states and peoples since the beginning of the crisis cascade, no longer on small hapless countries like Greece, but on a member state that fits the bill more perfectly still.

For a start, for this unconscious scheme of forgetting and blaming to work, we need a reliable key to distinguish between categories of people – or types of countries – apt or not for sacrifice. For a category to serve properly as sacrificial it must resemble as closely as possible those for whose benefit it is being sacrificed, while at the same time being distinct enough to avoid some dangerous confusion between the scapegoat and the rest of the group, the very same group seeking to deflect violence. Even if it's invisible, its malevolent influence must be fleshed out. Those people who are marginal within the community offer prime material – groups that have lived amongst us but have not woven the same ties as the rest. Something exceptional must designate the scapegoat, be it foreignness, age, servility, weakness, boastfulness, or its quality as the eternal Trojan horse.

To be sure, the scapegoat is not alien to us. Biblical and Greek myths tend not to be about solitary heroes, but about brothers – not loving siblings but *frères ennemis,* fraternal, intimate enemies or brothers at war, symbiotic antagonists. But it is not always possible to channel their reciprocal violence onto third parties for the sake of social peace. According to some Midrashic interpretations of the Torah, Cain's tragedy starts not with his jealousy of his brother Abel, but with the fact that they both yearned for the same sister, before God chose between them. Alas for Cain, he will have no other sacrificial outlet for his mighty resentment than Abel. The first man to be born kills the first man to die, fount of all sacrifices.

The scapegoat needs to be dispensable enough to be sacrificed, yet precious enough to be sacrificed meaningfully, precious all the more because the crisis is acute. She must serve as a dumping ground for all our rivalries, petty blames and jealousies, yet remain capable of protecting the whole community from its own violence. It might be a crime to get rid of her because she is sacred, but she would not be sacred if she was not meant to be got rid of.

Yet no one in particular need be responsible for designating the scapegoat. Better to let it designate itself, elect to climb the pyre all on its own. And the ritual disposing of the scapegoat must ensure that it will not in turn seek revenge or be joined by others supporting its cause.

The sacrificial safety valve is all the more effective when the whole process appears dictated from above, through eternal laws of some kind, dictated by gods or by some secular *acquis communautaire*. This does not mean that the law is impartial; nobody and nothing can be. Nor does it take away the agency of our protagonists. But for the cycle of violence in our societies to be broken at times of crisis someone needs to have the last word. Destructive ambivalence is the name of this game.

The problem with all this is that our clever scapegoating mechanisms cannot be acknowledged without losing their power. Think back to the Oedipus story. Freud only scratched the surface when he teased out from the story his famous theories of parricide and incest, the irresistibility and monstrosity of it all. There was something in Freud's thought, but it did not do justice to what was truly going on. For, in Sophocles' tragic vision, Oedipus is the quintessential story of social scapegoating.

Here is a city, Thebes, awash with fake news and controversy about who to blame for the city's plague and whose truth we must buy into. The plague – echoing that of the Exodus – has spread violence to the whole city, a city obsessed with one question: who started it? The investigation dresses up the scapegoating process. Oedipus is found guilty but in fact he is only made responsible, a true scapegoat candidate. He is responsible for the crisis not because of his terrible deeds but for the more general fact of indiscriminate and reciprocal mayhem – as if somehow he had done away with difference itself and had thus become himself monstrously different. He reassures the inhabitants of Thebes that he alone will bear the consequences, that the whole city will be freed through this transfer.

Crucially, this version of the facts can only become true thanks to a crucial ingredient in the collective brew: unanimity. Each against each becomes all against one. Thebans may be divided on all fronts – easterners versus westerners, old versus young, creditors versus debtors – but, with the sacrificial ritual of Oedipus their king, only one single division remains. Trying to woo any of them is futile. Animosity is no longer interchangeable. The myth gives us a community united in its culprit. For Oedipus' subjects there will be no resolution to their crisis, the plague, without unity.

The city must demonstrate to itself that the verdict is unanimous, and it must demonstrate to itself that the verdict is believed by all. There will be no resolution without universal faith in the scapegoat's guilt. And indeed, with Oedipus gone, the city recovers – although, unsurprisingly, only until the next crisis. That is another story.

In fact, unanimity is such that even the accused shares in the accusations. But in a similar story, Job, a kind of Jewish Oedipus afflicted by a terrible fate, refuses to accuse himself, and thus breaks the scapegoating cycle.

As a scapegoat, Oedipus serves as the pivot between a generalised paroxysm of

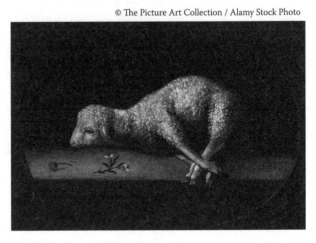

© The Picture Art Collection / Alamy Stock Photo

...Animosity is no longer interchangeable... *The Sacrificial Lamb*, Josefa de Ayala, *c.* 1670–84

reciprocal violence and peaceful consensus by providing a single magnet for all the aggression and rivalry in his world. The road from chaos to peace is painted with the blood from his eyes. But the magnet's force is also a function of the man's previously celebrated powers. This is the monster-slayer after all who confronted the Sphinx, which itself required sacrificial victims.

'When did it all start?' We asked in the previous chapter. Oedipus becomes king as a result of vanquishing a Sphinx who had been punishing the city for some ancient, all-but-forgotten crime, one which pre-dated his own birth in this same city. Oedipus' fate harks back to his own father's crime, yet he can only serve as scapegoat if the river of cause and effect can be truncated: all the trouble started when Oedipus committed parricide. There is no 'before', there are no prior causes that have consequences, causes that would show that he is not the only one to blame.

And, of course, if the scapegoat does not die, we must worry about what happens next. Will he be exonerated, rehabilitated, forgotten? In his exile in Colonus, Oedipus learns that, once he is dead, his body will confer great power on those who are his hosts

– from beneficent to malevolent and back to beneficent, the circle is complete. This does not mean that he will be forgiven. Beneficent Oedipus can succeed but not annul malevolent Oedipus. It only means that, as with so many stories, one that generates mayhem inside the family or fellow men can be redeemed outside the circle, and one that has faced inadmissible truths can be redeemed thereafter.

The circle is complete in the greater scheme of things, too, for it is Theseus, king of Athens, the Minotaur-and-Sacrifice-slayer, who welcomes Oedipus at the end of his long journey and gives him the redemptive death he so craves.

Unity Amor, Unity Terror

Sacrifice is part of the cult of oneness. A European Union which cannot unite against Xi, El-Sisi, Putin or Erdoğan has done so against one of its own even as it still sat around the common table. Should we be surprised? Shaken at its core, the polity must demonstrate to itself that the verdict is unanimous, believed by all, even Oedipus. From Thebes to Brussels, it is hard to resist redemptive Sacrifice. With all the plagues testing it, European unity can only be recovered thanks to a scapegoat that is one of us, *pas tout à fait le même, pas tout à fait un autre.* Isn't the UK both distinct and similar enough, dispensable and precious enough, to serve as the perfect scapegoat? What have the British ever done for us anyway (apart from sacrifice for our freedom and all that)! Great Britain might have prided itself for centuries on its capacity to sow divisions among us, its European neighbours, all the better to protect its own interests. Not this time!

Unity Amor. Love of redemptive unity, the EU's primary creed, expresses itself through unanimous delegation to a single negotiator. But from Warsaw to Rome, from Oslo to Tallinn, I have heard it as a guilty whisper: Unity Terror, that is what it feels like sometimes. On Brexit, Brussels does not even allow us to agree to disagree, as we usually do. Unity over Brexit is the price we have to pay if we want concessions elsewhere. Not only are we losing a partner, but we must pretend that we agree to its treatment. It does not feel to us like 'Europe one, whole and at peace'.

Unity Terror, can we speak of thee? Can we admit that our yearning for unity is only matched by our desire for separateness? After the original sin, Adam, the first hermaphrodite and a self-sufficient being like his creator, is divided into two imperfect sexes incapable of reproducing on their own. But no one hears Adam complain about Eve's existence. Plato tells us how each half of the primitive androgynous being, split into male and female by Zeus, will forever be looking for the other half to become one again. Yet, he passionately praises love of an Other. Sustained togetherness usually rests on continued autonomy.

We are told that our European states, peoples and citizens crave unity, but if our divisions are ever to be overcome, we might want to learn to better live with our differences instead. We could start by proclaiming loud and clear that Europeans with different material interests, historical memories or symbolic attachments relate to Britain and its withdrawal differently. Unity will need to be forged from other fires.

Self-reflexive Sacrifice

Europe cannot have its perfect scapegoat cake and eat it too; Britain cannot be sacrificed for a little while and still be redeemed as our closest friend at the end of the journey.

'Of course not,' everyone seems to swear in this mad Brexit saga, 'scapegoating will not do.'

For we sophisticated and civilised *Homo sapiens* learned this lesson a long time ago. Girard tells us that it was thanks to the story of Jesus' resurrection, which offers humanity the first collective awareness of its violent tendencies and of its urge to scapegoat. Indeed, the Bible may be full of sound and fury but it also distances itself radically from Sacrifice. Cain's story is about the innocence of the victim, Abel. Not so for Romulus and Remus a few centuries earlier. The cycle is broken. The self-reflexive Sacrifice serves as the Sacrifice to end all sacrifices.

We know that we have become self-aware societies. It is only when the mechanism of scapegoating is made visible that ritualism ends and politics starts. Britain will not restore peace and unity to Europe by leaving. Brexit will not channel our reciprocal violence. For Brexit to change the EU for the better rather than the worse, it needs to happen away from the sacrificial pyre.

Can Brexit come to embody the hallmarks of self-reflexive Sacrifice? A political wake-up call for the rest of Europe? An ironic Sacrifice whereby all sides share in the awareness of what is going on and seek to invent another way? Could it be what Macron meant early on when he vowed not to have red lines, but only horizons? What if, in short, European citizens and their leaders conducted their democratic conversation about the meaning of Brexit without embracing sacrificial delusions?

To be sure, such an attitude requires much sangfroid on the part of continentals after having endured three years and more of put-downs from the other side of the Channel. But Europeans can never forget that almost two-thirds of the British electorate and more among the young, did not vote for leaving. And that many of those who did were moved more by pan-European realities. Certainly Europeans can hope for genuine proof of recognition from UK officialdom of the EU's proud achievements and not-so-secret vulnerabilities, recognition that sticking to one's foundational principles is not an act of bullying, and that it is unreasonable to ask for everything to change on the other side in order to make sure everything can stay the same in a freed UK. Who can blame the keepers of the flame on the continent who passionately want rearguard sovereigntists on the UK side to face the bloody consequences.

Nevertheless, for Brexit to serve as a self-reflexive Sacrifice, tragic choices must be debated in the European agora. What does it mean to accept the consequences of one's choices and actions? What does it mean when the choice was made blind, from ignorance of the real and present strictures of EU membership, for sure, but also because these consequences would be defined in Brussels?

For Oedipus' story reminds us that there are no fixed beginnings in history, only an arbitrary fixing of the dial to deflect alternative truths. Depending on our side of a conflict, we each start the cause-and-consequences chain where it suits us, so we can say: they started it! This will happen for Brexit too. The dial can be turned back to the UK's entrance in a legal and budgetary system not attuned to its own parameters, or back further still to De Gaulle's Nos which prevented the UK from co-shaping these institutions in the first place, or even to Churchill's bailing out at the foundation. Some of us will continue to choose February 2016 as our key counterfactual. What if the EU had indulged the British government when it sought to conjure up European reform and re-foundation as a way to address its dilemma rather than offering a special deal for Britain instead? What if Cameron and Macron had overlapped? And what if the British-only deal had included a temporary but meaningful exception on free movement on the grounds that Britain had been more royalist than the EU king, with its open-door policy during the transition period for Eastern Europeans – ill-judged on numbers but not on principles? After all, Merkel's 'welcome refugees' a decade later was also ill-judged by an order of magnitude, and yet right. What if Merkel's open-door moment had overlapped with Blair's? What if Germany and Britain had given each other some slack on their fateful decisions to open their respective borders?

Some say: we must let them suffer for a while as a much-needed reality check and only when the point is made can we detoxify the cost of leaving. But surely there are points of no return. It cannot ever be a good idea to demean the other side as a political reprimand. Even if this is not the intention, care must be taken. Who is glorified by the thought of Britain kneeling at last to Brussels, perfidious Albion humiliated and banished from Thebes once and for all? Does it make sense for the EU to be the one to push the British Isles towards the Atlantic when it still has so many anchors on the continent? And what would this do to Europe's moral reputation and free-trade credentials? What is there to lose in generous conciliation? If the EU is as normatively righteous as it presents itself to the world, can it contemplate banishing one of its own, all the while wishing the pariah to eventually return?

Even if Brexit is about damage control, escalating the mutual losses may not serve to control the damage. A butchering of the City may not truly benefit Paris, Frankfurt, Dublin or Amsterdam, as Europe loses out to New York's financial dominance. Separate sanctions policies could serve Putin and Assad well. Does it make sense to hurt oneself for the sake of proving that the other side is worse off when leaving? And who decides how much disruption is the price to pay?

We should ask about the motives and methods of unanimity. Do we truly believe that the remaining member states will not renew their vows with the European Union as a result of Brexit? The British do need to abandon their old idea that salvation in Europe will always come from other capital cities rather than from Brussels. But does the EU truly need the glue of Sacrifice – Thebes demonstrating to itself that the verdict is unanimous – to show that the old UK 'divide and rule' does not work?

...Tragic choices must be debated... *Caïn venant de tuer son frère Abel*, Henri Vidal, 1896

We must not shy away from honouring all the bilateral stories that constitute the fabric of Europe itself.

Does the value of membership have to be measured against the cost of giving it up? Is it not better to make sure a withdrawing state is worse off only in terms of EU rights rather than all round? It may be better for each side to save the other from itself, understand the other's internal challenges and collude in conjuring up coping tactics. We shouldn't assume that a 'better deal for Britain' could collapse the entire EU if it only goes to showcase the EU at its best, an admirable piece of machinery capable of transforming destructive tensions into productive solutions.

Perhaps EU leaders are learning this lesson, in the face of imploding British politics, and even applying it to themselves.

Thus, in the process, Brussels may be able to resist the temptation to brand some in the south or east of Europe as pariahs, spoiler nations free-riding on the EU, when these nations were sacrificed yesterday on the altar of realpolitik where the crimes of Nazism and Stalinism converged.

How long can the EU invoke the ideal of 'integrity', integrity of its laws and single market, without agreement on what it means? It may mean internal consistency – you cannot have this without that – but is this also legal, economic or political consistency? Does it involve staying whole and undivided, in which case Brexit must be resisted at all costs, or does it refer to the older meaning of the word, as adherence to moral and ethical principles? But then whose morality shall we follow?

And what of scapegoating in the end. If the UK did too badly out of Brexit, would this prove that Brexit was wrong or that the UK was wronged? And if the EU did too badly out of Brexit, would it prove that it was wrong to wrong the UK? Would the EU escape the blame? Can it let its institutional insecurities aggravate the day-to-day insecurities of its citizens? There is no doubt that the pervasive scapegoating of the EU has poisoned European politics for decade, in the UK and elsewhere. But we also know that for the EU always to be blamed for Europe's woes did serve the Faustian bargain that made it possible for governments to give up sovereignty. Brussels may be tired of upholding its end of the bargain, but it will not help to reverse the logic by claiming credit for positive developments in member states or blaming them for trying to address their own problems in their own way. That is a lesson courtesy of Brexit.

And in the end, what is the right balance between mutual deference and mutual interference in relations between countries? How can we let each other be when what we each do so affects the others? This is a question that has haunted our continent for much longer than the existence of the present European Union or even the Westphalian era.

If these and many other questions can be debated openly and without taboos across Europe, if in the process sacred cows were to be slaughtered as some kind of replacement Sacrifice, Brexit 2.0 could turn out to be a pivotal moment, moving from heroic Sacrifice to ironic Sacrifice, whereby neither side plays a part in the scapegoating of the other.

Revolutionary Defeatists

We are not there yet, and we won't be until we have overcome the seductive power of 'revolutionary defeatism' that has pervaded the Brexit saga, a label for Lenin's century-old idea, which led to countless controversies at the time of the First World War and inspired socialist firebrand Rosa Luxemburg to give up her life in Germany in 1919. According to this theory, an imperialist war, hatched in secrecy and against which ordinary workers were helpless, had to be answered by revolutionary action against one's own government to hasten its defeat on the battlefield – a wartime revolution in order to convert war between imperial powers into a civil war. My French compatriots call this *la politique du pire*, or bringing about the worst, presumably to harvest the best.

Wherever one turns in the Brexit play, one encounters revolutionary defeatism of the peacetime variety: the urge to make things as bad as possible in the hope that the worse they get, the greater the chance that the result will turn out in your favour. No vulgar agent of the enemy there. Simply a calculated belief that your cause justifies the means, justifies the risk that all will be lost. In the UK, Leavers, of course, hoped for their government's defeat, a very bad deal to justify no deal at all and thus their better, cleaner, purer revolution in the end. Purists on the other side hoped for the worst deal possible so that reversal would become the only desirable option. A friendly happy Brexit would not make these Brexiters happy and a terribly sad Brexit would not make these Remainers sad. Both sides seemed to welcome a terribly uncivil war in pursuit of their aim.

Revolutionary defeatists on the continent have conspired with arch-Brexiters in this game. They too spoke the language of zero-sum games, whereby gains are sought through the other side's losses, or, worse, the language of negative-sum games, where all that matters is to lose less than the other. Us versus Them. 'It is not the EU's duty to help the other side', they said, as if both sides were not on the pyre together, offered up as sacrifices to the gods of small differences while the rest of the world waits to bury the European remains.

The revolutionary defeatist does not shy away from cheap *Schadenfreude*, scoring points whenever possible against all those who fail to understand that there is no middle ground. Accordingly, Brexit means that everyone must understand that 'out means out': a British city can no longer become a European capital of culture, the British standard setter can't take part in European agencies after Brexit, kids in Britain can no longer pursue a European baccalaureate. It's all or nothing, not only for the country but for everyone within it.

The revolutionary defeatist will never be wrong, never to blame for the defeat he himself helped to precipitate. Whatever happens, he will fall prey to Karl Popper's bête noire, verificationism, the way people tend to seek out evidence for what they already believe, whether in science, in politics or in everyday life. In the end, Brexit is like Communist Russia; if it fails it will only be because it wasn't done properly.

In a clash of revolutionary defeatists, each believing that the other side does not just have a different opinion but is morally wrong, the perplexed individual in between has little room to breathe. She is not a relativist who believes that all sides are equally flawed in this epic battle. But she does ask herself how one side's self-righteousness can be deflated without giving ground to the other side's alternative brand of self-righteousness. Can it ever be right to worsen people's lives for the sake of proving a point? Each side's drive to prove that they were right all along narrows the space for agreement. Trust is destroyed along with the potential for self-reflexive Sacrifice.

Many Worlds

As we stand wondering what the hell will happen next, we can console ourselves with the thought that everything will happen one way or another. There are quite a few physicists and philosophers of physics out there who believe in many worlds. As they see it, the world continuously branches into new worlds, at every moment of our lives, every probabilistic fork in the road, with the worlds thus created existing in parallel universes. There exists a universe where you did not miss the bus this morning; one where Lyra Belacqua does meet Will Parry again; and one where the EU is saved. Perhaps, as in Iain Pears' dazzling *Arcadia*, what we thought was a parallel universe is in fact our future, shaped by our fears of some alternative dystopia. Perhaps it is all in the mind, our Platonic worlds of ideas where we can roam freely. Perhaps we can even pick a ripe cherry from the tree of branching-out worlds, call it a realistic utopia and assume others will buy it. It could be that a utopia is not, as John Stuart Mill believed, something too good to be practicable, but the other way round: our only way of redefining what is practicable. If we could peek into parallel universes, I am sure we could discover fragments of practicable post-Brexit EUtopias, little and broken but still good. Shall we have a peek?

Sacrifice for Moral Influence

In this particular parallel universe, we find that Europeans already miss the departed Brits, perhaps because Leavers have landed back on earth, or left it altogether for their own parallel universe.

Here, the very control given up by sacrificing Britain's voice around the table serves to exert another kind of influence, akin to what Hugo Grotius in the 1600s called moral government, or what the Enlightenment view of Christian theology understood as Sacrifice for the sake of greater moral influence. Through his sacrificial death Jesus allowed God to forgive rather than punish humanity and to continue justly to rule over the universe. Grotius was preoccupied with taming the religious conflicts of his time on the basis of a broad moral consensus, and thought to ground such a consensus in the promise of moral government.

The great temptation on the EU side will be to state that something can be done – say, create an embryo European army or harmonise corporation tax – *because* of the UK's absence. There will be some truth to this. It will be harder to admit that British influence ought to be sustained *in spite of* this absence.

Yet, in this universe, four decades of co-creating Europe's legal and political order means that this EU is not what it would have been without the UK. The UK is responsible for its own creation, even as it abandons it, just as Saint-Exupéry's Little Prince was responsible for his rose.

This is a universe in which the UK aspires to demonstrate its worthiness in the manner in which it leaves and acts after withdrawal, thus reminding its fellow Europeans of those bits of British exceptionalism that make good on such moral influence, concerning the right of the ruled to limit power, a stubborn adherence to legal commitment, a relentlessly inquisitive powerlessness, and restraint from arbitrary interference with people's lives, otherwise known as the rule of law.

But, of course, in order to remind others of these great British gifts to the world the British first need to remind themselves what they are. As the withdrawal progressively takes shape in transition, will we judge Brexit in the years to come by the yardstick of these great collective qualities? Will UK democracy, reinvigorated by Brexit, lead by example, showcasing once again the unique democratic spectacle of an English parliament 'where England speaks to itself', as Walter Bagehot once said, and the world listens in? Or will we see these values wither instead in order to unmask EU illegals? The very un-British consequences of Brexit.

In such a universe, Westminster helps to shape Brussels as Britain ends up taking on the mantle of Her Majesty's very loyal opposition, bringing the political back to the EU in parliamentary scenes replete with cries of despair or irony at EU presidents' questions. Britain's goal is not to regain power over the continental system, or to subvert it. It does not side with the continent's governments and parties who, having found it impossible to mount a classic opposition to EU policies, have turned to an existential opposition to the EU regime itself. Instead the old reformist reflex has kicked back in.

Moral influence, then, will mean respecting the EU spirit of cooperation forged after all by Britain too, and thus upholding past commitments to refrain from the kind of competition that hurts rather than serves citizens. And it will mean continuing to negotiate, in the spirit of 'sincere cooperation', a principle enshrined in the treaties which admittedly is Europe's best shot at a British invention. Perhaps the tabloids were on to something when they pointed out that the EU would betray its own commitment to good neighbourliness and compromise with a no-deal, an ironic insight given their contempt for these treaties in the first place.

For the EU to better avail itself of some of the British virtues it still cherishes, the drive to union among the peoples of Europe will need to be checked by a concern that many see as very British, a value in jeopardy in Europe and beyond, a value which may seem to have been betrayed by the Brexit vote, but a British value nevertheless, namely pluralism.

The unlikely bet in the promise of moral influence is that Britain will promote through its very absence the promise of pluralism in the EU. It will certainly be hard for Westminster to live up to it and for Brussels to recognise the promise in the first place. And so it is a bet that others will uphold, from Amsterdam to Stockholm, Prague, Lisbon, Paris or Berlin, first among those the Scandinavian or Hanseatic countries orphaned by Brexit.

The bet will best be upheld if the EU resists the temptation to downgrade English from its pedestal as the lingua franca of the Union, given the more than 200 million Europeans who use it as their common language of communication, and the other 300 million others who wish they could. In an imitation of true British pragmatism, the EU will finally share a truly non-discriminatory language once it is nobody's first tongue.

And in this parallel universe, the EU will rediscover the spirit of mutual recognition that has animated it since the foundation and which has been championed by the UK throughout its membership, an ethos much beyond a single-market technology which emphasizes the horizontal ideal of mutual engagement between peoples over and above the vertical pooling of resources and authority. Let us not fear emotional engagement with our neighbors in our multiple connected theaters of recognition if out of conflict a greater familiarity can be born.

The irony in a Brexit Sacrifice for the sake of an EU truly living up to the challenge of diversity is that its victim is among the most pluralist countries of them all – even while Europeans quarrel over whose brand of pluralism works best. And ironically too, in order to succeed, the bet needs to avail itself of all that is good about British exceptionalism – all that reminds us why the Sacrifice should not have happened in the first place.

Or as the McVitie's biscuits slogan for the French market goes, '*C'est Anglais, mais c'est bon!*' (It's English, but it's good!)

Exit Interruptus

In this other universe, spiked by the jolt of Exodus, chastened by the long shadow of Reckoning and committed to the virtues of radical pluralism, our EUtopia is becoming a union that the British would not have wanted to leave or might one day want to rejoin. Brexit has redefined the nature of EU membership. Inspired by the Holy Roman Empire which survived, more or less, for a thousand years, the EU has devised a strategy fit for the purpose of accommodating every hue of exceptionalism within the bounds required by togetherness. Our newly anointed pluralist-in-chief calls it *exit interruptus.*

Exit interruptus is about refining the best possible proxies for EU exit to ensure against an ever-shrinking Union.

The pluralist's *exit interruptus* resists looking around for a renewed European story and proclaims instead: let a hundred European stories bloom! We each have our European story, each our ways of dreaming or rejecting Europe, of endowing it with all sorts of goods and evils, all sorts of pasts, pedigrees and prejudices. The European story can only be about weaving a plethora of individual plots into a patchwork fabric.

The pluralist's *exit interruptus* prefers the idea of union to unity. For unions rehabilitated voice over exit. Unions join different bodies that remain autonomous, while unity conveys the obsession with oneness which feeds on stigmatising others outside Europe. Her problem is not with 'ever closer union' since the complete motto reads 'ever closer union of the *peoples* of Europe' – in the plural (my emphasis). Her problem lies with the unwillingness of Europe's official sphere to allow Europeans to decipher, each in their own way, the true meaning of 'ever closer union of the peoples of Europe'.

The pluralist committed to *exit interruptus* is very partial to the motto of unity in diversity, and wishes even more radically to see Europeans united in relativity. Her theory of EU relativity is inspired by the economist Stephen King, who compared the structural flaws of a German-centric

...Let each country set its own frame of reference... *caroselli di maiali,* Robert Delaunay, 1922

eurozone to Ptolemy's theory of a universe centred around the earth. Everyone but Germany has to do the adjusting to protect the interests of German taxpayers against imbalances which only others seem to be responsible for. Why, he asked, has all the Copernican scrutiny bestowed on Berlin's Euro-theories failed? Perhaps, says the pluralist, because an alternative Copernican system for Europe would not be very palatable, either, if it were to establish Brussels as the new Sun King. Better to establish the European Union relativity principle: let each country set its own frame of reference by which it determines its relationship with every other country. No frame is preferred as each is as objective as any other. Our new motto is: Unity in Relativity! Admittedly, when it comes to a theory of real gravity, or general relativity, larger masses will determine space–time curvature and space–time curvature will determine what counts as free fall. Not all gravity is born equal in this alternative universe. As a minimum, Britain could benefit from the insight of astrophysicists devoted to identifying the Goldilocks zones around stars in which planetary life might develop, being neither too hot, nor too cold.

Our pluralist may leverage her theory of European relativity to question the EU's unavowed commitment to ubiquitous convergence. If we are not able to converge, she asks, we should not blame Europe's many separate orbiting masses which exhibit such a variety of varieties: varieties of constitutions, capitalisms, modernities, politics, societal mores, legacies. How could we ever wish them away? Heed Shakespeare's Ulysses in *Troilus and Cressida,* for whom it is not difference but its loss which creates violent confusion. 'O, when degree is shaked/Which is the ladder to all high designs/Then enterprise is sick!'

The pluralist knows that there is a long way to go. She rejoices in the renewed praise for flexibility in today's EU, sits back and applauds all the talk about differentiation, enhanced cooperation and coalitions of the willing. Of course, one size no longer fits all. It never did, really.

But she may still feel uncomfortable with the resurrection of the old stories about circles and speeds. Forget the Europe of concentric circles, she exclaims, with its echoes of hierarchies, peripheries and second-class citizenship. Hierarchies of power will always exist in Europe as elsewhere, but let us not formalise them.

Forget multiple-speeds Europe, she insists, with its connotations of fast and slow countries heading towards a single finishing line. Instead rebuild an EU of overlaps, overlapping circles with a shared core: the single market, especially on the web; common values, especially tolerance; and shared institutions, especially accountable ones. Encourage lighthouse projects like free roaming on the web on a train or on campus, to be shared by all but implemented in different ways. But much else will be done in country or regional groupings, from currency to defence, refugees, borders, fiscal rules or employment. As a result, everyone will come to accept that countries like Switzerland, Norway and, yes, Britain are not in a waiting room but in a common house, with multi-functional rooms.

Call it a club of clubs, multi-track, poly-creeds or variable geometries. And since configurations fluctuate over time, call it intermittent togetherness. Support the edifice with polycentric governance where we start from the premise that intelligence is distributed across our societies, and that it can be gathered, aggregated and dispersed again so that our social systems continuously learn about themselves. Nurture decentring technologies and mindsets.

This pluralist rethink is not just about virtual architecture. It reverberates all the way down. Differentiation, which is already the rule more than the exception, will no longer be thought of as exceptional. It stems from interpreting the requirement of equality through sophisticated doctrines of non-discrimination. 'Treat like cases as like' in fact means 'Treat *only* like cases as like', said Aristotle. If discrimination is defined as a different treatment that results in a disadvantage, it obviously follows that if an equal treatment results in a disadvantage we must discriminate in order to treat different people equally.

This is not a free-for-all. Our pluralist-in-chief moulds the Union to the diverse circumstances of its member states with ample and transparent allowances for compensation and conditions, derogations and safeguards as long as these are agreed together and in good faith. Well-designed international institutions always contain escape clauses, if only to make sure the rules will be bent not broken. As the most advanced of them all, the EU ought to be the most yoga-savvy of them all. With more member-state discretion, say on their budget or their frontiers, will come more responsibility, to handle their own default or to compensate others for taking on shared burdens. This is after all consistent with this paradoxical virtue that was the EU's original *raison d'être*: obligation by choice.

The pluralist believes in cycles of power. She does not buy the concern that the EU is stuck in a halfway house, in a permanent disequilibrium, having blunted the tools of statecraft of its member states but deprived itself of these same tools that would allow, for instance, to save thousands of refugees in the Mediterranean. The tools will always be shared. They should be so according to the needs of the time, with sunset clauses when possible and a reverse gear if necessary.

The pluralist Union is committed to mutual recognition between the many perspectives, histories and social fabrics of its member states as they open vistas onto each other's realities. It is committed to overcoming the denials of recognition that have plagued it in the last decade. Differentiation helps accommodate the different integration proclivities of its populations by providing a wider variety of democratic choices regarding integration than in the pre-Brexit era.

In this political universe, EU pundits and politicians resist the Manichean temptation to turn the Union into a battleground between warring cosmopolitans and nationalists, new variants for the old tyranny of dichotomies: are you for more or less Europe, for more powers to Brussels or for returning power to national governments? Instead, wise European publics will respond: it depends, because politics is more complicated than that.

When asked what is the glue that binds us together, the pluralist would have liked to invoke justice or solidarity. She knows that 'crisis' refers in Greek to the sharing of the booty, as when Achilles and Agamemnon quarrelled over the women they would make their slaves. And thus Europe's crisis materialises when Europeans fail to agree on how to share the costs and risks associated with either shocks or the structural violence of globalisation. She believes in a duty of risk-sharing. But she is reluctant to produce a formula and would prefer to rely on a cocktail of differentiated obligations, compensations and exceptions. Chosen solidarity will be at that price.

The pluralist will sigh that subtle compromises worked out over the years between the UK and its EU counterparts were pretty close to the mark, and that this is why it has been impossible to extract more 'positive-sum' solutions for the exit deal. For a Greek or a Hungarian, the UK's EMU-free, Schengen-free status could hardly be improved upon. *Exit interruptus*, however, would have meant preferring even more differentiation over departure. In this universe, differentiated integration would have been the EU's response to the British propensity (at least in some areas) to over-apply EU laws and thus become over-burdened with their effects. As it is, the European nation most committed to the single-market legal order decided to leave it.

The pluralist is a cautious proselyte. She wears her regional hegemony lightly and is relaxed about the selective engagement by non-members with some of its regimes and rules. She hopes to apply her strategy outside as well as inside Europe. For the rest of the world, the EU's unlikely embrace of radical pluralism is good news, leading it to abandon once and for all talk of Europe as a gentle civiliser of others, the obsession with speaking with one voice and the resort to Euronationalism. It makes it more likely for others to receive the British Sacrifice, not as a sign of European weakness and decline, but as a sign of Europe's welcome maturity and its continued relevance as a fascinating, if flawed, experiment in pluralist transnational governance. Maybe in the process we can learn fruitfully to disentangle the material regionalisation of markets and territories, regional cooperation between states and regional awareness as a feature of people's minds. In its external dimension, this ambitious version of flexibility is still very much in its infancy.

The irony, then, is that the UK is leaving the EU precisely at a time when many European leaders are starting to see the need for more subtle interpretations of European law and when even Germany is starting to appreciate the beauty of shades of grey. What an ironic Sacrifice it would be if Brexit manages to make the EU more British.

Will it also make Britain more European?

On the Importance of Being Former

In the story of Exodus, we asked what it could mean to arrive from the desert in a sprawling EU suburb called 'Europe-not-the-EU', and whether the EU could pretend that British citizens, civil servants and industries had not for so long contributed to building its pyramids. In the story of Reckoning, we asked with Sisyphus whether we could ever imagine a happy Brexit. In the story of Sacrifice, we ask what it would mean to abandon the ever-powerful temptation to sacrifice a state that is not any old third country. A country that should not be treated better or worse, just differently. Perhaps this is a message we can read in the infamous political declaration.

There will be many parallel universes where this is a fact: the departing member state will have become a former member state, the very first animal of its kind in the international system, a subset of one in the general category of third country. But this fact will be subject to various interpretations. Will the EU continue to be determined to treat third countries as third countries, period? How will Britain live with the consequences, rights and responsibilities of being an ex?

Brexit 2.0 will no longer be a choice between radicalising Brexit or reversing Brexit. Each side will recover the belief and confidence that it has taken back control. But the importance of being former goes beyond the fact that the UK will be the EU's most important trading and security partner and that a special relationship will be needed as befits the country's size and proximity. The EU must overcome its strategic myopia.

There is no legal status entitled 'being a third country which used to be a member and therefore ought to be treated differently than other third countries'. It has yet to be invented. In time, we will develop grand theories of disassociation and the requisite policies to suit this inversion of enlargement. We will ask what a disassociation covenant should entail. We will build the edifice on principles, not ad hoc improvisation, and this edifice might become a template.

These principles will not fall from the sky. They will follow from the route we take from Brexit 1.0 to Brexit 2.0, a voyage of many years. As such it should be, will be, about inventing a new status for Britain, perhaps for others to follow, that of the 'former' member state.

A former member state will not be a half-member, a partial member, a member *ad honorem* or a Trojan horse. Instead, this status should recover the ontological intuition that, if leaving is a

A mark manifesting itself in the form of a microchip implant as required by frictionless trade,
that very same condition desired by most Leavers and Remainers.
The Mark of the Beast is 666, William Blake, 1810

How often do humans actually deserve the disasters that befall them? Why should invisible forces,
antique gods or otherwise, dictate our destiny?
The Last Judgement, Michelangelo, 1536–41

Sacrifice

We remain haunted by Iphigenia's fate: Should our sacrificial victim truly suffer or be seen to suffer?
Why? What is the point of sacrifice anyway? To demonstrate to ourselves and to the world the real and tangible
strategic advantage of an EU status that our victim has scornfully rejected? Or would it not be enough for Britain to
retreat from our shores, serving the EU cause by virtue of its absence?
The Sacrifice of Iphigenia, François Perrier, 1632

Fraternal, intimate enemies or brothers at war, symbiotic antagonists... Alas for Cain, he
will have no other sacrificial outlet for his mighty resentment than Abel.
Caïn venant de tuer son frère Abel, Henri Vidal, 1896

For we do need scapegoats. All great ancient texts, from the Aegean to the Middle
East to China, place sacrifice at the very core of social order.
The Sacrificial Lamb, Josefa de Ayala, *c*. 1670–84

But remember also that the king's daughter Ariadne, none other than *Europa*'s granddaughter, provided Theseus with a thread to retrace his route, a thread of meaning that would write the end of all sacrifices to come.
The Combat of Theseus and the Minotaur, Klimt, Gustav (1862–1918): Poster for the First Art Exhibition of the Secession Art Movement, 1898 (uncensored version). From a private collection.

The play takes place in a cherry orchard. The old owners are having their last picnic on the grass, leaving cakes uneaten on an immaculate cloth. You may not pick the cherries, the child is told.
Le Dejeuner sur l'Herbe, Édouard Manet, 1863

The pluralist committed to *exit interruptus* is very partial to the motto of unity in diversity, and wishes even more radically to see Europeans united in relativity.
Caroselli di maiali, Robert Delaunay, 1922

'Distance yourself from falsehood,' the Torah commands. Perhaps both sides need to debate the meaning of this injunction running through the story of Exodus all the way to us today, and explore through their disagreements a way between the Scylla of absolute truths that plagues modern barbarism and the Charybdis of post-truths that dramatically unhinges our politics today.
Odysseus in Front of Scylla & Charybdis, Henry Fuseli, 1794–1796

Perhaps, just perhaps, the spirit of pan-European mutual recognition will linger forcefully enough here, there and everywhere, so that in the dark, when they are not looking, we will continue to weave and reweave the fabric of our shared future.
European Stories, Debra McEachern, 2010

Could it help our conversation, then, to explore the meaning of Brexit as ancient mythology? To juxtapose parallel and incommensurable meanings under the shadow of great archetypes, and treat Brexit, like all such archetypes, as a dramatic pivot around a moment, with a before and an after (before and after the parting of the Red Sea, before and after Oedipus knew, before and after Icarus fell)? And in so doing, to somehow connect a feature of *being* – to be or not to be European – with a feature of *doing* – to stay or not to stay in the EU. It is in making this connection between past and future visible that myths acquire meaning, allowing for an infinite retelling in infinite circumstances, and yet serving as metaphorical beacons for our collective imagination.

The Flight of Icarus, Gabriel Picart, 2004

right, countries should not be punished for leaving. The strategic advantage for being an EU member ought to be demonstrated by what the EU actually does *for* its members, not by what it does *to* Leavers. Why fear that accommodation would encourage leavers elsewhere? Surely, a magnanimous EU will be more attractive than a vindictive one.

This is however a reciprocal contract. A former member state will not be punished if and because it will consider the future Europe's peace and prosperity as a shared responsibility.

In fact, a former member state knows and feels what it is losing, hence its desperation over time to replicate membership advantages. Having gone through withdrawal pains, its population will have learned more about the EU than most in the remaining countries. Its citizens will have learned that they cannot have it all, that the trade-off between cooperation and control is real and that it is impossible to choose entirely one or the other. They will have learned that cooperation comes with connectors, norms, courts and the like, to the point where the EU will serve as a reference point in debates over the internal UK single market and institutions. The UK will learn to tolerate margins of differences between its constituent parts and like (hopefully) the EU jettison dogmatic talk of constitutional integrity for engagement with its own constitutional intricacies. The difference may be small from semi-detached to semi-attached, from in-almost-out to out-almost-in, but the former member state will have learned the most important difference beween the two: a seat at the table.

The former member state will repurpose its EU baggage and respect its makers, shadowing membership without aping it. It will understand the complex ways in which trade is predicated on layered and dynamic regulatory cooperation and will know to respect the EU's unique autonomous legal order, since it long defended it from the inside. It will not abdicate its loyalty to the EU, a very close union of which it knows so much. It will recognise that Union withdrawal is not like leaving a golf club but more like leaving a family, a web of intimate relationships, a commitment to what has been made together. It will feel responsible for its co-creation and understand that the old EU requirements of good faith and sincere cooperation are not perfunctory, even for outsiders.

The former member state will expect the EU to do the same,

and recognise the former state's integral role in the success of its ongoing ventures, its championing and design of many EU rules, and its past contribution, not just in money but also in expertise and intelligence, to its toys, such as Galileo. It will trust the EU not to abuse its greater power in the new relationship and instead creatively rewrite its rule to serve citizens on either side of the Channel (read: why not let the UK continue to deliver a European Bac if its government pays for it?). And it will trust the EU to heed voices from around the world demanding a right not to have to choose between the UK and the EU.

In return, the former member state will know to act in the long shadow of its membership deeds and own up to its sins as a member state, which are sadly less tolerated outside – such as the embarrassing evidence of UK fraud on imposing tariffs on Chinese imports, which emerged during the Brexit saga.

A former member state which has left the EU ecosystem cannot indulge in regulatory war or make regulatory discretion and divergence an end in itself. It must recognise that to dump regulations it has itself designed (for example, the infamous MiFID II in the field of finance) does not look good. Different assessments over good or bad rules that may emerge in time ought to be treated organically, not as an article of faith. It may readily allow EU regulators to stick their noses into its operations if that allows it in turn to write some of its own rules.

By the same token, the former member state cannot be treated as a potentially hostile state, barred from the EU's criminal extradition system or the high-security parts of its satellite programme when the world's ever-evolving security threats continue to be shared by all Europeans and participation is operationally rational.

Instead, the former member state will require a holistic relationship, reciprocity perhaps less diffuse than for full-blown members, but surely less targeted than in global politics. It would be foolish to escalate trade disputes into security disputes on the European continent. The kind of linkages between economics and security that have emerged with Brexit have nothing to do with threats, as when British negotiators argue that excluding Britain from criminal data-sharing might increase our joint exposure to terrorists. Instead they look more like legitimate calls for a pragmatic approach – how on earth can we disentangle the defence, intelligence, industrial, commercial and scientific implications of Brexit? And they are about politics – Europeans cannot ask Britain to risk the lives of their military personnel in, say, Africa, if exclusion from EU markets has destroyed their livelihood back home in the UK. As we heard in the courtroom discussion previously pitting the EU and its questioner, Brussels, Paris or Frankfurt cannot say: 'Give us your Chinook helicopters and your bankers, too!' Let us instead create a status where Britain can remain one of Europe's anchors in multilateral diplomatic forums.

A former member state understands the EU's desire for autonomy – after all, it defended it inside the tent. It should not expect full symmetry, as it interacts with a system rather than a country. But it needs a more symmetrical relationship than a state expecting to eventually enter the tent. Both sides ought to aspire to mutuality in their relationship. And it will need to earn a right of participation through active contribution to collective European initiatives, to dispel any fears about free-riding.

The former member state is continuously engaged in an exercise in translation, from EU law to international law, and probably frustrated with the limitations of the latter. It will need a new legal basis and deep commitment to organise its solidarity with the continent from outside.

The former member state will no longer be able to afford to rest on its peace laurels. The EU has allowed its member states to become lazy, to sit around tables without bothering with one-on-ones, among themselves or with the outside. Not so the former member state, which will discover the virtues of neo-bilateralism while the rest of the world will greet it: welcome back!

Paradoxically, the former member state will need to rediscover the value of others in its midst. London may certainly be a centre of the world but that is because the rest of us have made it our own. And the British state will engage creatively with its many European communities within to foster ties in the EU, looking inwards the better to turn outwards.

In the meanwhile, citizens of the former member state will also overcompensate and become more European. They too will no longer be able to leave it all to the EU. They will reinvent the kind of bilateral networking – between schools, universities, cities, organisations – that was so fashionable in the early days of European integration. They will become experts in European standards and learn to repurpose them, in their own way. And they will make sure to be ready when they cross the Channel: the appetite of British nationals for learning foreign languages has increased significantly since the Brexit vote.

Former member-state citizens will experience normative stickiness too. Unlike the simple image of reverse enlargement, losing rights is not symmetrical with acquiring rights, be it for individuals, corporations or groups. The entrenchment of citizens' rights on both sides will do justice to the felt experience of individuals and the EU mission to expand, not shrink, a zone of shared rights. Nevertheless, if European citizenship serves to outlaw discrimination on the basis of nationality, necessity will drive identity sharing. Brexit means the destruction of rights on a grand scale, turning a Brit overnight from Lithuanian to Ukrainian status. The EU will not break the link between EU nationalities and EU citizenship if it is to respect its member states' constitutional identities. To get their rights back short of restoring their country's EU membership, British citizens more than any others in Europe will embrace dual citizenship.

Hybridity will be contagious. Hopefully, Germany, Denmark, Cyprus, Malta, or Ireland, which disenfranchised their residents living outside the EU, will make an exception for those residing in the UK who never decided to move to a third country. At the same time, many UK residents in the EU and EU residents in the UK will give up the idea of post-nationality, the idea of a Europe world where super-diversity extends not just to race, ethnicity or origin but to ways of belonging, a world where you can belong without pledging allegiance to the British queen or the French Republic. Hopefully, the UK offer for EU nationals to keep their rights to vote in local elections will be matched by EU countries bilaterally. But we can be more ambitious and perhaps in the process will recover something precious: the incentive to become British (or French) for good, to acquire the right to vote in national elections and thus responsibility for the politics animating the country in which we live. Perhaps if we do so we will in turn better enrich our country of adoption and encourage the most other-regarding politics possible.

Precedent, Unprecedented

What happens to the EU's relationship with the rest of the world, in a universe blessed with the new species of former member state? And what does this mean for the negotiations to come, Brexit 2.0? How will the EU exploit its even greater leverage once the UK is out?

Up to now, precedents invoked by the EU have tended to play bad cop in this story. If Britain is privileged we have been warned that the EU's many other partners will cry foul play and ask for what she is having. In the worst case, as with the parallel negotiations with Switzerland, concessions to the Swiss or the Brits were both treated as potential bad precedents for the other.

But the story can be told differently. After all, the EU has made it its great mission in life to save free trade, battling against its detractors, all the while overcoming the devastating perverse effects of globalisation denounced by Europhobes. Will Brexit not be the measure of the EU's free and fair trade credibility?

In this universe, negotiators and regulators, scholars and politicians will continue to examine the lessons offered by the history of the single market, which provides subtle guidelines rather than fixed rules for the future. There are two lessons in particular.

Lesson one is that the single market has been built over time in a piecemeal and pragmatic way around the principle of mutual recognition, underpinned by rigorous adjudication of disputes where they arise. Countries of destination are asked to trust the home state to provide the right stamp for goods and services crossing borders.

But because trust is never blind between states, there is no such thing in the EU as pure mutual recognition. Instead, the EU single market has become a complex and layered system of managed mutual recognition, a recognition which can be partial, conditional and reversible, and involve more or less alignment. Even when more harmonisation is introduced, we still need mutual recognition of how the rules are enforced.

This is an ingenious dynamic process, involving trade-offs that may change over time. Ironically, it was devised to a great extent by Brits in Brussels precisely to avoid 'one size fits all' standards and supervision, allowing for a high degree of national regulatory autonomy. By constantly invoking mutual recognition out of context, Brexiters have failed to acknowledge that they have set out to reinvent the EU wheel but without the gears and spokes that make it work, otherwise known as institutions. They have failed to recognise what it means to access an entire regime of mutual recognition rather than a single country that would simply recognise you.

Conversely, the EU might consider the idea that to take away recognition ought to be harder than to grant it initially. It might thus decide imaginatively to explore a new dynamic version of regulatory managed mutual recognition for Britain.

Lesson two is that the EU has been seeking to export the single-market model to the rest of the world for decades. It is fair to say that this ambition has worked better as an asymmetrical exercise, for example in Norway, than a symmetrical exercise, as in the United States. And that the so-called mutual recognition deals the EU did manage to strike with outside partners are but pale imitations of the original, involving the recognition that exporters certify to the importing country standards – a kind of regulatory subcontracting. If every external trade deal negotiated between the EU and third countries in the last two decades has included a chapter on regulatory cooperation, these have remained long-term horizons. With Brexit, the EU can now experiment with a country that could live on these horizons.

Here is the thing. As a former member state the UK will not simply be a new exemplar of EU Story Two. It will have been an integral part of EU Story One. If there is no precedent for such a state of affairs, we should not start again with the pros and cons of Norway versus Canada, but invent a new paradigm consistent with the EU's own history and principles.

Can we assume that the former member state will remain EU-compatible, not only on day one but thereafter, probably more so than many less developed member states? Can the new relationship build on the extraordinary level of supervisory collaboration and trust that already exists between regulators on both sides? The compatibility model involves acknowledging on both sides that access to the EU's single market is neither about 'managing convergence' as with enlargement, nor about 'managing divergence' as the Brexiters dream and the EU fears, but about 'managing differences'. Compatibility is not conformity. The compatibility paradigm suggests that it is wrong to decide a priori that potential future differences in regulatory approaches will necessarily overshoot the bounds of legitimate differences. The European legal imagination has for many decades populated the space between regulatory independence and subservience with numerous notions labelled approximation, inter-operability, regulatory coherence, proportionality, balancing and functional equivalence, which apply differently to different sectors. Why should it be afraid of a new legal story?

Because Brexit bridges EU Stories One and Two, it will need to respect the spirit of internal EU law, which is not about accommodating ad hoc and idiosyncratic exceptions but about refining a principled approach over time.

And because things change over time, including levels of trust, the deal needs to involve a good dose of contingent contracting, predicated on accommodating different expectations. Evolutionary clauses are the bread and butter of international law and can provide the basis for a dynamic Brexit. Managed mutual recognition relies heavily on conflict management, remedies in case of disagreement and political decisions on whether to reverse incompatibilities that may arise or take the hit in terms of market access. Because the UK will be only partially involved in the EU's ecosystem of recognition management, these technologies of conflict will need to be robust and operate in the shadow of the European Court of Justice. The EU should not fear a UK ready to take the hit on market access by 'cherry-picking' areas where it will choose to diverge. It will have the power to manage the costs when the problem arises. To be sure, it is wrong to think that mutual recognition from outside can look and feel the same as mutual recognition for members of the club (there will be more asymmetry, reciprocity and reversibility). But it is not clear why it should be denied altogether or reduced to bare-bone unilaterally granted and revoked equivalence.

Can the EU contemplate a UK both on the outer fringes of its own managed mutual recognition system – Story One – and as the new frontier of its external mutual recognition ambition – Story Two?

Would other trade partners consider this a precedent to follow suit? Not if they are not as EU-compatible as this uniquely compatible former member state. Global non-discrimination clauses do not apply if you are different. It is not true that anything offered to the UK must be offered to Canada, South Korea and others. And these countries will understand that the unique status of the UK justifies a special partnership.

Nevertheless and paradoxically, the most unprecedented of events could come to serve as a precedent which may one day inspire the EU's relations with a broader circle of countries, starting with its neighbours, which over the next decades can progressively be brought within the ambit of the EU's managed mutual recognition system. This could in turn inspire new post-colonial EU thinking on reciprocity when dealing with third countries. And the compatibility model could eventually inspire global partnerships for economic governance.

'Different but compatible' is a motto fit for purpose. In this spirit, the compatibility paradigm can turn on its head the narrative that Brexit is a bad precedent. Brexit could come to stand in the court of history not as a disastrous internal precedent but as an ambitious external precedent, a reinvention of the EU's managed mutual recognition approach to fit its role in the world as a reliable hub in a turbulent world. Does the EU want to convince the world of its commitment to free trade, cooperation and openness? If so, its future relationship with the UK will be the test.

The Ultimate Proof

But perhaps in the end none of this matters...

Whether you believe that it is the first and last withdrawal because Britain is the only member to have the propensity and capacity to engineer such an extraction, or whether you believe that in spite of the new *exit interruptus* EU Brexit will be followed by others, what happens if Brexit, like Iphigenia, was never truly a sacrifice on the altar of the EU principles of integrity, indivisibility and autonomy, but rather a sacrifice of a higher order to demonstrate an even greater EU principle: the principle of free association?

Too many in Brussels have got the precedent story the wrong way round: if we demonstrate how hard it is to leave, they say, no one else will want to. But Brexit should stand as a more elevated precedent. Brexit is a demonstrative Sacrifice, making manifest the EU's essence: we are together by choice.

In this spirit, the meaning of Sacrifice is entirely contained in its very fact, the ultimate proof of the EU's fundamental theorem.

If this is true, it has been wrong to make it so very painful for the UK to leave, so internally divisive, so externally conflictual.

For whatever our differences, should we not all rejoice in the most paradoxical answer to the meaning of Brexit: *Britain sacrifices its membership in order to demonstrate, for all to see, that you can leave the EU.*

Thus, the Sacrifice will bolster the EU, not by allowing it to become ever more state-like and coercive, but by demonstrating that it isn't. Brexiters must face the contradiction: the EU cannot be a supranational Leviathan clipping its member states' sovereign wings if it is leavable by a simple majority vote. And if that is the case, no country should want to leave, in the knowledge that they could. *Brexit means that you can leave the EU – and therefore you shouldn't.*

Welcome to the Brexit paradox.

Think of this paradox as a case of positive deterrence. The more credible the promise that you can leave, the less likely that it will be acted upon. We know that our preferences can change in the face of changing alternatives, even irrelevant ones (say, inverting your choice for veggies over fish at the restaurant when you learn they have seafood on the menu). So if citizens believe that leaving is in the cards, they might turn against it. Witness how EU support shot up, including in the UK, after the vote (although this may have been a desperate outcry for stability amid Brexit chaos).

This version of the Sacrifice story starts with the idea that the essence of a union is defined by the way one may or may not leave it. That you *can* leave tells us something about the EU irrespective of who leaves or the circumstances of this leaving.

This was not necessarily the intuition that led to the drafting of Article 50 in the first place in 2002 during a European convention busy writing a new constitutional treaty for the EU. At the time what 'leaving the EU' could actually mean was up for grabs. Only Algeria and Greenland have accomplished it before, in radically different circumstances and not as member states but as part of one. In truth, the convention delegates were primarily concerned with how to deal with a rogue state which might have its voting rights suspended for bad behaviour incompatible with EU rules and values, but could not stay indefinitely in purgatory. It would either have to return to the fold chastened or leave voluntarily. Article 50 was to be the polite invitation: please leave voluntarily if you persist.

Not everyone liked the idea. Many Eurofederalists saw the draft exit clause as a sovereigntist ploy and opposed it vehemently. For in their minds, proper states generally do not have prenups (even the UK had to improvise its secessionist option for Scotland and it is the exception). Introducing an exit clause in European treaties meant that the EU would never cross the Rubicon to become a state as did the United States in 1865, the crucial moment when 'secession' was redefined as 'civil war', and ceased to be an option for the discontented. If these delegates were to support an exit clause it would only be as an expulsion clause for misbehaving countries. Otherwise, the clause was not meant to be used.

Not everyone on the convention floor agreed. For instance, I belonged to another brand of Europhiles who defended the idea of exit as the key to articulating a third way for an EU that would neither become a federal state, nor fall back to mere inter-state alliance, but would remain a third way, a federal union, a demoicracy in the making; that is, a union of peoples who govern together but not as one, and who remain together by choice. This is what Kant meant by *Völkerbund*. I have long believed that true Euro-idealism lies with perfecting this demanding equilibrium rather than following an uncreative credo of ever more centralization.

Obviously, something that makes sense in theory may not be desirable in practice. I may love the *idea* of orderly exit but I never wished for my country of adoption to make such a Sacrifice for the sake of proving that the EU could be left! The very thought may be the luxury of those like me who belong to both sides of the channel...

Nor have the proponents of the 'rogue state' interpretation of of Article 50 rejoiced. With Brexit, the EU is losing one of the most respected democracies in the world, while two member states, Poland and Hungary, even though they are playing havoc with the rule of law at home, can flout their immunity even to having their EU voting rights suspended as a result.

Nevertheless, Brexit demonstrates that the EU is not too sacred to be left, but is too precious to be predicated on anything else than the continually and freely affirmed will to live together. It stands as the ultimate proof of the idea of auto-limitation: if a state agrees to subordinate its sovereign powers to a higher authority through an international treaty, the state still retains the final say. In the EU however, this final say cannot be unilateral, for undoing the ties that bind is a shared responsibility. The serious contemplation of 'no deal' not only by British backbenchers but by EU authorities betrayed everything this Union is about.

If Brexit is to serve as the ultimate demonstrative Sacrifice all sides need to play their part, as the UK lingers in a state of neither in nor out.

Article 50 saw to it that the departing country could not be held hostage. Leaving would be facilitated and no member states would be able to veto it. It would not even be necessary to come to an agreement with the EU, since the treaties would simply lapse after two years. The two-year time limit was wildly unrealistic, but to be fair, it was never meant to apply to one of the largest European states in the face of huge internal turmoil.

There is not much glory in the 'Hotel California' night man's words that you can check out at any time but you can never leave. They only remind us how the British are able to achieve what no other country could. A Europe that is not a story of free association but of resigned acceptance has little future. For this wondrous message to ring loud and clear, the EU should resist the temptation to show the world how impossibly difficult it is to say goodbye and demonstrate for all to see that this is a flexible union where the relationship of the parts to the whole can be redefined flexibly with the needs of the times. This is not about free riding but free thinking.

In the process, we find that the EU abandons the language of necessity for the language of choice, impermanence and evanescence. There is little chance of reconciling a majority of Europe's citizens with the EU project if European officialdom simply frames Brexit as evidence that the forces of selfish retrenchment and fragmentation, parochialism and nationalism have triumphed in the UK, Brexit as a British problem for the years to come. Europeans, starting with the Brits, still carry the antibodies to resist the dark side.

The conflict between the older universal ideal of reason and the romantic idea of self-assertion will never disappear. EU official history would have us believe that the former finally and thankfully won the day in the guise of our technocratic union after Europe's near-oblivion in the twentieth century, turning it into an island of peace in the midst of a Hobbesian world of anarchy. But if we believe in the irrevocable plurality of European stories, that every European citizen relates to the European project in her own idiosyncratic way, we ought to remain attached to the nineteenth-century romantic declaration that man is independent and free, provided that political pluralism successfully tames the dark side, the exaltation of singularities *against* others. After all, isn't it this romantic spirit of indestructible regard for what a man himself believes to be true that led countless human beings to give up their lives in the resistance to Nazism, to rise in the name of ideals that might have been universal or local, collective or personal, but that ultimately did not belong to some grand overarching truth but to each one's inner calling, romantic as that may sound. There cannot be a single path in history, notwithstanding Marx or Hegel's metaphysical intimidation. But there may be a different kind of cunning in history, a cunning which recovers the force of multiplicity, diversity, tolerance and creativity from the clutches of its nationalist perversions, not only in Europe but ultimately everywhere as our children turn their gaze to the shared obligations of humanity.

Ultimately both ideals, the romantic many and the enlightened one, are but abstract poles between which we seek the flourishing of individual human beings.

With the likes of Isaiah Berlin, we may now hope to ground our *living together* in the idea that the essence of man is the power of choice and the history of mankind the play in which all men improvise their parts, searching for a compass, knowing full well that every choice sacrifices a path not taken. And we can now live together with this intuition contained in all our myths that the improvisation is not random, for the essence of humanity is also what keeps the great majority from acting outside the bounds of common decency.

The EU will remain too clumsy, too complex, too obscure to become popular. What do you expect when you try to create the impossible: eternal peace between quasi-sovereign nations on an overcrowded continent in a hostile neighbourhood? But the EU is a highly resilient conflict resolution machine. These days, those at the helm tend to be pragmatists seeking the rewards of working together, not idealists or ideologues. But they should not lose sight of our realist utopia, the ideal of a union of peoples who retain their capacity for self-determination while learning to be radically open to each other through genuine political dialogue about everything. If it can help us renew our European contract – more autonomy for states, more loyalty to the Union – an amicable Brexit could be Europe's saving grace.

Let us ask for the impossible and recover the evanescent charm of *Europa* riding her bull, an idea in movement, an idea without borders which belongs to the world at large, the spark for a theatre of recognition where we truly seek to know each other's minds, with a little help from our shared mythological landscapes.

> So Abram rose, and clave the wood, and went,
> And took the fire with him, and a knife.
> And as they sojourned both of them together,
> Isaac the first-born spake and said, My Father,
> Behold the preparations, fire and iron,
> But where the lamb for this burnt offering?
> Then Abram bound the youth with belts and straps,
> And builded parapets and trenches there,
> And stretched forth the knife to slay his son.
> When lo! an angel called him out of heaven,
> Saying, Lay not thy hand upon the lad,
> Neither do anything to him, thy son.
> Behold! Caught in the thicket by its horns,
> A Ram. Offer the Ram of Pride instead.
>
> But the old man would not so, but slew his son,
> And half the seed of Europe, one by one.

> Wilfred Owen, 'The Parable of the Old Man and the Young'
> Excerpt from *Wilfred Owen: The War Poems* (Chatto & Windus, 1994), edited by Jon Stallworthy.

Conclusion

'When I use a word,' Humpty Dumpty said in rather a
scornful tone, 'it means just what I choose it to mean –
neither more nor less.'

Lewis Carroll, *Through the Looking-Glass*

Words, Worlds and Myths

We started this journey wondering about meanings. In the end,
dear Alice, this is the only certitude: a word CAN mean so many
different things – not just full Brexit, smart Brexit, mean Brexit,
pretend Brexit or no Brexit at all. The word may find a master who
freezes its meaning against the flow of time. But there will still be
contradictory facts of the matter, there will be what-ifs and what-
nexts, and there will be arguments and perspectives exchanged
through frowns and fury. We will find that there is no last word, no
infallible ultimate interpretation in this story, but only the first word,
that initial uttering of endlessly contested meaning. What matters,
what *will* matter, is the way we conduct our democratic conversation
and break through the walls of our infamous echo chambers. We
must reinvent the way we talk to each other.

In my own early attempts to navigate the many Brexit narratives,
I found myself in the predicament of Richard Rorty's liberal ironist
who faces up to the contingency of her beliefs and desires, desires
such as that humiliation of human beings by other human beings

may cease. Ironically agnostic about the vocabulary she uses, and impressed by other vocabularies taken as final by people or books she has encountered, this liberal ironist finds that the argument phrased in her present vocabulary can neither underwrite nor dissolve her doubts. And insofar as she philosophises about a certain situation (say, Brexit) she cannot convince herself that her habitual vocabulary is by necessity any closer to reality than the vocabularies of others.

As she understands that she must look elsewhere, she remembers the stories that enchanted her as a child – the stories of Oedipus, Ulysses, Antigone, Prometheus or Sisyphus. And then there are the stories she encountered in other people's books – Eve, Moses, Isaac, Jesus. Borrowing from their sublime meanings may not be a bad way to scrutinise the mundane politics of our times.

If, as Wittgenstein suggests, meanings are justified by their use, it is for each of us to use them wisely. For my part, by inviting the reader on a journey through Brexit mythology, I have not tried to sell an enchanted version of Brexit, or even to provide a menu, a set of meanings among which to choose. I have neither commended nor condemned particular versions. Instead, this invitation rests on the ideal of mutual recognition – or the ideal not only of understanding the other, however alien to me, but of giving her status and respect for what she is and thinks.

And if words are the currency of politics, grand old myths are the currency of our political imaginaries. By appealing to our fundamental intuitions, these stories can help us connect diverse democratic praxis through bottom-up reconstruction rather than top-down construction. And they can counter or at least supplement Habermas's idea of democracy as deliberative rationality, not because we cannot be rational, but because to be so together we need common languages, across generations, disciplines, ideologies and national cultures, languages in which we can passionately disagree with greater civility. The EU is also, at its best, an ethics of translation.

At the same time, and perhaps paradoxically, thinking through the prism of myths may help us recover the ironic stance of modernity, by supporting a critical distance from whatever story we tell ourselves, and by placing question marks around our collective self-righteousness. For if agonistic politics remind us that conflict must be handled rather than denied, and that values can remain incommensurable and thus unamenable to liberal compromises, then myths appear as better templates for the conversation than technocratic blueprints. By flirting with tragic choices, the absurd and the desperate ironies entangling human beings, myths contain their own epistemic limits, at least in our contemporary eyes, provided we do not patronise our past selves. And they remind us that ambivalence is our birthright not just as individuals but also as collectives.

In the spirit of Hayyim Nahman Bialik, the Jewish poet who inspired Kafka and so many others a century ago, I believe that we ought to try to bring together in a kind of creative fusion Halakha and Aggada, or the normative and the narrative, law and legends, action and speech, justice and mercy, constrained and freed at the same time by timeless storylines, jazzing up our political ethics. Myths reassure us that we ought not to feel compelled to resolve the tension. They speak of the conditions of our world that are not readily available to scientific facts. They are malleable to contemporary normative prisms.

Allegorical interpretations of myth, from anthropology to psychoanalysis, assume that myths are really about something that is not made explicit in their content. But mythical interpretation of politics starts from explicit references to these stories as they have come to us in order to probe their connections with the here and now, each story requiring the interplay between inertia and yearning, obstacle and desire, constraint and opportunity. And in this interplay, we can each seek our own free thinking in the world.

If myths are, as the German theologian Julius Schniewind once put it, 'the expression of unobservable realities in terms of observable phenomena', when it comes to politics, these unobservable realities may refer to a sense, still, that the world is moved by grander logics than our petty day-to-day decisions. The purpose of telling stories is not to present an objective picture of the world as it is, but to express our understanding of ourselves in the world in which we live. Mythology and thought-worlds perhaps play a privileged role in this quest for meaning as they have moulded our modernity.

Can the multifaceted nature of myths prove to be contagious? Can we hope that with enough ironic liberals wandering around we might witness the birth of ironic populists capable of admitting to the infinite faces of the people they are claiming to read best? Can we imagine an ironic alliance of liberal populists who, freed from the univocal versions of familiar archetypes, stand ready to discuss in good faith their seemingly incommensurate and multi-coloured meanings?

‡

...A way between the Scylla of absolute truths that plagues modern barbarism and the Charybdis of post-truths... *Odysseus in Front of Scylla & Charybdis*, Henry Fuseli, 1794–1796

'Distance yourself from falsehood,' the Torah commands.

Perhaps both sides need to debate the meaning of this injunction running through the story of Exodus all the way to us today, and explore through their disagreements a way between the Scylla of absolute truths that plagues modern barbarism and the Charybdis of post-truths that dramatically unhinges our politics today.

If, as modern Ulysses, we fail to chart our course carefully between Scylla and Charybdis, the collateral damage could be those values that we hold dear and in whose name the battle is being fought in the first place: honesty, friendship, hospitality, decency, tolerance, and, yes, irony.

We can only steer the course between Scylla and Charybdis if we recover the force of empathy, that capacity to project oneself into the heads of others, giving up our little individualised canons without giving up our own convictions.

The Greeks probably did not literally believe in their myths, but myths were not fake news to them either (it all depends on what you mean by 'believe'). Even Plato did not believe myths to be false, only unfalsifiable, thus belonging to truth and falsehood simultaneously, depending on why and how they were heard. Thus he invoked his own myths to get at his most profound yet baffling truths, as we saw with the myth of Er. As our shared imagination, metaphorical shortcuts or paradigmatic clutches, myths can create meaning by distorting and deepening reality at one and the same time. They help us to make sense sensitively and provide structure to a fragmented narrative.

The onus is on us collectively not to let any one of these archetypal takes on Brexit crystallise as the new normal in our collective imagination. Whether or not they are eternal (well, we will never know, will we?) their claim to timeless validity should not distract us from their timebound readings, the great multiplicity of associated narratives reflected in our present.

Last but not least, she says almost apologetically, we have seen how more often than not it is women who connect the narrative threads, sometimes by sharing a secret or two, sometimes through their silence in the interstice of heroic action, the silence captured by Pat Barker in *Silence of Girls*, sometimes by soothing the wounds through the soft-spoken voice of moderation. From midwives to feminists, from weavers of truth to weavers of necessity, from women who make it to the Promised Land to women who wait, they endure. Their names can brand our Utopia as did Cretan *Europa*, our hubris as did Eve and Arachne or our redemption as did Antigone, Iphigenia or Ariadne. As Ece Temelkuran muses in *Women Who Blow on Knots*, it is their breath that gives life to the stories and sustains them from one generation to the next. Pandora, the beautiful first woman of antiquity we met alongside Prometheus, offered the ultimate riddle by keeping hope in her jar, the better to nurture it against the evils she had released and yet out of reach to the mortals roaming the earth. It will take a conspiracy of women to tilt the balance for hope to humanity's advantage. For we often know more intimately than blokes that to be fully citizens we need to be invested in utopian thinking, precisely because we have most to lose in careless improvisations. Thus, we carry out the impossible missions they abandon en route, bearing the risks and the scars, simply because we can.

Brexit Means Brexits

Perhaps we can try to imagine ourselves when we have eventually become a very distant past in our descendants' own imagination, when Brexit takes the form of just another myth clouded in the mist of history. Echoes of Exodus. Reckoning. Sacrifice?

In our moment in time, actors in the Brexit play often inhabit a single myth world, each a very real lens through which negotiators, politicians, entrepreneurs or the public at large understand what is going on. Listen to the passionate chatter. 'We must leave come what may'; 'The EU is doomed.' Some philosophers view myths as complete and closed tales about a person's insertion in the world demanding utter identification in exchange for an identity, one which dictates her behaviour consciously or unconsciously.

They are wrong. Myths are play worlds which allow us to come in and out of their landscapes, temporarily blinded by our imagination. For sure, we cannot ask myths to do all the work for us. And if we turn them into ideologies they will only narrow our gaze, as when true believers in the Exodus story on either side of the Channel betray their panicked rush to go or let go.

None of the three stories, or constellations of stories, I have told will have offered us incontrovertible interpretations that we can hang on to in order to claim later that we were betrayed or vindicated. Throughout this play in three acts, we have seen the triumphant simplicity of each theme eclipsed every time by the unfolding of contradictory meanings in the myths themselves, compounded by the unrelenting twists of our history of the present.

In telling these stories I have resisted the temptation to deny or demonise others' narratives. In doing so, I had to first make the stories my own and probe their meanings through my biases, unceremoniously stripping them of their supernatural qualities. I had to ask why at the end of their long march, it is only the Hebrew women who make it to the Promised Land. But I still wonder why it is right for liberation to entail so much suffering on all sides. Having lived all my life in Ulysses' company, I had to ponder anew why he so passionately refused to leave Ithaca in the first place, resisting the Exodus that was to make him one of humanity's most beloved heroes. I understood that it may have been fair in the end to see him punished for the deeds of others, his Greek companions in Troy. And I recognised how myths can help us overcome rather than entrench the sacrificial mindset, to slay the minotaurs lurking in the underbellies of our societies.

Throughout, I wrestled with Oedipus' fate, unsatisfied with

the simple tale of tragic Freudian self-discovery, the story of a destiny foretold at birth about how we deal with our parents. Nor is this a simple story of punishment for hubris and overconfident leadership leading to despair and destruction, however topical this may seem. Yes, there are three acts in the old Greek play, from Oedipus' birth, to triumph against the Sphinx in Thebes twenty years later, to reckoning with the truth during the plague after another twenty years. But the deeper message lies with the before and after, the mysterious chain of cause and effect which escapes our present moment. Why does everyone rest content with the idea that Oedipus himself is the cause of the plague in Thebes? Why has everyone forgotten that he is sacrificed for the sins of his father Laius and forefather Tantalus, committed many years earlier? How far back do we have to go in the relationship between Britain and the European continent to find the sources of Brexit? Does Reckoning not entail rejecting any claim that *this* or *that* is the ultimate cause, the original trigger? If we do reject such claims, we may find that the future is still open for the UK–EU relationship after Brexit, as it is at the other end of the Oedipus saga, when his Exodus guided by Antigone leads him to a new beginning. In spite of the prophecy, Oedipus the righteous does become the author of his own destiny.

If these mythical stories can serve as compass, they cannot chart a destination, but only take us to an open sea of meanings where we may accept the incompleteness of our narratives and open them up to each other. If we appear to be inconsistent in the process, we can console ourselves with the banal thought that consistency is the virtue of small minds. Better still, let's recognise inconsistency in all its glory, as the primary material of the pluralist democratic encounter. True democracy is about all of us accessing the overlapping and contradictory meanings of the stories we tell each other. In this, no answer should have the power to silence the questioners.

As with an M. C. Escher drawing, we can simultaneously see the meaning of Brexit through many prisms. Brexit will be all things: May Day on the road to the Promised Land, Mayhem in the eye of the storm and Maybe to a new Europe. But it can be so in countless permutations.

Each of us may desire a particular narrative to be true, false or irrelevant. We may admit to it or not. I don't know about you, but for my part I see the scraps of truth in every story.

But I do admit to being partial to some of their variants more than others. I dream of the adoption of a 'do no harm' principle in the way Britain and the EU deal with each other in the coming years. I prefer an Exodus-lite in the hope that the bright side of British exceptionalism will continue to enliven our European debates and its dark sides be tamed. I believe neither that this moment is the EU's last judgement nor that it can be its salvation, but that the EU's Reckoning calls for embracing the transformative potential offered by its detractors. And if enough people on both sides of the Channel contest the meanings of Brexit with gracious humility and self-deprecation, the British Sacrifice will not have been in vain.

I hope to have offered the thought that the ultimate gift from the UK to its fellow Europeans is to have demonstrated how the freedom to leave defines the very essence of the EU. Is this not an amazing feat! Plato may have been his master but Aristotle did not believe in the Philosopher King knowing our political desires better than us, the hoi polloi. If the ultimate goal of human life is simply happiness, then we only ask our politics to oblige. Even as the Exodus of biblical times will continue to inspire us forever, Brexit invites us to shun all messianic impulses in our modern world.

Leave to Remain

Meanwhile, Britain too will reckon with its demons, whatever happens next. We can hope that the Brexiters' mystified 'one people' becomes a multitude again, and that its many nations remain one. And we can hope that its many European aliens are all granted their 'leave to remain', a phrase of characteristic English linguistic genius for the baffled non-native who never understood that 'I hear you' means 'I disagree' or 'it's my fault' means 'it's yours'. Leave granted.

Perhaps the whole country will follow our lead and, in the end, leave in order to remain, remain more securely in the EU's ambit than if it had actually remained as a member. After all, Ulysses was bound to Ithaca by his Odyssey more securely than if he had never left.

If the EU is up to the challenge, Brexit may not even be forever.

...The times that bind
cannot be broken...
European Stories, Debra
McEachern, 2010

In order not to let the dead tie the hand of the living a decade or
two from now, those in charge today must imagine and negotiate a
relationship between the EU and the UK which leaves open different
future worlds, including one where a transformed UK rejoins a
transformed EU. We owe this much to our children on both sides
of the Channel whose projects and networks are deeply intertwined.
Paradoxically, the UK will have produced more committed European
citizens than anywhere else in Europe. Can we envision the return
of the prodigal son to a transformed EU in a couple of decades? A
return chartered by all those in this modern play clamouring for the
right not to be forgotten?

Exit from Brexit is of course part of all the stories in our journey.
Exodus can be a two-way street, Reckonings are about eternal
returns, and our myths usually bring the sacrificial victims back
from the brink, alive and almost well. Provided we hold on to our
commitment that the EU project is a journey, not a destination, a
new Odyssey is bound to unfold.

I hope that this journey to come will celebrate our salutary
ambivalence, the hidden motif in Homer's grand epic where both
humans and gods endlessly wrestle with their confusion about who
and what is right or wrong. As we recalled at the outset of the book,
Ulysses wore his ambivalence, not the love of glory, as a badge of
honour.

And so in the end, if we heed the ultimate message of our tragic
stories – that we must choose hope over optimism – we may find
solace in the story of his dear wife Penelope, who for twenty years
after this fateful day of salt and song, unwove at night her day's

labour to placate her suitors while awaiting Ulysses. Can it be the other way around? In our twenty-first-century version of the story, we can count on some fanatics to frantically continue to unweave the ties that bind in broad daylight. But perhaps, just perhaps, the spirit of pan-European mutual recognition will linger forcefully enough here, there and everywhere, so that in the dark, when they are not looking, we will continue to weave and reweave the fabric of our shared future.

Picture Credits

I would like to thank the artists who allowed me to use their wonderful work.

Preface

Ulysses and the Sirens, Otto Greiner, *c.* 1900, Bibliothèque des Arts décoratifs, Archives Charmet, Paris, France

Introduction

Mythomania, Ari Saunders, 2018, Oxford, courtesy of the artist
The Flight of Icarus, Gabriel Picart, 2004, Verhoeven private collection, New Zealand

Exodus

Exodus, Mel Brigg, 2010, Wentworth Galleries, courtesy of the artist
Seventh Plague of Egypt, John Martin, 1823, Museum of Fine Arts, Boston. Photograph © 2019 Museum of Fine Arts, Boston.
Joseph Dwelleth in Egypt, James Jacques Joseph Tissot, *c.* 1896–1902, gift of the heirs of Jacob Schiff, Jewish Museum, New York
Pharaoh Notes the Importance of the Jewish People, James Jacques Joseph Tissot, *c.* 1896–1902, gift of the heirs of Jacob Schiff,

Jewish Museum, New York

The Exodus, Horace William Petherick , 1839–1919. Image courtesy of Croydon Art Collection, Museum of Croydon

Eve, John Collier, 1911, Bonhams, London

The Rape of Europa, Valentin Aleksandrovich Serov, 1910, State Tretyakov gallery, Moscow. Photo credit: SPUTNIK / Alamy Stock Photo

The Passage of the Red Sea, G.H. Phillips after Francis Danby, Sanders of Oxford, 1829. Sanders of Oxford, Antique Prints & Maps www.sandersofoxford.com

The Departure of the Israelites out of the Land of Egypt, David Roberts, 1829, Birmingham Museum and Art Gallery, UK

Moses Forbids the People to Follow Him, James Jacques Joseph Tissot, 1896, gift of the heirs of Jacob Schiff, Jewish Museum, New York

Wanderer above the Sea of Fog, Caspar David Friedrich, *c.* 1817, Kunsthalle, Hamburg

Dante's Inferno, Sandro Botticelli, from *Divine Comedy Illustrated by Botticelli*, 1485 © bpk

Moses and the Messengers from Canaan, Giovanni Lanfranco, 1621–1624, The J. Paul Getty Museum, Los Angeles. Digital image courtesy of Getty's Open Content Program.

Visions of the Daughters of Albion, William Blake, 1793, Plate 1, Frontispiece. Image credit: Yale Center for British Art, Paul Mellon Collection

Egyptian hieroglyphs of Hebrew slaves making bricks, collage and elaboration from engravings of Tomb of vizier Rekhmire, *c.* 1450 BC. Image © gameover / Alamy Stock Photo

The Egyptians Drowned in the Red Sea, Gustave Doré, 1866, *La Grande Bible de Tours*

Reckoning

The Deluge, *c.*1837, Francis Danby (1793–1861), Tate Gallery, © Tate, London, 2019

The Last Judgment, Hieronymus Bosch, *c.* 1500–1510, Academy of Fine Arts in Vienna, Austria

Oedipus, 2014, poster, courtesy of Elysium Conservatory Theatre, California

The Mark of the Beast is 666, William Blake, 1810, courtesy of Rosenbach Museum and Library

Oedipus and the Sphinx, Jean-Auguste-Dominique Ingres, 1808–27, Museé du Lovre, Paris

Prometheus, Nicolas-Sébastien Adam, 1737, Louvre, Paris

Sisyphus, Franz von Stuck, 1920, Galerie Ritthaler, Munich

Arachne, Otto Henry, 1884, The Met, New York, gift of Mrs Otto H. Bacher, 1938

Oedipus and Antigone, Charles Jalabert, 1842, Musée des Beaux-Arts, Marseille

Rosa Celeste: Dante and Beatrice gaze upon the highest Heaven, The Empyrean, 'Canto XXXI' in *The Divine Comedy by Dante Illustrated, Complete*, Cassell & Company, London, Paris & Melbourne, *c.* 1890

The Last Judgement, Michelangelo, 1536–41, Sistine Chapel, Rome . Photo © Vatican Museums. All rights reserved.

Oedipus and His Daughters, Henry Fuseli, 1784, inv.833.1.30, courtesy of Musée des Beaux-Arts de Troyes.

The Deluge, Gustave Doré, 1866, *Illustrations in The Holy Bible: Containing the Old and New Testaments with Illustrations*, Cassell Company Ltd, London, Paris and Melbourne.

Sacrifice

The Sacrifice of Iphigenia, François Perrier, 1632, © Musée des Beaux-Arts de Dijon/Hugo Martens

Monty Python's Life of Brian, 1979, © HandMade Films/Python Pictures/Warner Bros/Ronald Grant Archive/Mary Evans

Poppies: Wave and Weeping Window, Paul Cummins and Tom Piper, 2014, Tower of London

Le Dejeuner sur l'Herbe, Édouard Manet, 1863, Musée d'Orsay, Paris, donation by Etienne Moreau-Nelaton in 1906, France. Photo © Musée d'Orsay / rmn

The Awful Fight between Theseus and the Minotaur, George

Wharton Edwards, in *Myths from Many Lands*, 1912, © UniversalImagesGroup/ Getty Images

The Sacrificial Lamb, Josefa de Ayala, *c.*1670–84, The Walters Art Museum.© The Picture Art Collection / Alamy Stock Photo

Caïn venant de tuer son frère Abel, Henri Vidal, 1896, Tuileries Gardens, Paris

Caroselli di maiali, Robert Delaunay, 1922, Musée National d'Art Moderne

Conclusion

Odysseus in Front of Scylla & Charybdis, Henry Fuseli, 1784, Aargauer Kunsthaus

European Stories, Debra McEachern, 2010, Book cover for "European Stories," Justine Lacroix and Kalypso Nicolaidis (eds), Oxford University Press, courtesy of the artist

Additional Centre Plates

Visions of the Daughters of Albion, William Blake, *c.* 1795 © Tate, London 2019

The Delivery of Israel out of Egypt – Pharaoh and his Hosts overwhelmed in the Red Sea, Francis Danby, 1825, © Harris Museum and Art Gallery, Preston, Lancashire, UK/Bridgeman Images

Pharaoh's Army Engulfed by the Red Sea, Frederick Arthur Bridgman, 1900

The Death of Oedipus, Henry Fuseli, 1784. Courtesy of National Museums Liverpool, Walker Art Gallery

The Combat of Theseus and the Minotaur: Poster for the First Art Exhibition of the Secession Art Movement, Gustav Klimt, 1898. From a private collection. © 2019. Photo Fine Art Images/Heritage Images/Scala, Florence

Bibliography

Core references

Introduction

Barthes, Roland, *Mythologies*, Editions du Seuil, Paris, 1957.

Conrad, Peter, *Mythomania*, Thames & Hudson, London, 2016.

Fry, Stephen, *Mythos*, Penguin Books, London, 2017.

Keum, Tae-Yeoun, *Plato and the Mythic Tradition in Political Thought*, PhD thesis, Harvard University, 2019.

Exodus

Levinas, Emmanuel, *Quatre Lectures Talmudiques*, Les Éditions de Minuit, Paris, 1968.

Zornberg, Avivah Gottlieb, *The Particulars of Rapture: Reflections on Exodus*, Schocken Books, New York, NY, 2001.

Reckoning

Aeschylus, *Prometheus Bound*, New York Review Books Classics, New York, NY, 2015.

Bernard, Williams, *Shame and Necessity*, University of California Press, Berkeley, CA, 1993.

Camus, Albert, *Le Mythe de Sisyphe: Essai sur l'Absurde*, Éditions Gallimard, Paris, 2016.

Hamilton, Edith, Huntington Cairns and Lane Cooper, *The Collected*

Dialogues of Plato, Princeton University Press, Princeton, NJ 1961.

Homer, *The Iliad*, Penguin Classics, London, 2003.

Homer, *The Odyssey*, Penguin Classics, London, 2003.

Kafka, Franz, 'Prometheus', in *The Great Wall of China and Other Short Stories*, Penguin, London, 2007.

Plato, *The Republic*, Penguin Classics, London, 2007.

Sophocles, *The Three Theban Plays: Antigone, Oedipus the King, Oedipus at Colonus*, Penguin Classics, London, 2000.

Veyne, Paul, *Les Grecs ont-ils cru à leurs mythes?*, Seuil, Paris, 1983.

Sacrifice

Aeschylus, *The Oresteian Trilogy*, Penguin Classics, London, 1977

Euripides, *Iphigenia at Aulis*, Oxford University Press, Oxford, 1992.

Euripides, *Iphigenia in Tauris*, Oxford University Press, Oxford,1992.

Girard, René, *La violence et le sacré*, Grasset, Paris, 1972.

Girard, René, *Le bouc émissaire*, Grasset, Paris, 1982.

Other references

Adonis, Andrew, *Prime Ministers on Europe, Half In Half Out*, Biteback Publishing, London, 2018

Alexandre-Collier, Agnés, '*Près d'Oxford, l'école européenne de Culham vit sous la menace du Brexit*', Le Monde, 20 Janvier 2019.

Appiah, Kwame Anthony, *Cosmopolitanism: Ethics in a World of Stranger*, W. W. Norton & Co., New York, NY, 2006.

Azmanova, Albena, 'The European Left's Machiavellian Moment: Notes on Costas Douzinas' "Syriza in Power", *Open Democracy*, 27 April 2018.

Balibar, Étienne, *Nous, Citoyens D'Europe?: Les Frontières, L'État, Le Peuple*, La découverte, 2013

Barker, Pat, *The Silence of the Girls*, Hamish Hamilton, London, 2018

Barnett, Anthony, 'Why Brexit Won't Work: the EU is About Regulation Not Sovereignty', *Open Democracy*, 25 June 2018

Bauman, Zygmunt, *Liquid Modernity*, John Wiley & Sons, 2013.

Beck, Ulrich, *The Metamorphosis of the World, How Climate Change is Transforming our Concept of the World*, John Wiley & Sons, 2016.

Behr, Rafael, 'So How does Brexit Britain Look to the World Now? Urbane but Unhinged', *The Guardian*, 16 August 2017

Bejan, Teresa M, *Mere Civility: Disagreement and the Limits of Toleration*, Harvard University Press, Cambridge, MA, 2017.

Bellamy, Richard, and Dario Castiglione, 'Between Cosmopolis and Community: Three Models of Rights and Democracy within the European Union', *Filosoficky Casopis*, vol. 47, no. 4, 1999.
Ibid, Joseph Lacey, and Kalypso Nicolaïdis, eds, *European Boundaries in Question*. Routledge, 2018.

Benner, Erica, *Be Like the Fox: Machiavelli in His World*, W. W. Norton & Company, New York, NY, 2017.

Berlin, Isaiah, *The Crooked Timber Of Humanity: Chapters In The History Of Ideas*, Princeton University Press, Princeton, NJ, 2013.

Bickerton, Christopher. 'Europe in Revolt', *Prospect Magazine*, January 2017.
Ibid, and Richard Tuck, 'A Brexit Proposal', *Thecurrentmoment Blog*, 3 December 2017.
Ibid, and Carlo Invernizzi Accett, 'Populism and Technocracy', *The Oxford Handbook of Populis*, Oxford University Press, Oxford, 2017.

Bischoff, Lisa, *Dys-EUtopia, British Novels and the European Union*, PhD thesis, Bochum: Ruhr University, 2018.

Blatter, Joachim, Samuel D. Schmid, and Andrea C. Blättle, 'Democratic Deficits in Europe: The Overlooked Exclusiveness of Nation States and the Positive Role of the European Union', *JCMS: Journal of Common Market Studies*, vol. 55, no. 3, 2017.

Bliesemann de Guevara, Berit, ed, *Myth and Narrative in International Politics: Interpretive Approaches to the Study of IR*, Springer, 2016.

Bloch, Ernst, *Le Principe Espérance*. Éditions Gallimard, Paris, 1976.

Blumenberg, Hans, *Work on Myth*, MIT Press, Cambridge, MA, 1985.

Bodenheimer, Aron, *Why? On the Obscenity of Questioning*, Stuttgart University Press, 1984.

den Boer, Andrea, 'Messianic Moments and the Religious (Re) turn in International Relations', *Meaning and International Relations.*

Advances in International Relations and Global Politics. Routledge, 2015.

Bostrom, Nick, 'The Vulnerable World Hypothesis 1', *Future of Humanity Institute*, vol. 3, no. 11, 2018.

Bottici, Chiara, and Benoît Challand, *Imagining Europe: Myth, Memory, and Identity*, Cambridge University Press, Cambridge, 2013.

Bourke, Richard and Quentin Skinner, eds, *Popular Sovereignty in Historical Perspective*, Cambridge University Press, Cambridge, 2016.

Brexit [Special Issue], *British Journal of Politics and International Relations*, 2017.

Bultmann, Rudolf, *Kerygma and Myth*. Harper, New York, NY, 1961.

Burke, Anthony, Stefanie Fishel, Audra Mitchell, Simon Dalby, and Daniel J. Levine, 'Planet Politics: A Manifesto from the End of IR', *Millennium*, vol. 44, no. 3, June 2016.

Burke, Edmund, *Reflections on the Revolution in France*, Macmillan, London, 1790.

Butler, Judith, Ernesto Laclau and Slavoj Žižek, *Contingency, Hegemony, Universality: Contemporary Dialogues on the Left*, Verso, London, 2000.

Buxton, Richard GA, *Imaginary Greece: The contexts of mythology*, Cambridge University Press, Cambridge, 1994.

Calamur, Krishnadev, 'Brexit: What would George Orwell Do?', *The Atlantic*, 23 June 2016.

Cassirer, Ernst, *The Myth of the State*. Yale University Press, New Haven, CT, 1946.

Chakrabarty, Dipesh, *Provincializing Europe: Postcolonial Thought and Historical Difference – New Edition*, Princeton University Press, Princeton, NJ, 2009

Chalmers, Damian, Markus Jachtenfuchs, and Christian Joerges, eds, *The End of the Eurocrats' Dream: Adjusting to European Diversity*, Cambridge University Press, Cambridge, 2016.

Chryssogelos, Angelo, 'The EU Must Realize that Populism is a Symptom of Real Policy Failure', *Chatham House*, 31 May 2018.

Cohn-Bendit, Daniel, et Edouard Gaudot, *Pour La Planete*, Dalloz, Paris, 2009.

Collignon, Stefan, 'Brexit has the Semblance of a New English Civil

War', *LSE Brexit Blog*, 9 March 2018.

Coltrin, Chris, 'Picturing Political Deliverance: Three Paintings of the Exodus by John Martin, Francis Danby, and David Roberts', *Nineteeth Century Art Worldwide*, vol 10, issue 1, spring 2011

Craig, Paul, 'Brexit: A Drama In Six Acts', *RRDE*, 2016.

Crouch, Colin, *Post-Democracy*, Polity, 2004.

Dahl, Robert Alan, *Democracy and Its Critics*, Yale University Press, New Haven, CT, 1989.

Debating Europe, *Is the EU Irrelevant to You?* 11 October 2018.

Demertzis, Maria, Jean Pisani-Ferry, André Sapir, Thomas Wieser, and Guntram B. Wolff, 'One Size Does Not Fit All: European Integration by Differentiation', *Bruegel Policy Brief*, vol. 3 September 2018.

Denton-Borhaug, Kelly, *U.S. War-Culture, Sacrifice and Salvation*, Routledge, 2014.

De Vries, Catherine E, *Euroscepticism and the Future of European Integration*, Oxford University Press, Oxford, 2018.
    Ibid. and Kathleen R. McNamara, 'How Choice Can Save Europe: Why EU Needs Less Technocracy and More Democracy', *Foreign Affairs*, 14 May 2018.

Dodds, Eric Robertson, *The Greeks and the Irrational*, University of California Press, Berkeley, CA, 1966.

Douthat, Ross, 'The Myth of Cosmopolitanism', *New York Times,* 2 July 2016.

Duff, Andrew, *On Governing Europe: A Federal Experiment*, CreateSpace Independent Publishing Platform, 2018.

Ehrenberg, Victor, *From Solon to Socrates: Greek History and Civilization during the 6th and 5th Centuries* BC. Routledge, 2010.

Eliot, Thomas Stearns, *The Love Song of J. Alfred Prufrock*, Poetry magazine, Chicago, 1915.

Eliot, Thomas Stearn, *Murder in the Cathedral*, vol. 72, Houghton Mifflin Harcourt, 1963.

Elster, Jon, *Ulysses Unbound: Studies in Rationality, Precommitment, and Constraints*, Cambridge University Press, Cambridge, 2000.

Esposito, Roberto, *A Philosophy for Europe: From the Outside*, John Wiley & Sons, 2018.

Evans, Geoffrey, and Anand Menon, *Brexit and British Politics*, John

Wiley & Sons, 2017.

Ferguson, Niall, 'The Degeneration of Europe', *Prospect Magazine*, 15 October 2015.

Ferrante, Elena, *Neapolitan Novels*, Penguin, London, 2012–2014.

Ferry, Jean-Marc, *La Question de l'État Européé*, Gallimard, Paris, 2000.

Ferry, Luc, *Oedipe, La Sagesse des Mythes*, Glénat BD, Paris, 2018.

Fisher, Roger, William L. Ury, and Bruce Patton, *Getting to Yes: Negotiating Agreement without Giving in*, Penguin, London, 2011.

François, Étienne, and Thomas Serrier, 'Europa, Notre Histoire', *Le Débat*, vol.1, 2018.

Frazer, Elizabeth, 'Political Power and Magic', *Journal of Political Power*, vol. 11, no. 3, 2018.

Freud, Sigmund, *Moses and Monotheism*, Leonardo Paolo Lovari, 2016.

Fry, Stephen, *Mythos: The Greek Myths Retold*, Penguin, London, 2017.

Fukuyama, Francis, 'The End of History', *The National Interest*, vol.16, summer 1989.

Furedi, Frank, *Populism and the European Culture Wars: The Conflict of Values Between Hungary and the EU*. Routledge, 2017.

Galbraith, James K, *The Predator State: How Conservatives Abandoned The Free Market And Why Liberals Should Too*, Simon and Schuster, London, 2008

Gamble, Andrew, *Between Europe and America: The Future of British Politics*, Macmillan International Higher Education, 2017.

Garner, Oliver, 'A Joint EU-UK Court for Citizens' Rights: A Viable Option After and Beyond Brexit', *European Law Blog* 3, August 2017.

Garton Ash, Timothy, 'A Humiliating Brexit Deal Risks a Descent into Weimar Britain', *The Guardian*, 27 July 2018.

Gély, Véronique, 'Pour une Mythopoétique: quelques propositions sur les rapports entre mythe et fiction', *Bibliothèque Comparatiste, Revue Vox Poetica*, 21 May 2006.

Ghemawat, Pankaj, 'The History of the English-Speaking People', *The Economist*, 15 March 2018.

Goodhart, David, *The Road to Somewhere: the Populist Revolt and the Future of Politics*, Oxford University Press, Oxford, 2017.

Grant, Charles, Sophia Besch, Ian Bond, Agata Gostynska-Jakubowska, Camino Mortera-Martinez, Christian Odendahl, John Springford, and Simon Tilfrod, 'Relaunching the EU', *Centre for European Reform Report,* 7 November 2017.

Greenhall, Jordan, 'On Sovereignty', *Deep Code – Medium,* 19 February 2018.

Grimm, Dieter, *The Constitution of European Democracy,* Oxford University Press, Oxford, 2017.

Habermas, Jürgen, *The Lure of Technocracy,* John Wiley & Sons, 2015.

Harari, Yuval Noah, *Sapiens: A Brief History Of Humankind,* Random House, 2014.

Hassan, Gerry, 'Darkest Hour – What Does a Rash of Winston Churchill Portrayals Tell Us About Brexit for Britain', *Open Democracy,* 18 January 2018.

Hobolt, Sara, Thomas Leeper, and James Tilley. 'Emerging Brexit Identities', in *Brexit and Public Opinion.* from The UK in a Changing Europe, London, 2018.

Holmes, Martin, ed. *The Eurosceptical Reader,* Springer, 2016.

Horkheimer, Max, Theodor W. Adorno, and Gunzelin Noeri, *Dialectic of Enlightenment: Philosophical Fragments.* Stanford University Press, California, Palo Alto, CA, 2002.

Ipsos MORI Report, *Shifting Ground,* 2013.

Joffe, Josef, 'Brexit Britain Has Displaced Germany as the Land of Dreamers', *Financial Times,* 15 August 2017.

Johnson, Boris, *The Dream of Rome,* Harper Collins, London, 2006.

Johnson, Dominic, and Dominic Tierney, *Failing to Win: Perceptions of Victory and Defeat in International Politics,* Harvard University Press, Cambridge, Massachusetts, MA, 2006.

Johnson, Dominic, *God is Watching You: How the Fear of God Makes us Human,* Oxford University Press, Oxford, 2016.

Jones, Lee, 'Charlottesville and the Politics of Left Hysteria', *Thecurrentmoment Blog,* 26 August 2017.

Kahneman, Daniel, *Thinking, Fast and Slow.* vol. 1., Farrar, Straus and Giroux, New York, NY, 2011.

Kálmán, György, 'Kafka's Prometheus', Neohelicon, vol. 34, no. 1., 2007.

Kant, Immanuel, *To Perpetual Peace: A Philosophical Sketch,* Hackett Publishing, Indianapolis, IN, 2003.

Keynes, John Maynard, 'National Self-Sufficiency', *The Yale Review*, vol. 22, no. 4, June 1933.

Khong, Yuen Foong, 'The American Tributary System', *Chinese Journal of International Politics*, vol. 6, no.1, 2013.

King, Stephen, 'What Ptolemy Tells Us about Germany and Greece', *Financial Times*, 20 February 2012.

Kochenov, Dimitry, 'Misguided "Associate EU Citizenship" Talk as a Denial of EU Values', *Verfassungsblog*, 1 March 2018.

Koenig, Gaspard, *Time To Philo: Notre Monde Vu par la Philosophie*, Larousse, 2017.

Krastev, Ivan, *After Europe*, University of Pennsylvania Press, Philadelphia, PA, 2017.

Lacoue-Labarthe, Philippe, 'De Holderlin a Marx: Mythe, Imitation, Tragedie: Entretien Réalisé par Bruno Duarte', *Labyrinthe*, vol. 22, no. 3, 2005.

Lacroix, Justine and Kalypso Nicolaïdis, eds., *European Stories: Intellectual Debates on Europe in National Contexts*, Oxford University Press, Oxford, 2010.

Landry, Charles and Margie Caust, *The Creative Bureaucracy & Its Radical Common Sense*, Comedia, 2017.

Leach, Edmund Ronald, *Genesis As Myth: And Other Essays*, vol. 39, Cape, 1969.

Lenin, Vladimir Illich, *The Right of Nations to Self Determination: Selected Writings*, Greenwood Press, Westport, CA, 1977.

Lévi-Strauss, Claude, *The Raw and the Cooked: Introduction to a Science of Mythology*, vol. 1, Harper & Row, New York, 1969.
Ibid. Myth and Meaning, Routledge, 2013.

Lincoln, Bruce, *Theorizing Myth: Narrative, Ideology, and Scholarship*, University of Chicago Press, Chicago, IL, 1999.

Lord, Christopher, 'Polecats, Lions, and Foxes: Coasian bargaining theory and attempts to legitimate the Union as a constrained form of political power', *European Political Science Review*, vol. 3, no. 1, 2011.

Machiavelli, Niccolò, *Discourses on Livy*, Oxford University Press, Oxford, 2009.

Mair, Peter, *Ruling the Void: The Hollowing of Western Democracy*, Verso Books, London, 2013.

Margetts, Helen, Peter John, Scott Hale, and Taha Yasseri, *Political Turbulence: How Social Media Shape Collective Action*, Princeton

University Press, Princeton, NJ, 2015.

Marsili, Lorenzo and Niccolo Milanese, *Citizens of Nowhere: How Europe Can be Saved from Itself,* Zed Books Limited, London, 2018.

Mishra, Pankaj, *The Age of Anger: A History of the Present,* Farrar, Straus & Giroux, New York, NY, 2017.

Morales, Helen, *Classical mythology: a very short introduction,* , vol. 167, Oxford University Press, Oxford, 2007.

Mouffe, Chantal, *Agonistics: Thinking the World Politically,* Verso Books, London, 2013.

Mounk, Yascha, *The People Vs. Democracy: Why Our Freedom is in Danger and How to Save It,* Harvard University Press, Cambridge, MA, 2018.

Murdoch, Iris, *The Sea, The Sea,* Penguin, London, 2001.

Muthu, Sankar, *Enlightenment Against Empire,* Princeton University Press, Princeton, NJ, 2009.

Müller, Jan-Werner, 'Can Liberalism Save Itself?', *Social Europe,* 13 April 2018.

Nicolaidis, Kalypso, 'A Letter to my British Friends: for Europe's Sake, Please Stay!', *Open Democracy,* 8 March 2016.

Ibid. 'Brexit and the compatibility paradigm: A Guide for the Mutual Recognition Perplexed', *The UK in a Changing Europe,* 15 March 2018.

Ibid. 'Brexit Arithmetics', *Negotiating Brexit,* Munich: Verlag C.H. Beck, 2017 and Hart Publishing, Oxford, 2017.

Ibid. 'Mutual Recognition: Promise and Denial, from Sapiens to Brexit', *Current Legal Problems,* December 2017.

Ibid. 'Sustainable Integration in a Democratic Polity: A New (or not so new) Ambition for the European Union after Brexit', *Brexit and Beyond,* Cambridge University Press, Cambridge, 2017.

Ibid. 'The Political Mantra: Brexit, Control and the Transformation of the European Order', *The Law and Politics of Brexit,* Oxford University Press, Oxford, 2017.

Ibid. and Juri Viehoff, 'Just Boundaries for Demoicrats', *Journal of European Integration,* vol. 39, no. 5, 2017.

Nougayrede, Natalie, 'Macron Had a Good Year In 2018, He Could Even Stop Brexit', *The Guardian,* 30 December 2017.

Orgad, Liav, *The Cultural Defense of Nations: A Liberal Theory of Majority Rights,* Oxford University Press, Oxford, 2015.

Orwell, George, *England Your England & Other Essays*, Secker & Warburg, London, 1953.

Østergaard, Uffe, *Europa's Ansigter (Faces of Europe)*, Rosinante Paperbacks, 1992.

Ostrom, Elinor, *Governing the Commons*, Cambridge University Press, Cambridge, 2015.

O' Toole, Fintan, 'Britain: The End of a Fantasy', *New York Review of Books*, 10 June 2017.

Pears, Iain, *Arcadia*, Faber & Faber, London, 2015.

Piketty, Thomas, *Capital in the Twenty-First Century*, Belknap Press, Cambridge, MA, 2014.

Pisani-Ferry, Jean, Andre Sapir, and Guntram B. Wolff, 'The Messy Rebuilding of Europe', *Bruegel Policy Brief* 719, 2012.

Pullman, Philip, *His Dark Materials: Complete Trilogy*, Scholastic, 2000.

Quatremer, Jean, 'Brexit: Pour Bruxelles, les Jeux Sont Faits', *Liberation*, 18 June 2017.

Ricoeur, Paul, *Oneself as Another*, University of Chicago Press, Chicago, IL, 1992.

Roddy, Nicolae, *The Particulars of Rapture: Reflections on Exodus*, Doubleday, New York, NY, 2001.

Rodrik, Dani, *The Globalization Paradox: Democracy and the Future of the World Economy*, W. W. Norton & Company, New York, NY, 2011.

Rorty, Richard, *Contingency, Irony, and Solidarity*, Cambridge University Press, Cambridge, 1989

Rosset, Clément, *La Philosophie Tragique*, Presses Universitaires de France, Collection Quadrige, 1961.

Sansone, David, 'Iphigeneia changes her mind', *Illinois Classical Studies* 16.1/2, 1991.

Sarmiento, Daniel, 'The EU's Constitutional Interpretation of Article 50 TEU: Be Careful What You Wish For', *Despite our Differences Blog*, 6 September 2017.

Saunders, Ari, *Id*, Kindle Edition, 2014.

Schérer, René, 'Cosmopolitisme et Hospitalité', *Communications*, vol. 65, 1997.

Ibid. Zeus Hospitalier: Éloge de l'Hospitalité, 1993.

Schmitt, Carl, *The Concept of the Political: Expanded Edition*, University of Chicago Press, Chicago, IL, 2008.

Schuman, Robert, '*Reformier l'Union Europeenne: Un Imperatif*

Politique et Democratique, *Question d'Europe*, no. 463, 19 February 2018.

Shakespeare, William, *As You Like It,* Wordsworth Editions, Ware, 1993.

Simms, Brendan, *Britain's Europe: A Thousand Years of Conflict and Cooperation*, Penguin, London, 2016.

Sinn, Hans-Werner, *The Euro Trap: On Bursting Bubbles, Budgets, and Beliefs*, Oxford University Press, Oxford, 2014.

Sørensen, Catharina, *Danish and British Popular Euroscepticism Compared: A Sceptical Assessment of the Concept*, DIIS Working Paper, no. 25., Danish Institute for International Studies (DIIS), Copenhagen, 2004.

Sternberg, Claudia Schrag, Kira Gartzou-Katsouyanni, and Kalypso Nicolaidis, *The Greco-German Affair in the Euro-Crisis: Mutual Recognition Lost?*, Palgrave Pivot, Oxford, 2017.

Streeck, Wolfgang, 'The Crises of Democratic Capitalism', *New Left Review,* no. 71, September–October 2011.

Ibid. Buying Time: The Delayed Crisis of Democratic Capitalism, Verso, London, 2014.

Ibid. How Will Capitalism End?, Verso, London, 2016.

Temelkuran, Ece, *Women Who Blow on Knots*, Parthian Books, Swansea, 2018.

Thompson, Helen, 'Inevitability and Contingency: The Political Economy of Brexit', *The British Journal of Politics and International Relations*, vol. 19, no. 3, 2017.

de Tocqueville, Alexis, *The Old Regime and the Revolution*, Harper & Brothers, New York, NY, 1856.

Tomasi di Lampedusa, Giuseppe, *The Leopard*, Pantheon Books, New York, NY, 1958.

Tuck, Richard, 'Brexit: A Prize in Reach for the Left', *Policy Exchange,* 19 July 2017.

Van Parijs, Philippe, *Linguistic Justice for Europe and for the World*, Oxford University Press, Oxford, 2011.

Varoufakis, Yanis and Benoit Hamon, 'Our New European Party Can Unite Britain's Feuding Remainers and Leavers', *The Guardian,* 18 April 2018.

Verhofstadt, Guy, *Europe's Last Chance: Why the European States Must Form a More Perfect Union*, Hachette, London, 2017.

Vernant, Jean-Pierre, *Œdipe sans Complexe*, Éditions Rationalistes,

1967.

Vimont, Pierre, 'Flexibility is not Europe's Miracle Solution', *Carnegie Europe*, 26 June 2018.

Wade, John, 'Negotiation Lessons from the Book (Not The Film) of Exodus', *Bepress*, March 2015.

Ibid. 'Systematic Risk Analysis for Negotiators and Litigators: How to help clients make better decisions', *Bond Law Review*, vol. 13, no. 2, 2001.

Wade, John and Christopher Honeyman, 'A Lasting Agreement', *The Negotiator's Fieldbook: The Desk Reference for the Experienced Negotiator*, ABA, Chicago, IL, 2006.

Walzer, Michael, 'Liberalism and the Art of Separation', *Political Theory*, vol 12, no. 3, August 1984.

Walzer, Michael, *Exodus and Revolution*, 1985.

Warner, Marina, *Fantastic metamorphoses, other worlds: ways of telling the self*, Oxford University Press, Oxford, 2004.

Weatherill, Stephen, 'What "Mutual Recognition" Really Entails', *EU Law Analysis*, 4 March 2018.

Weiler, Joseph H.H, 'Europe in Crisis – On "Political Messianism," "Legitimacy", and the "Rule of Law"', *Singapore Journal of Legal Studies*, December 2012.

Ibid. 'Editorial: The Case for a Kinder, Gentler Brexit', EJIL:Talk! (February 6, 2017).

Williams, Bernard, *Shame and Necessity*, vol. 57., University of California Press, Berkeley, CA, 2008

Wolf, Martin, 'Brexiters Misunderstand the European Project', *Financial Times*, 4 October 2018.

Žižek, Slavoj, *Against the Double Blackmail: Refugees, Terror and Other Troubles with the Neighbours*, Allen Lane, London, 2016.

About the Author

While writing this book, Kalypso Nicolaidis changed status twice. She became a (very) friendly alien with settled status in Britain, after living in the country for twenty years as a mere European citizen. Married to a Brit and living in Brexitland, she then decided to become a British citizen and thus fully partake in the body politics of her country of adoption, come what may. Of French and Greek nationality, she sees herself as a rooted cosmopolitan, in Kwame Anthony Appiah's felicitous phrase. This of course implies not that you are from anywhere, but that you belong to several somewheres, a village in Oxfordshire and one in Kassandra, almost any shore on the Mediterranean Sea or any street corner in Paris, and other secret places. She says, 'While I dislike all nationalisms, I do like the sense of anchoring that comes with national belonging – and feel extremely lucky to have so many anchors.' She teaches at Oxford. More can be found on her website: kalypsonicolaidis.com.

What's in a name? We know that Ulysses beats all the odds to come back from the Trojan War to his native Ithaca where for twenty years his wife Penelope has faithfully waited for his return. His longest adventure on the way is with the half-goddess Kalypso, whose name means 'I shall hide'. When Ulysses lands on her island, shattered by his encounters with the Cyclops and other monsters, having lost all his men and all his ships, and having almost lost all his courage and wit as well, she takes him in for seven years. She wavers on whether to keep him for herself or help him move on. In the end, she gives him a choice: stay with me and become immortal, or return home a mortal. She probably hides from him the simple truth: she already knows the answer and she approves. Her ironic gift will be to let him believe that he, all by himself, has recovered mastery of his destiny.

Index

Unbound is the world's first crowdfunding publisher, established in 2011.

We believe that wonderful things can happen when you clear a path for people who share a passion. That's why we've built a platform that brings together readers and authors to crowdfund books they believe in – and give fresh ideas that don't fit the traditional mould the chance they deserve.

This book is in your hands because readers made it possible. Everyone who pledged their support is listed below. Join them by visiting unbound.com and supporting a book today.

Julie Adams
John Alderdice
Beverly Ames
Philipp O. Amour
Othon Anastasakis
Merih Angin
Barbara Arroyo
Albena Azmanova
Daniel Baer
Marq Bailey
Rana Baladi
Abhijit Banerjee
Nicholas Barber
Petra Bárd
Davide Barile
Anthony Barnett
Marija Bartl
Gloria Bartoli
Ezgi Başaran
Joxerramon Bengoetxea
Bill Best

Paul Betts
John Beyer
Lorenzo Bini Smaghi
Lisa Bischoff
Brad Blitz
Sarmila Bose
Nicolas Bounet
Bruce Bowie
Lorna Boyd
Nathalie Brack
Bjoern Bremer
Matthew Broad
Harvey Brown
Claire and Richard Bruce
Anthony Bunge
Andy Buschmann
Daniel Butt
Jeremy Butterfield
Marina Calculli
Emre Caliskan
Jane Carey

Howard M G Carr
Daniela Caruso Micali
Bertrand Casalis
Dario Castiglione
Teresa Castro
Valerie Caton
Fikret Čaušević
Paul Chaisty
Kaukab Chaudhry
Francis Cheneval
Dimitris Chryssochoou
Valerius M. Ciuca
Molly Cochran
Cary Coglianese
Barry Colfer
Jamie Collier
B Vasilis Constantatos
Luke Cooper
Olivier Costa
Finn Costello-Dermis
Laura Coyne
Paul Craig
Roger Crisp
Ben Crum
Krisztina Csortea
Andrew Curry
Elln Dahrendorf
Chad Damro
Gareth Davies
Richard Davy
Sam Daws
Grainne de Burca
Armand de Mestral
Anne Deighton
Graciana del Castillo
Raffaella A. Del Sarto
Erin Delaney
Vincenzo Della Sala
James Dennison

Faisal Devji
Thomas Diez
Hugo Dixon
Phillip Dove
David Doyle
William Drake
Sophie Duchesne
John & Ella Eades
Mary Eagleton
Geoffrey Edwards
Kjølv Egeland
Nadia El Meliani
Alexandros Eleftheriadis
George Ellis
Scilla Elworthy
Bill Emmott
Richard Escritt
Dana Eyre
Cecile Fabre
John Farnell
Alexandre Fasel
Samuel Faure
Adrian Favell
Kevin Featherstone
Jean-Marc Ferry
Massimo Fichera
Adriana Filip
Financial Markets Policy
    Foundation
Nora Fisher-Onar
Paul Flather
K E Fleming
Stewart Fleming
Fondation Jean Monnet pour
    l'Europe FJME
Rosemary Foot
John Erik Fossum
Eleanor Fox
Jeremy Fox

Jim Franks

Elizabeth Frazer

Michael Freeden

Steven French

Joerg Friedrichs

Roman Frigg

Matteo Garavoglia

Frank Garcia

Timothy Garton Ash

Kira Gartzou-Katsouyanni

M W Gehring

Sassan Gholiagha

Oleg Giberstein

Daniele Gibney

Dorothy Gietzen

Cedric Gilson

John Gledhill

Claire Gleitman

Matthias Goldmann

Jean Gonie

Giuseppe Greco

Jonas Grimheden

Yaprak Gursoy

Daniel Halberstam

Thomas Hale

Peter Hall

Todd H Hall

Wayne Hall

Gabor Halmai

Ruth Harris

Sissy Hatzichristou

Vassilis Hatzopoulos

Richard Hay

Jarrod Hayes

Ronald Heifetz

Daniela Heimpel

Tammy Hervey

Dougald Hine

Richard Hitchman

Jessie Hronesova

Kira Huju

Achim Hurrelmann

Johari Ismail

Maciek Jastrzebiec-Pyszynski

Ayse Kadioglu

David Kalfon

Eirini Karamouzi

Kostis Karpozilos

Anthony Kasozi

Ruth Kastner

Zachary Kaufman

Lucas Kello

James Ker-Lindsay

Dimitris Keridis

Stephan Keukeleire (University of
    Leuven)

Dan Kieran

David Francis TaeSeok Kim

Uwe Kitzinger

Eleanor Knox

Elena Korosteleva

Alexey Kostyanovsky

Andrei Krasnyansky

Nadiya Kravets

Hanspeter Kriesi

Damjan Kukovec

Pierre L'Allier

Cécile Laborde

Joseph Lacey

Justine Lacroix

Paulina Lampsa

Matteo Legrenzi

Irene Lemos

Carol Leonard

Peter Lindseth

Denise Line

Clare Lockhart

Astrid Loiselet

Matthew Longo
Sonia Lucarelli
Gjovalin Macaj
David Madden
M Magninn
Imelda Maher
Rama Mani
Antigoni Manolidou
Petar Markovic
Robin Markwica
Anna Marmodoro
Judith Marquand
Benjamin Martill
Dorte Sindbjerg Martinsen
Matthias Matthijs
Hartmut Mayer
Geraldine McAllister
Robin McConnachie
Nick McDonell
Anne McNaughton
Mario Mendez
Adis Merdzanovic
Sophie Meunier
Marily Mexi
Virginie Michelet
Frédéric Misrahi
John Mitchinson
Richard Montagu
Marco Moraes
Christopher Morris
Jonathan Morris
Manuel Muniz
Cosmo Murray
Karma Nabulsi
Mikael Hiberg Naghizadeh
Carlo Navato
Ilhan Nebioglu
Ulla Neergaard
Helene Neveu Kringelbach

Brooks Newmark
Dimitri Nicolaidis
Stelios Nicolaidis
Fadela Nicolaidis Sadaoui
Kerem Oktem
David Oppenheimer
Federico Ortino
Marius Ostrowski
Christos Panotopoulos
Yannis Papadopoulos
Richard and Robin Parker
Craig Parsons
Gregory Paschalidis
Roberta Pavone
Iain Pears
Lyana Peniston
Risto E J Penttilä
Simon Pfeiffer
Simona Piattoni
Justin Pollard
Poly & Chris
Alex Pravda
Patrick Quinton-Brown
Tariq Ramadan
Manjeet Ramgotra
Rahul Rao
Dr Guevara Rauldiaz
Jeanne Reagan-Gordon
Jose Reinhardt
Louise Richardson
Armin Riess
Adam Roberts
Alasdair Roberts
Paul Rosenberg
Élise Rouméas
Muriel Rouyer
Carlo Rovelli
Lillian Rozin
Andrea Ruggeri

Alison Ryde
Lora Sabin
Andrea Sangiovanni
Daniel and Gail Saunders
Simon Saunders
Alexander & Rama Schieffer -
    Mani
Frank Schimmelfennig
Giulio Schinaia
J Schmitz
Christina Schneider
Gilg Seeber
Avi Shlaim
Alison Shore
Anthony Simon
Thomas Sinclair
Dorian Singh
Samuel Singler
Anne-Marie Slaughter
Michael Smith
Duncan Snidal
Katarzyna Sobieraj
Julie Songer
Guillaume Soto-Mayor
Debora Spar
Uta Staiger
John Stein
Zofia Stemplowska
Claudia Sternberg
Ioannis Stivachtis
Imola Streho
Brendan Strong
Francesca Strumia
Ezra Suleiman
Rebecca Surender
Sam Sussman
Oisin Suttle
Stefan Szwed
Michal Tamir

Jean-Bernard Tanqueray
Véronique Tappenden
Rosemary Taylor
Tom Theuns
Anja Thomas
Charles Simon Thomas
James Tilley
Gabriele Tonne
Emanuel V. Towfigh
Malcolm Townsend
Bosko Tripkovic
Dimitris Tsarouhas
Tanya Tsikas
Katherine Tyson
Lidia Usami - John Ikenberry
Paolo Vacca
Milada Anna Vachudova
Lieve Van Woensel
Julia Vassileva
Juri Viehoff
Leïla Vignal
Dr. Vaira Vike-Freiberga
Anthony Viscusi
Dustin Voss
Virginia Walker
David Wallace
Jim Weatherall
Stephen Weatherill
Gloria Webster
Clara Weinhardt
Hannah Whelan
Alastair Wilson
Derek Wilson
Erika Wise
Jonathan Zeitlin
Theodore Zeldin
Bohan Zhang
Michael Zürn